BEAR WRANGLER

Bear Wrangler

*Memoirs of an Alaska
Pioneer Biologist*

WILL TROYER

UNIVERSITY OF ALASKA PRESS
Fairbanks

University of Alaska Press
P.O. Box 756240
Fairbanks, AK 99775-6240

ISBN: 978-1-60223-043-9 (cloth)
         978-1-60223-044-6 (paper)

Library of Congress Cataloging-in-Publication Data

Troyer, Will (Willard A.)
Bear wrangler : memoirs of an Alaska pioneer biologist / Will Troyer.
     p. cm.
ISBN 978-1-60223-043-9 (cloth : alk. paper) — ISBN 978-1-60223-044-6 (pbk. : alk. paper)
1. Troyer, Will (Willard A.) 2. Biologists—Alaska—Biography. 3. Natural history—
Alaska. I. Title.
  QH31.T765T76 2008
  591.9798092--dc22
                              2008009913

Cover design by Dixon Jones, UAF Rasmuson Library Graphics

This publication was printed on acid-free paper that meets the minimum requirements for
ANSI / NISO Z39.48–1992 (R2002) (Permanence of Paper for Printed Library Materials).

Contents

Chapter 1

North to Alaska

Huge white-capped combers slammed into the *Sablefish*, periodically causing its bow to sheer left and right. The skipper, Gene Stubb, throttled back the engine and spun the wheel to face each onslaught. "Looks like a real nor'easter coming down the strait," he said to me.

My queasy stomach began to really churn. I knew I was in for another siege of seasickness. I gripped the portside window ledge tightly and braced my legs as wave after wave broke over the bow. A small chair slid across the wheelhouse floor and crashed into the wall. It was getting too rough! The skipper spun the wheel to starboard, and the *Sablefish* slowly responded. A moment later the waves were on our stern and we were running with the raging seas.

"We better get out of this storm while we can," Captain Stubb shouted. "We'll run behind that island ahead and hole up in Alert Bay until it blows itself out."

I wholly agreed, as I was sweating profusely and swallowing to keep everything down. But to no avail. I ran for the head and got rid of breakfast and lunch. It was the third time I had been seasick in as many days, and now my voyage of adventure did not seem to be so much fun. I dove for my bunk and lay there, wishing I were on solid ground.

The *Sablefish* continued to roll as the breakers surged into our stern, but after thirty minutes we gained the leeward side of the island and the waters calmed. I crawled out of the bunk and went to the wheelhouse, where I cracked a window for some fresh air. Captain Stubb looked at my ashen face and grinned. "Not feelin' so hot?"

I did not answer, just frowned.

The FWS Sablefish *anchored along the British Columbia coast in 1951.*

The little *Sablefish* was only thirty-six feet long and heavily loaded with supplies and people, so it did not take very rough seas to make it buck and roll.

My real journey to Alaska had begun many years before. As a teenager during the early 1940s I had read many books about the Last Frontier. The stories
enthralled me: a vast land relatively uninhabited and teeming with exotic wildlife. It was a direct contrast to the Indiana farm life I knew. In 1948 I drove the
Alcan Highway to Alaska. After spending a few weeks in this immense northern land of high mountains, lakes, glaciers, and an unending taiga forest, I was
convinced it was the place where I wanted to live and work someday.

In 1951, during my junior year at Oregon State College in Corvallis, I heard
about a job in Southeast Alaska. The seasonal position was with the commercial
fishery research branch of the U.S. Fish and Wildlife Service (FWS). I was a
wildlife management major and not looking for a job in fisheries, but working in
Alaska caught my attention. I applied for the job, even though I would have to
miss spring term.

Now, here I was, fighting my way through rough seas along the coast of British
Columbia, seasick, but determined to see it through. We had left Seattle three
days earlier, bound for Ketchikan and anticipating a three- to four-day voyage.
Unfortunately, we had not yet reached the halfway point. I wondered if my weak
stomach would survive the long trip.

Three of us seasonal employees were aboard the *Sablefish*, along with Captain
Stubb, his wife, and their four-year-old son. His wife was an incessant talker and

constantly sought my ear. I was in no mood to talk when I was even slightly nauseated from the rolling ship, so I often retreated to my bunk to avoid her chatter.

We tied up at the dock in Alert Bay and spent two days in the Canadian fishing village before the storm subsided. The trip to Ketchikan continued to be one storm after another, and I became seasick at least four more times. We worked our way north along the coast, dashing for shelter when the seas got too rough and running when the weather permitted. I got a lesson in Canadian geography as we passed Bella Bella, the Queen Charlotte Islands, Prince Rupert, and various other islands and landmarks along the British Columbia coast. On the tenth day we finally reached our destination.

Ketchikan was a typical fishing town in Southeast Alaska, with its maritime businesses crowded along the seashore. Large seiners, trollers, gillnetters, and sailboats filled the local boat harbor and were anchored in every cove that offered protection from stormy seas. Numerous docks jutted into the salt water, and boardwalks lined many streets. A forest of huge spruce, cedar, and hemlock trees bordered the edge of town. Wet sphagnum moss hanging from the tree branches typified the rain forest that covered this part of coastal Alaska. Fishermen in knee boots and foul weather gear strolled along the boardwalks, contrasting sharply with the bankers in business suits. This fishing town was quite dissimilar to the small towns I was used to in the States.

We spent several days in town recuperating from our voyage and taking on more supplies. We then headed up the coast past Bell Island Hot Springs and anchored at the mouth of a small salmon stream. After hauling the equipment a hundred yards up the stream, we pitched our plywood tent frames on four feet of hard-packed snow that remained from winter. As spring progressed and the snow melted, the tent frames sometimes dropped a few inches, scattering our supplies on the floor.

We stayed two months at the first site and at Old Tom Creek in Skowl Arm on Prince of Wales Island, clipping the adipose fins from tiny pink salmon fry. We caught the newly hatched fish in nets and placed them in small, shallow pans of water mixed with a few drops of alcohol, which slowed their squirmy movements. We then held the subdued fish between two fingers, clipped the fins, and released them back into the stream. Pink salmon return to their parent stream to spawn after two years at sea. The adults with clipped fins would later be counted in salmon catches and in the streams to determine survival success and migration patterns.

After a few weeks of constantly clipping fins, the task became a bit boring. But I loved the evenings and off-duty days when I roamed the beaches and forests observing numerous deer, black bear, and other wildlife. Occasionally I found the tracks of a wolf in the sand or observed red fox feeding on clams. The bays were filled with various species of sea ducks, shorebirds, and bald eagles. I wandered the beaches and forests for miles and never saw the track of another human. I was captivated by the wildlife and by the massive wilderness in this wild, remote country. Where I had grown up in Indiana, the countryside was dominated by developed agricultural lands, people, and cities. As I experienced these wild lands I had so often read and dreamed about in my youth, I realized that I felt at home.

This early spring job near Ketchikan turned out to be only a prelude to a summer of adventure.

Chapter 2

Summer on the Situk

I hiked up the Situk River one morning, passing numerous small pools, riffles, and gravel bars. A few red salmon were already fighting their way upstream, harbingers of the hordes of salmon that would soon follow. A deep pool lay before me, and in the placid water I could see dozens of steelhead trout moving back and forth. Occasionally one rose to snatch an insect. My hands shook with anticipation as I attached a small lure to my fishing line. I cast the lure above the trout and slowly retrieved it, expecting an immediate response, but nothing happened. I cast again and again, without success. My euphoria faded, and I became frustrated and angry. This was not going to be easy after all. On about the tenth cast the rod was nearly jerked out of my hands. The line was ripped from the reel as I fought to slow the fish. The spool was almost empty when the steelhead turned and ran toward me. I thought it was gone until the huge trout leaped four feet out of the water in a cloud of spray. I was astounded at the size of the fish. I was reeling frantically to take in slack line when it leaped again, shaking its head violently in an attempt to throw the lure. The big fish raced across the pool several times before it began to slow its efforts. I worked it closer to shore, and when the steelhead gave up the struggle, I pulled it onto the gravel bar, dropped the rod, and ran forward to claim my prize. I held up the twenty-six-inch fish, hardly believing I had finally landed such a trophy. I was elated and yelled, "What a fish! What a fish!"

I turned and looked downriver. No one else was on the Situk, and in the distance I could see the weir, the structure through which I would count thousands of

Counting salmon through the fish weir on the Situk River in 1951.

salmon during the course of the summer. I looked at the fish in my hands again and said to myself, "Boy, there're sure some major perks to this job."

In May, after completing the pink salmon project near Ketchikan, I was offered a job as weir watchman on the Situk River near Yakutat. My boss, Gomer Hilsinger of the U.S. Fish and Wildlife Service, was the fishery management agent for this region. When I arrived at his office in Juneau, he briefed me on my duties, which were primarily to count the different species of salmon that migrated up the Situk River to spawn. Documenting the number of salmon in the major streams in Alaska helped the FWS monitor the health of salmon populations that were subject to intensive commercial fishing.

After Gomer trained me for the summer job, he smiled and said, "I probably shouldn't tell you this now, but for your information the Situk River is one of the best sportfishing rivers in Alaska. Remember, your first priority is to count the fish through the weir, but you should have plenty of time for fishing. I'll envy you while I'm sitting here in this office."

Gomer also informed me that I would be traveling to Yakutat aboard the vessel *Kittiwake*. It was one of the vessels the commercial fishery branch of the FWS maintained to assist them in carrying out their salmon management duties. I was not eager for another long sea voyage, as I had not forgotten the rough trip

Yakutat in 1951.

to Ketchikan on the *Sablefish* only a few months before. Gomer must have read the scowl on my face. "Oh, don't worry," he said. "It's only a one-day trip, and the weather forecast is good."

His comment relieved my fears temporarily, and the next day I boarded the *Kittiwake*. It was about fifty-eight feet long, with lots of cargo space and limited living facilities. Hank Museth, the skipper, met me as I stepped aboard. "Welcome to my ship, Will. Just take your gear downstairs and toss it on any empty bunk available," he instructed me.

Hank was a tall, lean man with a tanned leather face acquired from years at sea. A few hours after we left Juneau, his deep bass voice resounded through the wheelhouse when he got on the radio to let the Juneau office know of our progress. "Juneah, Juneah, dis is da *Kidd-ah-wake* approachin' Point Retreat," he informed Hilsinger's office.

Hank warned me to enjoy these relatively calm waters while I could, for once we passed Cape Spencer and entered the Gulf of Alaska, we could expect rough seas. I was not happy to hear those dire warnings, but I dismissed them for the moment. I was enjoying the scenic snowcapped mountains and the numerous green forested islands that surrounded us. The weather was pleasant and I stood on the deck of the *Kittiwake* with my binoculars observing the abundant marine life. Various species of seabirds rose from the water as the *Kittiwake* sent its wake rolling toward the shores of Admiralty Island. I spotted harbor seals lying on rocky islets and sea lions diving as we approached them. Several times I saw the white head of a bald eagle sitting on its nest in the top of a tall spruce tree.

Soon after we rounded Point Retreat and entered Lynn Canal, a pod of porpoises appeared on our port side. They swam along the bow of the vessel for a few minutes, occasionally breaking the surface; then they furiously pumped their tails and raced ahead before circling back to repeat the playful performance. In Icy Strait, near the entrance to Glacier Bay, a group of humpback whales became visible. I was enthused at the abundance of wildlife and often yelled at the crew inside, "There's a whale!" or "Look at the porpoises!" Hank only smiled at my exuberance.

Darkness was falling as we entered Cross Sound, and Hank decided to spend the night in Elfin Cove, a small, well-protected bay. He wanted to get a good night's rest before we entered the expected rough seas in the Gulf of Alaska.

The next morning I was awakened by the noise of the *Kittiwake*'s engine, and a few minutes later I heard the anchor chain being hoisted onto the foredeck. I quickly got dressed. The smell of brewing coffee permeated the air. Hank and Pete, who was the boat's cook and deckhand, were listening to the marine weather forecast when I entered the wheelhouse. The forecaster predicted winds from the northwest at fifteen to twenty knots and seas to eight feet. It was not the best forecast, but Hank thought we could make it.

Pete offered a breakfast of pancakes, bacon, and eggs, but I opted for two slices of toast, knowing from previous experience that my stomach would be churning when the *Kittiwake* started to buck heavy seas. Once we passed Cape Spencer, there would be no islands to duck behind along this rugged coastline. Hank figured the trip to Yakutat would take sixteen hours. The *Kittiwake* made a steady nine knots. Before long we entered the unprotected coast, and the *Kittiwake* charged straight into the swells. It did not roll from side to side, but the up-and-down motion was enough to upset my weak stomach.

Hank saw my uneasiness and asked me to take the wheel while he went to the galley for a snack. An old seaman, Hank possessed an appetite that was not curbed by the bucking vessel. To keep the *Kittiwake* on course, I quickly learned to not overcompensate on the wheel when the vessel wandered slightly. I also discovered that steering kept my mind off my upset stomach.

By midafternoon the seas had increased, and at times the water broke over the bow, slamming against the wheelhouse. Hank was forced to throttle back the engine to reduce the impact of the waves. Our forward speed slowed to about six knots. I was rather pale as I grasped the windowsill to steady my balance. Pete looked at my ashen face and suggested I eat a few saltine crackers. It seemed to help temporarily, but I had no appetite for food.

By nightfall the combers had become larger, crashing into the wheelhouse on a regular basis. My stomach was really roiling by then, and I ran to the head to upchuck what little food I had eaten in the last twenty-four hours. I was miserable and wondered how I could have signed on to this trip after the similar experience I had endured en route from Seattle to Ketchikan only a few months before. I vowed that if I ever got to shore, I would never set foot on a boat again. But I wanted the summer job on the Situk River and consoled myself with the thought that this trip would not last forever. I crawled into my bunk and hung on to the railing to keep from being thrown onto the floor.

The drone of the vessel's engine was often drowned out by the sound of waves slamming into the ship. After each onslaught the *Kittiwake* lurched and rolled. Sometime during the night the refrigerator door came open, spilling its contents. I heard the sound of breaking glass and rolling cans coming from the galley, but I was too sick to care what happened and only tightened my grip on the railing. I found out later that Pete was also seasick. Only Hank, the weathered seaman, seemed unaffected, but he later confessed he had felt a little queasy.

My misery seemed to last forever, but finally the *Kittiwake* quit rolling. It gave me some hope. An hour later I was feeling much better and decided to get up. I walked through the galley, where Pete was still cleaning up the mess, and said, "Good morning!"

"What's so good about it?" he answered with a couple of expletives. I ignored his obvious bad mood and continued to the wheelhouse.

Hank was at the wheel. He smiled and said, "Didja enjoy da ride?"

"Not exactly," I replied. "I had a pretty miserable night."

I peered out the window. Fog covered the ocean for as far as I could see. "Where are we?" I asked Hank.

"Wished I knew."

The *Kittiwake*, like most vessels in those days, had no radar or depth finder. Hank navigated by compass and dead reckoning. "We're somewhere in Yakutat Bay, but I don't know where."

He told me to get on the bow, take the lead line, and get some depth readings. The chill, fresh air smelled good, and I began to feel better. I took numerous soundings and yelled the information back to Hank. He took the data, looked at the charts, and figured we were close to Yakutat. I saw a faint shoreline through

Hauling fish on the railroad.

the dense fog. Hank dropped the anchor to wait for the fog to lift so he could see to enter the harbor.

I had eaten nothing but a few crackers for twenty-four hours, and the smell of frying bacon in the galley whetted my appetite. Pete was now in a good mood and had bacon, eggs, and hot biscuits ready. I ate a hearty breakfast, washed down with coffee and orange juice. The fog lifted after breakfast, and finally we were tied to the dock in Yakutat—twenty hours after passing Cape Spencer.

Yakutat had been a small Native village and a sea otter hunting center during the Russian era. It had since become a major commercial fishing port, and now the small town contained a fish cannery, stores, and other small businesses. The Federal Aviation Administration (FAA) maintained a modern airport a few miles out of town. It was a major stopover and refueling site for commercial airlines flying between Anchorage, Juneau, Ketchikan, and Seattle.

Numerous salmon streams flowed into the Gulf of Alaska along the coast from Yakutat to Dry Bay. Early in the 1900s, the canneries had built a railroad from town to the Situk River and beyond, for the purpose of hauling fish from the rivers to the canneries. It was still in use in 1951, but trucks mounted on railroad wheels had replaced the train. A well-built road provided access to the airfield, but past that point rail service was the only way to haul supplies to the

Our camp on the Situk River.

Situk River. The camp where I was to work was located on the west bank of the river, several hundred yards upstream of the railroad bridge.

Personnel already at the camp on the Situk consisted of Bob Bain, the FWS enforcement agent; his wife, Helen; and Larry Knapp, the fishery management agent. Two weeks after I arrived, George O'Neil joined the crew. A retired railroad employee from Michigan, One-Shot George, as we knew him, was the real character in camp. He had come to Yakutat to hunt brown bear several years before. The story was that he had killed several bears, needing only one shot each time. The local people initiated him into their tribe as One-Shot George. He was quite proud of this title and always introduced himself as One-Shot George. He was rather lean and agile for his age, and his prominent reddish hooked nose reminded me of the snout of a spawning male salmon.

We unloaded the *Kittiwake*, hauling the gear to the bridge and carrying it to camp. Next we installed the fish weir, which was stacked in pieces on the riverbank from the previous year. First we placed the horses, which were heavy wooden tripods, in the river and fastened them together with two-by-fours and heavy planks. We then nailed the smaller two-by-two weir pickets upright to the two-by-fours and sandbagged the bottoms in the water to help hold them against the strong current. The project took several days of hard labor.

The local barbershop on the Situk River.

A few red salmon had entered the river by the time we got the weir installed. They swam back and forth in front of the pickets looking for a way upstream. The weir contained several gates, each of which had a white board staked to the river bottom. When I opened a gate, the fish immediately passed through the weir. I sat and counted them as they passed over the white board. At first only a few hundred salmon a day passed upstream and I had ample time to take breaks and fish with One-Shot George. Later, during the peak of the run when thousands of salmon migrated upstream, I spent most of my time counting fish. Tabulating all the salmon became a bit boring, but as Gomer had said, "The job has one big asset—sportfishing on your time off."

The steelhead were already up the river spawning by the time we installed the weir. They, unlike salmon, do not die after spawning, but go back to the sea, returning to the river in subsequent years. Sometimes nearly one thousand steelhead swam back and forth behind the barrier, looking for a way back to sea. The law forbade fishing within three hundred feet of the weir, but several excellent pools, filled with these large trout, lay upriver. One-Shot George and I spent hours at the pools, hooking, playing, and releasing these salmon-sized fish. Usually the only sport fishermen on the river were One-Shot and me; on some weekends a few local FAA personnel showed up. Heavy rains later raised

One-Shot George and me with a morning's catch of king salmon.

the water level of the river, and I had to open all the gates to keep the weir from washing downstream. The steelhead all escaped back to sea.

One-Shot and I now turned our attention to the large king salmon that had entered the river. Many of these weighed thirty-five pounds or more. We spent many hours catching and releasing these giants at a hot spot above the bridge.

My first king was the most exciting to catch. One-Shot and I had reached the pool early in the morning. Occasionally the back of a large salmon broke the water surface. "Okay, Will, you try first," One-Shot said. I cast a lure across the pool and started the retrieve. When the bait got to the middle of the pool, the line went tight. For a moment I thought I had snagged the bottom, but then the fish turned and ran. I tried to slow its run. "Hold him! Hold him!" One-Shot instructed me. "Keep the line tight."

The rod bent double as I tried to stop the salmon. I slowed it down, but the fish continued to the far end of the pool. "Hang on, Will!" One-Shot yelled. "That's a big one."

He did not need to tell me. I had never hooked such a big fish. "He's a giant all right," I yelled to One-Shot, "but I'm not sure I can hold him."

One-Shot encouraged me to stay with the fish and gave me all kinds of advice. I put as much pressure on the line as I could, and whenever the fish gave me some slack, I reeled in line. I fought the monster for twenty minutes before it

We competed with the bears for wild strawberries.

began to tire. The king made several more runs, but eventually I got it near shore. One-Shot slipped the net under it and lifted the struggling fish out of the water and onto the gravel bar.

"Holy smoke," I said to One-Shot. "That's a big, big fish!" I ran over and pulled the flopping fish from the net and held him up to admire.

"He's big all right. I expect he will go close to thirty-five pounds," One-Shot predicted.

After admiring my first king, we both got back to fishing. We landed three more and decided that was plenty. We strung the four fish on a large pole and carried them back to camp. We saved one for eating, and I smoked and canned the rest. I planned to return to Oregon State College in the fall. The fish would be a welcome change from the cheap hamburger my roommates and I ate most of the school year.

Abundant wild strawberries were another benefit of the job. I picked and ate them every day for forty days. Strawberries with whipped cream, strawberry pie, and strawberries in tapioca were our favorite desserts. I also canned strawberries to take back to college.

We often ate fresh Dungeness crab after Bob discovered a small, shallow bay near Yakutat in which the crabs could be captured by hand on a low tide. I was learning the subsistence lifestyle in Alaska. It reminded me of my youthful farm days when we grew everything we ate.

Later in the summer silver salmon entered the river in large numbers. One-Shot and I fished them every day. They took every shiny lure we cast in front of them, and we caught plenty.

By late August the red salmon run was just about over. Gomer Hilsinger sent word to shut down the weir and remove it from the river. Larry and I spent several days at this task and in securing the camp for the winter.

My first summer in Alaska was coming to an end. I had enjoyed it immensely and hated to leave. The outstanding sportfishing, the variety and abundance of wildlife, the majestic mountains, and the vast unpopulated wilderness appealed to me. I was hooked on Alaska. As soon as I was back at college, I began to plan my return.

Chapter 3

Sand Point Summer

B ob and I were patrolling the southern side of the Alaska Peninsula with a twin-engine Widgeon. Near noon, as we approached Orzinski Bay, we spotted a large vessel with three small catcher boats at the head of the bay. Drawing closer, we saw that one of the small boats had its seine stretched across the mouth of a stream filled with salmon. Three fishermen were in the shallow water trying to drive the salmon into the net. Commercial fishing was not permitted within three hundred yards of the mouth of any salmon stream; large NO FISHING markers were on each side of the stream.

Bob looked at me with a grin. "We got 'em!"

I smiled back, but I was thinking, "Wow! So this is what it's like to catch an illegal fisherman. Now what do we do?"

I graduated with a bachelor of science degree in wildlife management from Oregon State College in the spring of 1952. I yearned to return to Alaska to start a permanent career in my chosen profession. I had learned during the previous summer, however, that wildlife management jobs were scarce. Alaska was still a territory then, and the U.S. Fish and Wildlife Service was responsible for management of Alaska's wildlife resources. Its emphasis was on enforcement and predator control. There were approximately twenty-five wildlife enforcement field positions in Alaska, while there were only about eight in wildlife management and research. I wanted to be a wildlife biologist, but it was obvious that if I wanted to work in Alaska, my best opportunity was in enforcement.

Sand Point in 1952.

During the winter Bob Bain had written me several letters encouraging me to apply to be his summer field assistant. I had accompanied him on some enforcement patrols in Yakutat, and he apparently thought I was a good enforcement agent candidate. He assured me that the job would probably lead to a permanent position. I decided to apply, and in late May, having been hired, I flew to Anchorage. Bob met me at the airport, and we drove to Seward, where he was now stationed with the FWS. He had a split permanent assignment: he served as a game warden on the Kenai Peninsula during the winter, and in the summer he was in charge of the commercial fishery enforcement program at Sand Point.

I spent a week in Seward, planning the summer program with Bob and buying supplies. Bob, a pilot, was assigned a twin-engine Widgeon to patrol the commercial fishery during the summer. We flew to Sand Point in the Widgeon the first week in June. Bob and his wife, Helen, had rented a house in the small community, and I stayed with them when not on patrol. Sand Point is a small fishing village on Popof Island, one of the numerous islands in the Shumagin Island group south of the Alaska Peninsula. During World War II, the military had built a small airstrip near the village to help defend the area against the Japanese, who had invaded and occupied several of the Aleutian Islands. Bob kept our plane on this airstrip.

Our enforcement district stretched 1,350 miles, from just north of Chignik Bay on the Alaska Peninsula southwest to the end of the Aleutian Islands. We never actively patrolled beyond Unimak Pass, so in reality our district was about

The FWS Teal, *our slow patrol vessel.*

three hundred miles long. But it contained both the north and south sides of the Alaska Peninsula. Low clouds often prevented us from crossing to the north side for aerial patrols.

In addition to the Widgeon, we had the *Teal*, a sixty-foot vessel with a crew of three, and three stream guards to help enforce the commercial fishery laws in this vast geographic area. The diesel-powered *Teal* was an old boat, built in 1923, and was extremely slow, with a top speed of seven knots—much slower than most commercial fishing vessels. With a slow patrol boat and only three stream guards, our enforcement efforts were quite limited; in addition inclement weather often prevented us from flying. The commercial fishermen were well aware of our restricted capabilities to enforce fishery regulations, and many thumbed their noses at our efforts. Creek robbing was rampant.

I soon found out how flagrant the violations were. Bob and I flew over Orzinski Bay in the middle of the day and caught the three fishermen in the process of robbing a creek shortly after I arrived at Sand Point.

After sighting the creek robbers, Bob circled over the scene as the culprits looked up at us and likely thought, "Oh shit, we got caught!"

Bob made several more passes as I photographed the illegal fishermen for evidence. He then landed on the water and taxied behind the large vessel, letting them know we intended to come aboard. I thought we would both go aboard to make the arrest and direct them to proceed to Sand Point to face the consequences. Instead Bob said, "You jump aboard and bring 'em in." Wow! I had never made an arrest in my life. I was unsure of myself and a bit scared.

The skipper stretched out his hand and helped me aboard. The crew members on deck looked rather glum, but the skipper smiled and said, "Well, you caught us!"

I heard the roar of the airplane as Bob took off for Sand Point. Boy, did I feel small! I was one young, inexperienced enforcement agent among a whole crew of unhappy fishermen. I knew they could throw me overboard if they wanted to, but I took comfort in knowing that Bob had witnessed my boarding.

I looked into the skipper's eyes and said firmly, "I'm going to have to take you in to Sand Point." He nodded.

"We won't have to bring in the small boat?" he asked. I had not thought of that; I was not sure of the rules when a large ship with small catcher boats was involved. I confidently informed him that it was not necessary to bring in the boat—only the men involved in the violation.

The fishermen were fairly friendly as we proceeded toward Sand Point, but I was a bit uneasy. They offered me a cup of coffee, and we chatted about fishing. They knew they had been caught breaking the law and would have to pay the usual fine of $250 to $300. Like many other fishermen, they planned to pay the fine and then make it all back on the first night they could find a creek full of fish.

The next day the magistrate convened court in her home, a common practice for magistrates in small towns. She explained the violation and asked the skipper how he pled. "Guilty, your honor," he said. Then he briefly explained that fishing had been poor and they were only trying to make enough money to pay expenses.

She gave them a short lecture about the evils of creek robbing, explaining that if fishermen did not let salmon escape up the rivers, there would soon be no salmon to fish. She paused for a few seconds and looked the skipper straight in the eye. "I find you guilty, and for this violation you are fined $700." She slammed down the gavel. The skipper got a sick look on his face. He had expected a maximum fine of $300, based on her past court actions. Too late—he had already pled guilty.

Afterward Bob questioned him about the length of the fishing net. The skipper told him it was legal, but Bob had doubts. He told the skipper he was sending me back out to measure the seine. Bob later informed me that I should have also brought in the small catcher boat that was used in the illegal catch. I was learning fast!

When I reboarded the vessel, the mood of the crew had changed. They were an unhappy lot. They felt the magistrate had given them twice the fine that others had received for the same violation. They implied that she had singled them out because they were from out of town—Anchorage. I did not feel too comfortable on their craft and began to wonder if this enforcement work was for me.

Our patrol plane lands behind the FWS Teal.

When we got back to Orzinski, I boarded the small catcher boat and measured the seine. I was relieved when it turned out to be legal. Bob arrived before long in the Widgeon and picked me up. He lectured me again to always bring in all the evidence I could. I was glad my first enforcement case was over. Bob, however, was enthused about our first arrest. He grinned and said, "We'll catch some more."

I spent the summer alternating my time between flying aerial patrols with Bob and doing vessel patrols on the slow *Teal*. The vessel patrols were long and often boring, as we spent many days at sea, but I rather enjoyed the eccentric crew. The skipper of the boat, Howard Marks, had a drinking habit. He always had a bottle of Scotch sitting in the wheelhouse, and he took regular nips. During the course of a long day he usually consumed the entire bottle. He held his liquor well, however, and I never detected that his drinking impaired his ability to carry out his duties. Before coming to Alaska, Howard had traveled with a large musical band on the East Coast and was an excellent pianist. I never discovered how he had made the transition from a professional piano player to a skipper of an Alaskan vessel.

Two other crew members were assigned to the *Teal*: Hank, the engineer, and Willie, the cook and deckhand. Hank was rather aloof and had problems pronouncing the various Russian geographic places along the coast. One day he stumbled over "Belkofski" several times. When I chuckled at his efforts, he looked at me in disgust and said, "Oh, I wished uh white man would haff got here fust!" He was from the South, had worked his way to Alaska aboard a freighter, and had been at sea most of his life. Once in a while he told me about his sea experiences, but most of his life remained a mystery.

Willie was physically small and rather quiet. He thought the sun rose and set on Howard and was fully devoted to him; both men enjoyed their alcohol. Willie brought the skipper a cup of coffee whenever Howard raised his finger to his lips, and he always referred to the skipper as Mr. Marks when in the company of others.

We often tied up at local docks and spent the night in small communities. Willie soon had dinner on the table and, after eating, he and Howard headed into the village to see the sights. Sometimes Hank and I accompanied them, but I usually preferred to wait a half hour or so, knowing things would have begun to liven up. If there was a bar in town, and there usually was, Howard and Willie quickly sniffed it out. The bar often had a piano, and after a drink or two Howard would sidle over to it. At first he fingered the keys lightly to check the sound and familiarize himself with the feel of the piano. Then suddenly his fingers would fly over the keyboard in a lively musical number. Boy, he could play! It was not long before a crowd, glasses in hand, gathered around the piano. Willie always stood at the end of the piano smiling, proud that his boss was such an accomplished pianist. Sometimes, like a conductor leading an orchestra, he waved his hand to get the crowd enthused.

Tune after tune erupted as Howard's fingers glided rapidly across the keyboard. When he fired up an old number that everyone knew, the place would explode with song. Howard never failed to keep the clientele entertained, and the musical evening often continued well past midnight. After he had played at a remote village, the people rarely forgot him. On future visits someone would board the *Teal* to ask if Mr. Marks were coming ashore to play. He always obliged.

Tarlton "Tee" Smith, the fishery management agent for the district, often boarded the *Teal* for extended trips. He loved to camp, fish, and observe wildlife. The *Teal* crew frequently dropped him off on some remote stream for a few days or more, later returning to pick him up. Howard and Willie considered him a bit weird because he was a loner and took very little food with him. They claimed he survived on popcorn during these trips. That was an exaggeration, for I noticed he did take compact items of food besides the popcorn. He also had some of the best lightweight camping equipment I had ever seen. Such equipment was rare in those days. I envied it and later ordered some supplies from his catalog sources.

Sea lions on Jude Island.

One weekend he told the crew he needed to check out Jude Island, a large sea lion rookery near Sand Point. He had little official excuse to go to the island, and Howard told him so, balking at the trip. Tee, however, convinced him that sea lions ate salmon and he should learn something about the status of these marine predators. Tee invited me to accompany him, and I jumped at the chance for a break from my routine patrols.

The day was clear and calm, and as we approached the rookery, Tee estimated there were about five thousand mammals on the island. We anchored on the leeward side. When Howard shut down the boat's noisy engine, we could hear a loud, constant roar coming from the mass of bellowing animals.

Hank took Tee and me ashore in the small skiff. As we neared the island, I was almost overwhelmed by the deafening din and the powerful stench. The sound of the roaring animals reminded me of a livestock yard that I had visited a few times with my dad in Indiana. The huge sea lion bulls fought constantly to protect their large harems. The brown adults contrasted with the nearly black juveniles, which lay sleeping on rocks near their mothers. Hundreds of animals dove and swam in the deep blue surf. Others clambered out of the water and moved up the rocky shoreline in slow, ungainly movements. I moved through the crowd, photographing the roaring, stinking animals. I made sure to keep my distance from the huge, menacing males. I had never before been surrounded by

The author in front of the house rented by the FWS in 1952.

such a mass of wild, bawling animals. I should have been intimidated; instead I was exhilarated and felt I was in my element.

After several hours on the island, Tee signaled for the *Teal* crew to pick us up. As we climbed into the skiff and pushed off from shore, several adult sea lions swam under it and one bumped the small boat, rocking it unsteadily. I grabbed the gunwales, afraid the skiff might swamp, but it stayed upright.

I had shot several hundred feet of movies and numerous slides while on the island. It was a tremendous experience, and as we were traveling back to the *Teal*, I said to Tee, "Man, this has been one of the greatest experiences of my life. I've never been surrounded by such a mass of wild animals. I sure appreciate being invited along."

Tee answered, "I've wanted to do this for a long time. It was also one of my best experiences. We will have to do it again someday."

After we got aboard the *Teal*, we sat in the galley, each with a cup of coffee, and relived our day on the island. Howard and Willie did not seem impressed and became bored with our chatter. A night in a bar seemed more exciting to them than a day on a sea lion rookery.

A week later I was invited aboard a local cannery's brailing vessel as it emptied the fish traps located on Popof Island. Fish traps were numerous along the Alaska

Fish traps were still in use in 1952. Salmon followed the long leads into the trap.

Peninsula, as they were in other parts of Alaska prior to statehood. The pile-driven traps, owned mostly by big cannery operators, were extremely efficient at catching salmon. The traps were strategically placed to intercept schools of salmon as they migrated from the open ocean to the spawning streams. The long, heavy-gauge wire leads extended a considerable distance into the sea, where a wing steered the fish into the trap by a series of progressively smaller enclosures. The fish were held in the trap until a salmon tender arrived, brailed the salmon from the trap, and hauled them to the cannery for processing. The small fishermen hated the traps because they captured a large portion of the salmon harvest. The owners were usually allowed to fish the traps from 6 a.m. Monday until 6 p.m. Friday.

As the brailing boat pulled alongside of each trap, the crew moved the nets to confine the salmon to a small portion of the enclosure. They then dropped their brailer, a long, heavy net with a weighted pole on one end, into the seething mass of fish, letting it sink to the bottom before hoisting it aboard with hundreds of flopping, squirming salmon. They dumped the fish into the hold of the vessel before dropping the brailer to fill it again. This process was awesome to see, and I was especially interested in documenting the practice with photographs. Fish traps were controversial and I did not expect them to last much longer. They were outlawed a few years later, so I actually documented the end of a historical era.

We continued our patrols the rest of the summer and arrested a few more fishermen. I became more confident in my duties, but I still did not get a thrill

Brailing salmon out of a fish trap.

out of arresting fishermen as Bob Bain did. I frankly wondered if I were going to make a good enforcement officer. I did not feel that we were very effective in preventing most of the unlawful fishing activities, but I did believe we thwarted a lot of illegal acts because of our presence in the general area.

In late August, at the end of the fishing season, we loaded up our gear, said goodbye to Sand Point, and returned to home base, flying along the shore of Cook Inlet. I was amazed at the number of fish traps along this long inlet. As I recall, they were spaced about one mile apart. Seeing such a vast number of efficient traps, I understood why the small fishermen hated them.

Bob dropped me off in Kenai and told me to drive a new patrol car to Seward. I drove through Soldotna, which consisted of a filling station, a coffee shop, and little else. Eleven years later I would live near this growing town. I continued down the all-gravel Sterling Highway to Cooper Landing. It was my first look at the small, picturesque community where I would retire at the end of my career. I reached Seward an hour later.

My Sand Point summer was over. I had enjoyed most of my experiences on the remote Alaska Peninsula, but now I was looking forward to my next assignment in a different geographic region of Alaska.

Chapter 4

Wrangell Game Warden

The day I arrived in Seward I was offered and I accepted a permanent position as assistant enforcement agent to Monte Clemmons at Wrangell, a fishing town of approximately 1,500 people located on the northern end of Wrangell Island. Bob Bain had been right. I now had a permanent job in Alaska.

I flew from Juneau to Wrangell with Ellis Airlines, one of the two airlines that served the smaller communities in Southeast Alaska with amphibious aircraft. Only four passengers were on the flight, and the pilot invited me to sit in the copilot seat, where I had an excellent view of the horizon. We passed over a multitude of islands, bays, and inlets. Solid old-growth rain forests covered the lowlands, and to my left I could see numerous glaciers and snowfields that lay along the Alaska-Canada border. In Frederick Sound the pilot pointed out Petersburg, which lay within my new enforcement district. We passed over the massive Stikine River delta, and then the plane circled over Wrangell.

Monte met me as I stepped off the plane. He was a fairly tall, lean, neatly dressed man. He took me to the FWS office. Standing in front of a large wall map of Southeast Alaska, he pointed out the boundaries of the Wrangell Enforcement District.

In 1952 there were four enforcement districts in Southeast Alaska, headquartered in Juneau, Sitka, Wrangell, and Ketchikan. Agents enforced game regulations during the fall and winter months and commercial fishery laws during the summer. The Wrangell district covered the geographic area from Bradfield Canal along the mainland coast to Cape Fanshaw, the northern portions of Prince of Wales and Etolin Islands, north to Frederick Sound, and west to Chatham Strait. It included

This small boat served as my living quarters while I patrolled the Stikine River flats.

all of Kupreanof, Kuiu, Mitkof, Wrangell, and Zarembo Islands and numerous smaller islands, bays, channels, and inlets. Monte said it would take several weeks of travel in a patrol boat for the two of us to cover the entire district.

He enthusiastically told me about his favorite part of the district, the Stikine River north of town. It had a large moose population, and the delta marshes attracted large numbers of waterfowl. "Do you like to hunt ducks?" he asked.

"Boy, I sure do," I answered. "I like to hunt about anything."

He smiled. "Well, you'll get your chance. We get a large migration of ducks and geese that stop on the Stikine marshes each fall."

By the time I had spent an hour with Monte, I was convinced I had landed one of the best jobs in Alaska.

I was in Wrangell less than a week when Monte sent me to the Stikine flats to patrol the waterfowl season. The flats were indented with numerous tidal sloughs and covered with grasses, sedges, and other plants favored by ducks, cranes, geese, and shorebirds. Waterfowl used the delta marshes as a major stopover while migrating to and from their northern nesting grounds. The multitude of birds created a favorite hunting area for residents of Southeast Alaska.

For waterfowl enforcement work I used a small boat with a covered cabin that contained a cookstove and a bunk. I anchored the craft in one of the deep sloughs, and it served as my living quarters while I patrolled the flats on foot. Weekends

The young game warden Troyer disguised as a duck hunter.

usually brought out a few hunting parties, and I checked their licenses and bag limits. Sometimes I would not see a hunter for days, but I wandered the marshes, learning the lay of the land and the favorite hangouts of ducks and geese.

As enforcement officers, we did not wear uniforms. Monte encouraged me to hunt while on foot patrol, which also helped to disguise my presence as a warden. I took advantage of this situation and killed my share of ducks and geese.

I issued a few warnings to hunters who opened the season a few minutes early, but I can remember making only one arrest that first fall. It turned out to be a bit humorous. I received a tip one weekend that a group of hunters using the Gucker cabin on the west end of the flats did not plan to pay much attention to bag limits. As I hunted and worked my way into their midst, I started checking their bags of waterfowl. I found that a hunter by the name of Pete had an extra duck in his possession. I wrote him a ticket, took his ducks, and ordered him to report to Magistrate Joel Wing in Wrangell. Pete received a small fine and returned to his home in Juneau.

The arrest received some added publicity because Pete was part owner of a large marine hardware store in Juneau and did a lot of business with the FWS. When word of his arrest got out, poor Pete took quite a ribbing from the FWS personnel. Juneau hunters learned to watch out for the young game warden disguised as a hunter on the Stikine flats.

Several weekends later, while I was checking the bag limits of a group of hunters, one man asked, "Hey, are you the guy who arrested Pete with an extra duck?" When I confessed to being that culprit, he chuckled. "Well, he had it coming. He has always bragged about getting more than his share of ducks."

Most of my hunting consisted of walking along the edge of tidal sloughs or ponds and jump-shooting ducks. I rarely missed, and I began to consider myself a good duck shot. My ego was about to be deflated.

In October Monte assigned me to work with Doyle Cissney, checking deer and waterfowl hunters in the numerous bays near Petersburg. Doyle was a predator control agent, but he had been sent to assist in game patrols that fall. It was common in those days for field agents to operate a patrol vessel, and Doyle was skipper of the FWS *Black Bear*. When I boarded the boat with my shotgun and small pack, Doyle asked if I had brought plenty of shells. I told him I had one box. He raised his eyebrows, but did not say anything. Since I was going to be on the trip for only ten days and there was a possession limit of ten ducks, I figured a box of twenty-five shells would be plenty.

Our first stop was Whale Pass. Doyle liked to pass-shoot birds as they flew through a narrow gut. We anchored the *Black Bear*, went ashore, and hid behind some rocks. Pintails and mallards flew through on a regular basis, and I estimated some were going sixty miles per hour with the strong tailwind. I raised my shotgun when the first flock approached, but they zipped past me before I could pull the trigger. I heard Doyle shoot, but nothing fell. In a few minutes four more pintails flew directly over me; I got off two shots without touching a feather. I then emptied my gun at a flock of mallards, and a few minutes later I fired two useless shots at a single. I missed thirteen ducks in a row! I had no idea how far to lead these fast flyers. In frustration I pulled at least six feet ahead of the next duck and when I shot, it folded. I now knew I was shooting far behind these speedy ducks, but even with this knowledge I continued to miss. I got only three ducks with that entire box of shells!

Doyle ribbed me a little when we got back to the boat and handed me two more boxes of shells. "Here, take these. I think you'll need them before the end of the trip!" He then told me, "You got to lead ducks with a tailwind a long ways. They're moving a lot faster than you think."

I took his advice and got a little better at pass-shooting ducks, but I decided I was not an expert duck shot after all.

Doyle also taught me the fundamentals of towing a skiff. The deck of the *Black Bear* was not large enough to carry ours, so we towed it behind the boat. One day, before entering Sumner Strait, he asked me to check the skiff. The small boat was sheering a bit, so I let out a little more rope and retied the line. Apparently I did not fasten it properly.

We got into heavy seas and I became seasick. I was thinking of lying down when Doyle discovered the skiff was missing. He immediately turned the *Black Bear* around. As it turned, the boat rolled violently, and for a moment I feared the vessel would capsize. We scanned the rough seas for twenty minutes before sighting the skiff bobbing on a high wave.

"I'll pass the skiff, turn around, and swing alongside," Doyle told me. "When I do, you go to the back of the boat and try to lasso it."

In my sickened state I had no desire to snag a boat in those pitching seas. The *Black Bear* again keeled far over when Doyle turned it around. That was too much for me; I leaned over a rail and upchucked. I recovered slightly, grabbed a rope, and stood on the stern of the boat. Like a sea cowboy, I tossed the lasso toward the stray boat several times, but I kept missing the cleat. I was ready to give up, but Doyle leaned out the window and yelled, "Try again!"

I was so sick I did not care if I fell overboard. Anything to escape my misery would have been a welcome relief. But the next time Doyle maneuvered the *Black Bear* near the skiff I steeled myself and threw the rope. Success! The lasso landed neatly around the cleat. I tied it temporarily to the back of the boat, grabbed a long-handled hook, and snagged the tow rope. After I secured the line properly, I climbed inside the *Black Bear*'s cabin and collapsed on my bunk. I rested a few minutes before continuing to the wheelhouse.

"You don't look too good," Doyle remarked.

I did not answer. The pallor of my face told the story. Doyle did not make any greenhorn jokes. He knew I had learned a lesson.

Doyle piloted the *Black Bear* across the strait and into a small, calm bay. We anchored and waited for the storm to subside. As bad as that experience was for me, it turned out well. I never got seasick again!

We continued going from bay to bay checking deer and waterfowl hunters. At times we did not see anyone for several days. We did arrest one hunter for shooting a doe, the most common deer-hunting violation. It was another learning experience for me.

We entered a small bay on Prince of Wales Island and found a small fishing boat anchored at the head of the bay. Doyle circled the boat with the Black Bear. Two hunters came out on deck to acknowledge us. Doyle waved a greeting and then said to me, "Those guys sure look suspicious to me."

I had no idea why he suspected them. After we anchored, Doyle said, "Come on, let's pay them a visit."

We boarded the boat, and they invited us in for a cup of coffee. They informed us they had been hunting deer but had not seen anything. Doyle asked, "Mind if we look around?"

We checked their skiff and the hold, but we failed to find anything. When we returned to the galley, Doyle started accusing them of shooting an illegal deer, which they vehemently denied. I was amazed at Doyle's sudden charges and a little embarrassed because they both seemed innocent to me. He relentlessly kept up the questioning. I was convinced they were innocent and Doyle was out of line; he did not have any evidence that they were guilty. They continued to deny any wrongdoing.

The interrogation went on for an hour. I was beginning to feel sorry for the old man whom Doyle was accusing. After a long silence Doyle suddenly asked him, "What's that blood doing on your arm?" He pointed to the guy's wrist.

The old man's face turned red, and he immediately confessed. "Yes," he said. "I shot a doe this morning and left it in the woods." He went on to say he needed meat for his family. He could not find a buck, so he shot the doe and planned to wait until dark to get the deer and take it home.

Doyle later told me he had seen a couple of fresh deer hairs on the railing when we boarded the boat. He also spotted blood on the man's sleeve when he served us that first cup of coffee. I had missed all the clues and thought he was innocent. Obviously, I had a lot to learn in becoming a game warden.

I did not spend much time in Wrangell that fall and winter. A fire had burned part of the business district the previous year, destroying the town theater and a few other businesses. Few single ladies lived in town, so there was not much social life for me. I therefore spent most of my time in the field.

The fur-trapping season occurred during the month of December, and we enforcement officers spent the middle of the winter on fur patrols. Fishermen trapped mink to supplement their income. In a good fur year they could earn an additional $1,000 or more—a good chunk of change in 1952. Each trapper claimed a section of beach to trap each year. We patrolled the area to make sure nobody trapped before or after the season. Most trappers were happy to see us around because a few outlaws always tried to get out early and swipe mink from someone else's grounds.

By my second year I felt I had quite a bit of Alaska outdoor experience under my belt, and I became confident navigating in the wilds. But a fall hunting trip reminded me that I was still a novice. I was on deer patrol with Thurston Orcutt, skipper of the *Harlequin*, the department's newly acquired fifty-foot patrol vessel. Thurston anchored the boat near Woewodski Island in Duncan Canal. Sig Olson,

In the 1950s, Wrangell was mainly a commercial fishing town.

the deer biologist for Southeast Alaska, had come on patrol with us, as he often did. Sig and I decided to make a short hunt on the small island that afternoon.

Thurston took us ashore in the skiff, and we followed a Forest Service trail to a small lake. We decided to hunt up a ridge to the top of the island. Sig and I got separated, so I continued on alone. I worked my way through the dense forest, but I did not see much deer sign until I got to the top. Many deer trails, several marked with fresh tracks, crisscrossed the muskegs that dotted the ridge. I sneaked along the muskeg edges but failed to see any deer. In the deepening dusk I knew I should be heading down, but I hated to give up. Ten minutes later a doe ran across an open muskeg with a buck in hot pursuit. The rutting season had begun, and the buck had sex on his mind. The doe stopped about sixty yards away from me, and the buck mounted her. I spoiled the romantic moment by raising my rifle and shooting the buck.

I had just taken my first deer in Alaska, a nice forked horn. I was excited! I dressed the animal quickly and made a gambrel pack by slipping each front leg through a slit I cut near the knee joint of each back leg. I hoisted the deer on my back using the joined legs as backpack straps.

My excitement at getting the buck was dampened by the rapidly falling darkness. I thought I could still make it to the lake and then follow the trail to the beach. I hurried on until I came to a stream. I unloaded the deer to look for a crossing point, but when I returned to where I thought I had put the deer, I could not find it. It was just too dark to continue the search. I did not want to lose the deer, so my only alternative was to spend the night in the woods and wait for daylight. Since this hunt was to have been a short one, I had no tent or sleeping bag. Already I was not looking forward to the night when rain began to fall and I discovered I had no matches.

I spent the night huddled next to a large spruce tree. When I periodically got cold, I walked around the tree to get warm. I kept up this routine all night. I thought about the nice warm bunk on the boat as I huddled under my raincoat. I wondered what Thurston and Sig were thinking when I did not show up. I vowed numerous times during the night that I would never get caught out in the dark again. At about seven in the morning, with enough daylight, I found the deer lying within forty feet of the tree. I was disgusted that I was so close and had not been able to find it. I loaded it on my back and continued down the ridge. I anticipated reaching the lake in less than an hour, but after an hour and a half of walking I had to admit I was lost. Discouraged, I consoled myself with the thought that I was on a small island; if I continued downhill, I would eventually hit a beach. A little while later I got below the fog line and saw salt water in the distance. It was a lovely sight. I now realized I had descended the wrong side of the ridge after I killed the deer. A half hour later I got to the beach and laid the deer on a log. I knew once I found the *Harlequin*, I could use the skiff to retrieve it. About an hour later I spotted the *Harlequin* at anchor. I fired several shots into the air, and eventually Thurston picked me up.

Sig and Thurston had been up most of the night looking for me. Sig had walked the trail to the lake where he had last seen me without finding any fresh tracks. He was worried something serious had happened to me, so he took the skiff back to Petersburg to organize a search party. Thurston radioed him that I was okay before the search got underway. Sig returned a few hours later. Boy, did I get razzed about getting lost on such a small island! I was embarrassed but took the ribbing. I never again went into the woods without a compass and matches.

Soon after I arrived in Wrangell, I became friends with Lee Ellis, a skilled woodsman. Some years before, Lee had spent the spring months trapping beaver on the Stikine River. He and some Canadians, who trapped farther up the Stikine and Iskut Rivers, gathered at the Canada-U.S. boundary each spring after the beaver season to wait for the river ice to go out. While they waited, they socialized, told stories of their winter experiences, and sipped a little whiskey. The gathering, known as the spring rendezvous, was a big social event for the trappers, who spent lonely winters in their remote cabins. When the ice broke, they floated to Wrangell in boats they had stashed at the boundary the previous fall and sold their catch.

Surveying the Stikine River from a mountaintop.

Lee later moved to Wrangell and became involved in guiding, commercial fishing, and trapping. During my second year in Wrangell he talked Senator Doris Barnes into getting a bill through the territorial legislature to fund additional predator control work in the Wrangell area. Of course Lee got the job that the bill created. That winter Monte asked me to make several trips with Lee to help him check his bait stations around the islands.

Predator control work, conducted by Lee and FWS personnel, was popular with the public in the 1950s. Most people felt that the more wolves killed using predator control measures, the more deer would be available for hunters. The most common method of taking wolves in Southeast Alaska was to poison them. The predator men first shot seals, also considered a predator, and skinned the animals. They then cut the heavy layer of blubber into one-inch squares and inserted a strychnine pill into each piece of fat. The bait was placed in strategic locations that wolves frequented. In addition to putting out strychnine bait Lee set out "coyote getters." These poison traps had bait fastened to the top of a small pipe containing an explosive. When an animal took the bait, the getter detonated the charge and shot cyanide into the animal's mouth. Getters killed a lot of coyotes and wolves, but wolverines also took the bait. I remember one weekend trip with Lee when we found seven dead wolves and two wolverines. Back then most people considered wolverines a nuisance, not a beautiful member of the weasel

Lee Ellis puts on his Native-made snowshoes.

family. I did not like poisoning wolves and wolverines, but I did enjoy being out with Lee. He was a good woodsman, and I learned many skills.

During another winter I helped Lee conduct a moose census on the Stikine River. We stayed at various cabins on the river and circled the area on snowshoes, counting moose tracks to determine population numbers. I was twenty-seven years old and in pretty good physical shape; Lee was in his late forties. I considered him to be an old man, but he snowshoed circles around me from the beginning. I did not understand how he did it until I lifted his snowshoes that first evening. They were light as a feather compared to my heavy commercial trail shoes. He told me that the Tahltan Indians, who lived farther up the river, made the light snowshoes. The frames were made of willow, and tanned moose-hide strips formed the webbing. I ordered a pair that winter and found I could move a lot faster on these handcrafted shoes. They now grace a wall in my log home.

My job as a game warden in Wrangell was varied, and I enjoyed it immensely. I spent most of my time in the field observing wildlife, checking hunters, and hunting during the appropriate seasons. The job was leisurely and gratifying. I was gradually learning new outdoor skills as well.

Chapter 5

Fish Cop

Commercial fishing dominated the Southeast Alaska economy in the early 1950s. Pristine old-growth forests reigned supreme throughout the region, but logging was limited. The Ketchikan Pulp Mill was still under construction. Shrimp, black cod, and halibut were sought-after species, but most commercial fishermen were after salmon.

Salmon fishing seasons were short and extremely competitive. Each boat crew was under a lot of pressure to get its share of the harvest and bring home adequate cash income.

Enforcement officers also felt unrelenting pressure. We were expected to be in the field day after day during the commercial salmon season with little rest or sleep. Gone were the leisurely days of hunting and fishing that we enjoyed during the fall and winter game patrols. Most of the salmon fishing seasons occurred from May through August; I was always glad when they were over so that I could relax again.

Fishermen used several different methods to catch fish. The Wrangell district had trolling, gill net, and purse seine fleets. Fish traps, owned mostly by the big canneries, were also scattered throughout the region.

Trollers were a rather independent group who fished for king and silver salmon. Trolling consists of dragging lures behind a boat and reeling in the fish as they strike. Trollers gave us few problems; their gear was not designed for creek robbing. They had long seasons and extensive fishing areas; they had, therefore, few incentives to break the law. Trolling vessels were usually operated by a single owner

The FWS Harlequin, *a fifty-foot vessel, was used for fish and game patrols in the Wrangell district.*

or by a husband-and-wife team. Many lived on the boats all year and did not own a home in town. They often invited me aboard for coffee.

The drift gill net fleet was confined to the waters near the delta of the Stikine River. Most gillnetters operated their own small vessels and lived in Wrangell or Petersburg when not fishing. The nets were made of mesh of a designated size to gill and hold a particular-sized fish when they swam into the net. Periodically the nets were reeled in and the fish picked. A few gillnetters violated laws by fishing during closed periods or in closed waters.

Purse seiners operated larger vessels with crews of five to seven people. When the crew sighted a large school of fish, they encircled it quickly with the net. They gradually closed the seine and eventually brought the fish alongside the vessel, where they brailed the catch aboard the boat. The purse seiners moved rapidly from area to area as fish runs developed. When the fishing was good, they made some large hauls—which meant good money.

Most seiners were law abiding, but Wrangell had its share of outlaws who constantly tried to outsmart us fish cops and swipe a few fish. Every salmon stream had a closed area near the mouth, where salmon formed schools before migrating upstream to spawn. Closed areas full of fish were a temptation, especially when no law enforcement people were around. Habitual creek robbers often painted their boats a dark color to conceal their night operations. Some worked in pairs or groups, with one vessel stationed at the entrance to a bay watching for fish cops while others were inside scooping up illegal fish. One group even used a small plane. The pilot located fish and kept track of our patrol boats and planes.

I used a small sixteen-foot skiff to zip in and out of bays while on fish and game patrols.

Fortunately, we were not completely alone in our efforts to catch the outlaws. Law-abiding seiners often tipped us off to illegal activities.

Fish traps were stationary. The operators were not allowed to fish them on weekends. It was our duty to see that the gates were sealed during weekend closures.

To enforce the fishing regulations in the Wrangell district, we had between twelve and fifteen stream guards, a large patrol vessel, and the occasional use of a patrol plane. The stream guards were stationed at the mouth of salmon streams to keep fishermen honest. We rotated the guards from one stream to another to protect the most productive fish runs. We used the fifty-foot *Harlequin* to patrol the waters throughout the district. Thurston Orcutt, the boat's young skipper, and I spent most of the fishing season aboard the vessel. My responsibilities included checking the stream guards periodically, keeping them supplied with groceries, and moving them from stream to stream as the salmon runs progressed. My boss, Monte Clemmons, spent most of his time in Wrangell supervising the entire operation and flying patrols. The FWS had a twin-engine plane in Ketchikan that was dispatched to the Wrangell district when needed.

We towed a sixteen-foot skiff with a twenty-five horsepower motor behind the *Harlequin*. The skiff was capable of speeds up to twenty-two miles per hour. I used this fast craft to zip in and out of bays and inlets to check fishermen. The *Harlequin* was capable of doing ten knots (nearly twelve miles per hour), and we roamed far and wide throughout the district. We kept in radio contact with Monte in Wrangell and used code numbers to represent geographic locations. This served to keep him informed of our location and progress and to keep our

Wrangell in 1954.

movements secret to outlaw fishermen. Monte, in turn, suggested where we should concentrate our efforts. The *Harlequin* had good living facilities, and Thurston and I frequently remained on patrol for several weeks at a time. We were constantly on the move, often operated at night, and got little sleep or rest during the peak fishing season.

Night operations were sometimes dangerous, as it was difficult to see logs, rocks, and other obstacles. The *Harlequin* was equipped with a compass, but no Fathometer or radar. One night at about two in the morning we were approaching Wrangell. The city and harbor lights were aglow, and we were anxious to get home. But it was extremely dark, and gillnetters were everywhere. They maintained night lights on their vessels and on the ends of the gill nets. Thurston had the engine throttled back and was maneuvering the *Harlequin* around the maze of gill nets when...grrrummp, we hit one. Before Thurston could stop the engine, the net had wrapped around the *Harlequin*'s propeller. The light on the end of the net had failed. We had not only ruined a fish net, but we had to radio for help and be towed into town. It took four frustrating hours to get to Wrangell. Later, the fisherman was compensated for the accident.

We spent most of that day getting the net out of the prop, refueling, and taking on more supplies. Early the following morning we left on another patrol. Neither our boss nor the honest fishermen wanted to see our patrol vessel in town at the height of the fishing season. We were under continual pressure to stay in the field. I was single, but Thurston had a family; he did not see much of them in the summer.

In addition to the pressure to stay out in the field as much as possible, I was under constant stress to learn the tricks of the job. Early in my enforcement career I decided to make a night skiff patrol to nearby Berg Bay. Monte had reported large schools of fish at the head of the bay, which was about twenty miles from Wrangell. I left town after dark, and in an hour I had reached Berg Bay. I stopped at a rocky reef and waited quietly. At about eleven o'clock I heard several fishing boats coming up the channel from Bradfield Canal. High tide would be near midnight, and I was convinced they were coming to rob the creek. I waited nervously. The air was still, and I could hear the boats moving into the bay. They were running without lights, and in about thirty minutes they stopped near the head of the bay. I heard a loud noise and assumed it was a net going into the water. I waited ten minutes and then jumped into the skiff, started the engine, and roared up the bay. I pulled alongside the nearest vessel, cut my engine, and jumped aboard. Several people were standing on deck and knew what I was look-ing for. But...no nets in the water! I realized my mistake; I had heard the anchor drop—not a net. I was embarrassed, but I did not want to show my error. "Just checking to make sure you guys are legal," I remarked.

"Well, for your information, we just moved up here to get an early start in the morning," the skipper replied, rather sarcastically. "By the way, it might not be healthy running around at night and jumping onto boats in the dark!"

I knew this was no idle threat. Some outlaw fishermen had criminal records and would no doubt harm fish cops if they thought they could get away with it. A few years after I left Wrangell, a stream guard mysteriously disappeared. His body was never found. The FBI strongly suspected one of the outlaw boats, but they never gathered enough evidence to convict the culprits. The disappearance was never solved.

I got back in the skiff and pulled into Wrangell at two in the morning, tired and disappointed. I crawled into bed as quickly as I could. We were scheduled to leave for another patrol at seven.

Despite many missed opportunities, we apprehended several seiners robbing creeks, but they were usually small vessels with poor equipment that obviously had not made a good catch in several seasons. I felt pity for them rather than disdain. I wanted to catch the illegal operators with the big boats and airplanes. Due to their organized methods and sophisticated equipment, however, we were rarely lucky enough to make an arrest. I felt like a small-town cop up against the Mafia, incapable of breaking up the illegal activities.

We also had to deal with Washington, D.C., politics that often resulted in bad fishery management decisions. One year, late in the season, we realized that many of the streams were not going to get an adequate escapement of fish to their spawning grounds. Monte and I recommended an early season closure. Dick Myron, the fishery management agent at Ketchikan, agreed with this plan, as did the regional fishery personnel in Juneau. When the big cannery operators heard about our proposal, they called their political pals in Washington. Our recommendations were rejected. Once again we were the little guys in the field getting dismissed by the powerful Washington lobby. It was discouraging. Most fishermen felt the same way we did, and they pressured the U.S. government to cede control of commercial fishing to the Territory of Alaska. Gaining local control of commercial fishing management was eventually one of the major factors that brought statehood to Alaska.

We were often undermanned and underequipped to handle certain enforcement situations. One weekend during my second summer in Wrangell, Monte sent me to Anan Creek, near Bradfield Canal, to oversee the season opening. Anan had a pink salmon run that reached large numbers every other year. Fishermen had taken over a million fish during the previous peak and were expecting another bumper harvest. The season opened at 6:00 a.m. on a Monday. I left Wrangell in a skiff before four o'clock and arrived near Anan at five-thirty. I could hardly believe the number of seiners that were waiting to fish. I estimated that a hundred or more boats were lined up along the bluffs or were maneuvering to get into position for the six o'clock opening. A few were still getting their gear ready. Numerous salmon were jumping, indicating that thousands of fish were present near the bluffs. It reminded me of crowds waiting for a circus parade.

Several fishermen stopped me and requested that I fire a shot to announce the opening so that everyone could let their nets go at the same time. I agreed and ran back and forth in front of the vessels to keep everyone legal. Alone in the skiff, I felt quite small and overwhelmed, trying to keep an eye on all those anxious fishermen. By 5:45 a.m. all were just itching to release their nets. The tensions were mounting, and I hoped no one would try to jump the gun. Some of the fishermen's nerves may have been tight, but mine were tighter. At 5:55 I saw a boat release its net. All eyes were on me, watching my reaction. I immediately roared up to the seiner in my small skiff and yelled at him to stop. I threatened him with arrest unless he pulled in his seine. The skipper cursed but began retrieving the net. I pulled out in front of the boats again. It was 5:59, and I immediately fired the rifle. The boats on either side of the one that had tried to jump the season let their nets go and cut in front of him. It was exactly what I hoped would happen. I could tell the fishermen that I stopped were angry, with one member shaking his fist, but several of the men on the other vessels waved at me and grinned, indicating their approval of how I had handled the situation. I whooped and raised my arms in celebration. I roared past the fishermen at full throttle and felt a big sense of relief as I sped back to Wrangell.

I worked as a fish cop for only three summers in Southeast Alaska, but they were three long summers—weeks and weeks of long days in the field, working under a lot of pressure. I was always glad when the commercial fishing season ended so I could get back to the more relaxed fall and winter game patrols. I usually celebrated the end of the salmon season with a physically demanding deer hunt in the high country. It served to relieve my stress and anxieties.

Chapter 6

Adventures with Goats

The mountain goats of Southeast Alaska are true wilderness animals. They thrive in remote mountain peaks characterized by precipitous slopes. They are sure-footed and adept at scrambling along sheer cliffs and leaping from ledge to ledge where few animals, including man, dare to follow.

I had read that mountain goats were the most difficult large animals in North America to meet on their own turf. This challenged me to want to do just that. Not long after I arrived in Southeast Alaska, I spotted a group of white goats standing like sentinels on a high peak above Horn Cliffs, near Petersburg. As I watched the majestic animals, I laid plans to meet them face to face in their lofty environment.

A few weeks later I took a skiff across Dry Straits to the bottom of the cliffs, drifted in the sea water, and gazed upward through rocks and ledges until I had selected a route that led to the goats. I anchored my boat and started the climb.

I carried a light daypack with only a camera, a telephoto lens, and a few sandwiches so I could move rapidly. The route followed a ravine for the first thousand feet, but it ended at the bottom of a cliff. I was disappointed when I reached this barrier that I could not scale. I paralleled the rock wall for a hundred yards, and when I found another opening, my spirits soared. The hiking was steep and strenuous, but in a few hours I was two or three thousand feet above the ocean. I studied the precarious slope I had climbed and got a sick feeling in the pit of my stomach. I realized I would eventually have to find my way down that tricky slope. I put these negative thoughts out of my mind and trudged upward.

After climbing another twenty minutes, I reached a ridge that I thought was nearly level with the goats, so I followed it. I pulled myself up over a high rock. When I peeked over the top, I was elated to spot a group of twelve goats: a mixture of nannies, kids, and a few yearlings. They were bedded down chewing their cud, as serene as a herd of cattle in a pasture. I cautiously raised my head higher to get a better look. An open meadow separated us and prevented me from approaching any closer without spooking the animals. It would be a long shot for the 200 mm lens, but I rested the camera on a rock and took a few photos. They were not the close-ups I had hoped for, but they were worth recording nevertheless.

I watched the goats for thirty minutes, hoping a few would rise and start feeding toward me, but it did not happen. I waited another twenty minutes, and then I impatiently began to inch toward them. A watchful nanny spotted me and jumped to her feet. That set off a chain reaction until the entire group stood and stared in my direction. "Oh no," I told myself. "You have ruined your chances." But there was no time for regrets. I snapped a few more photos before they turned and disappeared over a rise. I ran across the meadow just in time to see them cross a high snowfield. Following them on that slippery slope was impossible.

"You should have been more patient," I scolded myself.

Dejected, I turned to start back, but then a lone goat emerged on a ledge several hundred feet below me and moved slowly behind a rock wall. My hopes rose for getting some close-up photos. I descended quickly to the ledge and followed it around a cliff just in time to see the animal leap across a small four-foot gap. The wide ledge I was following narrowed to two feet just before the breach. It was considerably wider on the other side, however, so I jumped across. I assumed I had the goat cornered, but as I rounded another curve, the nimble animal sprang from the ledge and scrambled down a very steep mountainside. A slip on that sheer slope would result in a two-hundred-foot fall. I finally admitted defeat and turned to retrace my steps.

I now saw that I had to jump across the four-foot gap and land on the narrow two-foot ledge. There was no room for error. If I did not land exactly right, I would fall at least sixty feet. I was fearful and sat down for a few minutes to calm my nerves. I then stood up, removed my pack, held it in my right hand, and before I could have second thoughts, I leaped!

When my feet hit solidly on the other side, I moved rapidly off the narrow ledge and then sat down again to compose myself. I knew I had narrowly avoided disaster and vowed to never again get myself into such a predicament. While I was resting, I studied the landscape below and discovered a return route to the

I had some narrow escapes while trying to photograph or hunt mountain goats.

ocean that was much safer than the one I had ascended. I relaxed, and within an hour I was safely back at the skiff.

My second encounter with goats came later that fall. I was staying in a cabin on the Stikine River near the British Columbia border with two friends who were hunting moose. I wanted a mountain goat for my freezer and glassed the mountains for a likely prospect. On the second day I spotted a group in an alpine meadow above the cabin. It looked like an easy one-day hunt, and I decided to try the following day. I learned the hard way that hunting goats can be just as difficult as trying to photograph them.

I packed a few sandwiches, a hunting knife, a rifle, and a pair of binoculars and left camp the next morning before the sun rose over the mountains. I informed the moose hunters at camp that I would be back before dark. They had their doubts but wished me luck.

I followed a cascading stream that led steadily upward through a forest of spruce and alder. It was a gradual climb, and in a few hours I reached timberline and peered down at the cabin, which was now a mere speck on the river. I realized I had misjudged the distance to the goats. They were still a long way off and moving away from me. I watched them disappear behind a mountain. I hurried on, thinking it was still feasible to find them, complete the hunt, and return to the cabin before dark.

After another hour of hiking I reached the mountain where I had last spotted the goats, but they were gone. I climbed several more peaks and scanned the vast terrain without success. They had simply vanished. It was nearly midafternoon, and I was ready to give up. Discouraged, I started back by walking around a small mountain. There they were, resting peacefully on an open green slope, unaware that a predator was nearby. Most of them were relaxed and chewing cud. I debated about whether it was too late to shoot one and still pack it out before dark. Temptation overcame good judgment. I carefully glassed the animals and selected one. Slipping my rifle onto a rock, I aimed carefully and shot a medium-sized male. The rest jumped up and disappeared around the mountain. The billy was a beautiful specimen, and in many ways I hated to end its life. At the same time I was euphoric at my success. I wanted the supply of meat and the challenge of taking a goat in such difficult terrain.

The dead goat was much larger than I had estimated. I skinned it out carefully and split it into two separate packs. The 150 pounds of meat was too heavy to carry down the steep slope all at once. I packed it down the mountain by first carrying one load about three hundred yards and then returning for the other. I rested often and enjoyed the mountain vistas of snowcapped peaks and the winding Stikine River valley far below. It was immense, wild country.

The light faded fast after sunset, and I became aware I could not make it to the cabin before dark. I did not relish spending the night on the mountain without a tent and sleeping bag, but I set my mind to accept the inevitable. The numerous snowfields reflected enough light so I could see to walk, but with the heavy pack I had to move slowly over the rocky terrain. The exciting hunt now became drudgery; I was determined to finish the task, however. I was out of food, so I stopped several times to eat the abundant blueberries that grew along the route.

At about two in the morning it started to drizzle, and visibility became limited. I moved slowly with my heavy pack, carefully putting one foot in front of the other. Some hours later I reached the dark timberline; I could go no farther until daylight. I drew a light rain parka around myself and rested next to the goat meat. The rain and sweat had soaked my clothes, and I became chilly. I walked around in circles to increase my circulation and body heat. I longed for the cabin far below and thought about the big meal I would eat when I arrived. I kept up the routine of resting and moving in circles. After another two hours, it became light enough to follow the route down through the spruce forest. I stashed half of the meat near a huge boulder and started down with the rest. It was tough going with the heavy pack, and I moved slowly down the steep terrain. I spotted the cabin far below and knew each step was one closer to my destination. I made it to camp at about ten in the morning, twenty-seven hours after starting the hunting adventure.

I dropped the pack near the door. My two friends in camp were relieved to see me; they had been in the process of planning a search. A big pot of moose stew simmered on the stove. We exchanged hunting stories while I gorged. After the meal, I crawled into my bunk and slept the clock around.

The next morning after a big breakfast, I informed my friends I was heading up the mountain to get the rest of the meat. "Are you crazy?" one of them asked in disbelief. "The bears have found the meat by now and made short work of it. Don't waste your time."

But I was adamant about not wasting meat and determined to make an effort to salvage it. I followed the same route up along the mountain stream in a drizzling rain and arrived at timberline in two hours. The meat was undisturbed. I took a short rest, loaded my pack, and returned to the cabin in record time. Needless to say, I had no desire to hunt goats for a while, as it took me several days to recuperate from my marathon hunt. I was, however, gratified at challenging the goats again; this time I would enjoy some delicious goat steaks as compensation for my efforts.

My next mountain goat adventure was another photographic safari. It was a near disaster but ended humorously. I knew about a group of goats that stayed in the high mountains above Andrews Slough, a tributary of the Stikine. I wanted some 16 mm goat movies and waited for a suitable summer day. When one arrived, I took my skiff up the Stikine River and tied it to a spruce tree on the banks of the slough. I grabbed my pack and pushed through the alders to a long draw that led up the mountain; it was still filled with snow. The sun's rays sparkled like diamonds off the snowcapped peaks on this rare clear day in Southeast Alaska. I climbed the long, hard-packed slope by digging the toes of my boots into the firm snow for traction. Though a bit slippery, it beat fighting the alder brush and devil's club thickets that covered most of the slope. I made a rapid ascent and was soon in goat country.

I hiked around several mountain peaks and searched the slopes with my binoculars, but I failed to find the goats I had previously spotted. Like phantoms, they had simply vanished into the immense wilderness. I sat down to rest and ponder my next move.

The vistas themselves were rewarding. Several thousand feet below me the Stikine River wound like a giant serpent through a densely forested valley. Across the river, towering mountain peaks capped with snow thrust upward into clear blue skies. The alpine slopes were covered with a colorful array of wildflowers. I took a few photos, but I wanted goat pictures. After resting, I searched additional slopes in vain. Finally in midafternoon I gave up and headed down the mountain.

I again chose the snowy ravine for travel. The descent, however, was much faster than the climb had been. I whittled off a six-foot alder pole with my pocket knife to aid in going down. The snow was slick, but by sitting down, digging in my heels, and riding the alder stick, I managed to stay in control most of the time as I slid. It was a thrilling way to go down a mountain!

My braking heels threw tracers of snow into my face. I slid rapidly past the alders on the edge of the ravine. At times the pelting snow obscured my vision as I slid and spun down the precarious slick slope. Periodically I halted and took a brief rest before I shoved off again. Several times I caught myself saying, "Whew! That was a close one!"

As I approached the bottom in a particularly steep section, I lost control. My body spun in various directions, and I was unable to break my speed as I shot down the slope. At any moment I expected to crash into an alder, and I feared for my life. I fought to stop the desperate, fast slide. A few seconds later my pack slammed into several alder shrubs, but I ricocheted off. I dug my alder stick into the snow as hard as I could and managed to stop just before reaching a group of solid alders.

"Holy cow! You're going to kill yourself!" I thought.

I regretted my recklessness, but it had been fast and fun!

I had a few bruises on my legs but no serious injuries. I stood up shaking, knowing I had averted disaster by a hair. I soberly stepped off the snow and hiked the rest of the way to the skiff through alder and devil's club thickets.

The mosquitoes were atrocious near the water, and they attacked in swarms. My shirt became covered with the dark demons that bit unmercifully. In desperation I ripped off all my sweaty clothes, threw them and my pack into the skiff, and dove underwater. The cool water felt good and soothed the itchy bug bites, but every time I stuck my head above the water they attacked again. I was in a dilemma. How would I get dressed without trapping dozens of mosquitoes under my clothes? I pondered the problem a while, and then swam to the side of the skiff, jumped in, started the engine, and roared down the slough, naked as a jaybird! It may have looked rather odd, but it sure felt good.

I steered with one hand, batting and swatting mosquitoes with the other, until I lost most of the biting pests. About three hundred yards ahead I spotted a boat full of people coming up the slough; fortunately, the high alder thickets along the banks of the slough partially obscured their vision. I saw a narrow fork in the river that allowed me to veer to the right and disappear behind an island. I slowed down, quickly got dressed, and headed back to town.

Several days later, rumors spread around Wrangell that a crazy naked guy was seen boating on the Stikine River. I smiled to myself but kept my mouth shut, and my secret was never revealed.

During one of my last goat experiences I nearly lost an eye. Early in summer I again took my skiff across Dry Straits to Horn Cliffs, near Petersburg, to photograph the animals. I worked my way up through the spruce forest; near timberline I came to several stands of devil's club that had not yet leafed out. The spiny stems protruded through the snow, which still prevailed on a few shady slopes. I had climbed for nearly two hours to reach this high terrain. My legs were tired, and I became careless as I picked my way through the thorny devil's club. My foot slipped on the snow and I fell forward, my head smacking into the top of a spiny stem. A sharp pain shot through my right eye. I quickly placed a hand across the eyelid and felt for a thorn, but I found none. I forced my eyelid open and gently brushed my handkerchief across the eyeball. The pain continued, and I was unable to find the foreign object that was causing the excruciating pain. After carefully probing around my eyelid, I finally concluded that I probably had a very fine thorn in my eyeball, but I was unable to locate and extract it. I needed medical assistance, but I was all alone on a steep mountain slope far from any medical help. No one would look for me for at least a day.

I was unable to see clearly to follow the trail back to the skiff. My injured eye was the dominant one, and opening my left caused severe pain because it flexed the muscles of both eyes. I was in trouble and I knew it. In utter frustration I stood up and screamed, "Help!" The sound of my voice echoed off the mountaintops as if to mock my efforts.

Sweat soaked my shirt as I pondered my predicament. I sat down to compose my mind and spoke firmly to myself, "Troyer, get a hold on yourself. No one is going to look for you. The only way you're going to get off this mountain is by your own willpower."

After a few moments, calm and determination flowed through me. I clamped my hand over my right eye, squinted out of my left, and started slowly down the mountain. Every step I took was one closer to the skiff—my immediate goal. In several precarious places I had to crawl on my hands and knees, but I was making progress. I rested often and kept repeating to myself, "Come on, Troyer, you can do it."

Resting, slowly walking, and crawling, I gradually worked my way down the mountain. At least four hours passed before I reached the beach and spotted the skiff. I was now confident I would make it, though I still had to run back to Wrangell by boat. I knew the route well, but I had difficulty seeing the geographical features that guided me across the treacherous straits. It took me almost two hours to get to Wrangell. I tied the skiff to the FWS dock that contained my small wanigan home and found the telephone. I called some friends, and they rushed me to the hospital.

The local doctor diagnosed the problem as I lay on my back on the examining table. He spotted a tiny thorn stuck in my eyeball, and with a pair of fine tweezers he extracted it. I received immediate relief from the pain. The doctor was no eye specialist, but he thought that if I rested and kept a patch over my eye, it would heal in a few days. This I did, and on the fourth day, when the doctor reexamined me, he found I had lost part of the fluid in my eye.

"What does that mean?" I asked in alarm.

"I don't know, but I'd better get you to an eye specialist," he replied.

His comment really scared me. I was devastated just thinking about losing part of my vision. The only eye doctor in Southeast Alaska served many communities. By placing a few phone calls, my doctor located him in the small village of Klawock on the west side of Prince of Wales Island.

The next day I flew to the small medical clinic. After a thorough examination, the eye specialist concluded that the Wrangell physician had removed the thorn successfully but had made a mistake by letting me move around too soon. He informed me that I would have to stay on my back for at least three days and wear a patch over my eye for several weeks. He assured me, however, that my eye would heal and I would eventually regain my full vision. I was immensely relieved!

He requested that I remain in Klawock in the meantime so he could check the healing process. He told me that if the thorn had penetrated one layer deeper, I would have lost the sight in that eye. After a week the doctor released me from the clinic. I continued to wear the patch over my eye for several weeks and learned to judge distance with a single eye while driving. It took practice. My eye eventually healed, and the injury left no scar.

I admire mountain goats; I enjoyed the exhilarating highs I experienced when on their turf. These early episodes, however, taught me that recklessly pursuing them was dangerous. In the future I became more cautious when following these nimble creatures of the high cliffs.

Chapter 7

Sourdough Characters

In the 1950s many eccentrics led secluded lives in Southeast Alaska. The abundant forest provided a variety of trees and other materials for building log cabins and firewood for heating and cooking. Plentiful fish, shellfish, deer, and wild berries along with a small garden plot supplied most of the food these individuals required. They could obtain the modest amount of cash they needed to buy other essential items by trapping or doing a little commercial fishing.

I met many of these old-timers while on my rounds as a game warden. I enjoyed listening to them relate interesting episodes from their past. They were also knowledgeable about the wildlife in their area and often provided tips about any poaching activities. I therefore cultivated their friendship and visited them whenever I was in their vicinity.

Five old sourdoughs lived along the back channel between Wrangell and the head of Bradfield Canal. Commercial fishing friends delivered their mail during the summer, but few people traveled these waters in the winter. The local postmaster requested that we game wardens deliver their mail in the winter during our regular patrols.

The first character we would visit after leaving Wrangell was an ex-marshal, Earl West. He lived in a small cabin near the shore on the northeast side of Wrangell Island, and he was always delighted to see us drop anchor in front of his home. He invariably came out, waved, and shouted for us to come visit. The old marshal loved to talk. As soon as I handed him the mail, he would pour each of us a cup of coffee and start chattering nonstop. Occasionally, Earl would ask a question, but before any of us could answer, he would launch into another episode from his past, most of which I had heard before.

After the preliminaries were over, Earl would serve us glasses of home brew. It was terrible-tasting stuff, but we smacked our lips and pretended to like it. The ex-marshal would quickly down two or three glasses and then drag out several books of poetry he had written. He would begin reciting poems, and we pretended to enjoy each one; some were, in fact, quite clever and humorous. Once the effect of the home brew took over, the old sourdough began singing the poems. That was a bit too much, so we would find excuses to leave and continue our patrol. The partially inebriated marshal stood onshore and continued singing poetry as we pulled anchor and departed. Usually I would remember a few lines of Earl's poems and attempt to recite them. The others laughed at my poor impersonation as we continued down the channel.

The next old sourdough to whom we would bring mail was Albert in Berg Bay. He was a large man in his early seventies with a quiet demeanor. He had no front teeth, so he gummed his food and avoided anything too tough to chew. He lived in a simple ten-by-twelve-foot canvas tent. He kept saying he was going to build a cabin the next year, but he never did during my time in Wrangell. Albert would always invite us inside his crowded abode for coffee. A small stove at one end of the tent provided warmth and heat for cooking. A few cooking utensils and a limited supply of food were visible inside several Blazo boxes stacked near the stove. A low, narrow bed sat on one side of the tent, and the other side contained a neat stack of split wood. I am sure Albert had a few clothes and other items stashed under his bunk, but he seemed to have few personal belongings.

Albert, unlike most sourdoughs, was well informed on national and world affairs, gleaning news from a small battery-operated radio and from magazines supplied by fishermen friends. He often engaged me in conversations on these subjects. I enjoyed his viewpoints, especially since he was so far removed from the outside world.

Albert trapped a few furs for cash, but he never took an excess of wildlife resources. He talked enthusiastically about the deer, bear, otter, mink, and various birds that he had recently seen. It was obvious that Albert preferred watching wildlife to consuming them. In 1953 I purchased a wolverine skin from him for a few paltry dollars. I insisted on paying more, but he refused, saying that it was the price he would receive from a fur buyer. It is a beautiful pelt that still hangs on a wall in my house, reminding me of the kind old gentleman.

Our next mail stop was at the home of two Kentucky brothers, who lived on the north side of Bradfield Canal. They came to Alaska during World War I—some said to avoid the draft—and built a two-story cabin on the shores of the canal. Like the rest of the old-timers, they had a garden, gathered game and fish, and needed little else. Jack was dominant, and I have forgotten the name of his brother, but I will call him Jim. They loved to talk and tell stories. The longer we stayed, the more exaggerated the tales became.

"Yes sir, we have a big brown bear that comes around every week. He loves music, and when we turn on the Victrola, he stands on his hind legs and looks in our second-story window! Ain't that right, Jack?"

"Yep, that's right, Jim."

The more far-fetched the stories became, the more they called on each other to verify the exaggerated tales.

"Yeah, he sticks his head into our second-story window." This would have made the bear about sixteen feet tall, taller than any bear on record. "Then he sways to the music and starts to dance. Ain't that right, Jack?"

"Yep, that's right, Jim. We also have a black bear and a wolverine that are friends. The other day the black bear came walking down the beach with the wolverine riding on his back! Ain't that right, Jim?"

"Yep, that's right, Jack."

"And we have this black wolf that can talk to us…" The stories would continue unabated, each brother trying to outdo the other.

We would always pretend to believe the outlandish tales, but after departing we would laugh uproariously. It was good entertainment.

Not all the sourdoughs I met were part of our mail runs. Ham Island Slim (so named after an island that was once his home) lived a reclusive life in a remote cabin above the Bradfield Canal tidal flats. He tried to scare away strangers who came too close to him and frightened several people who accidentally stumbled onto his cabin while they were hunting brown bear in the area. He pulled a gun on Johnny Wendler, a friend of mine from Ketchikan, and threatened to shoot if he did not leave immediately. Johnny complained to the local marshal, but the marshal was reluctant to confront the eccentric isolationist.

I met Ham Island Slim through my friend Lee Ellis. Lee guided a few bear hunters in the upper Bradfield Canal drainage and always hired Slim as an assistant when hunting that area. Slim also trapped fur animals and came into Wrangell each spring to sell his catch and pick up a few supplies. He never lingered in town, immediately returning to his solitary life in the forest. Lee introduced me to Ham Island Slim the first spring I was in Wrangell. Slim had trapped a few beaver that winter, and in those days beaver were a major fur animal sought by trappers. The number of beaver taken by each trapper was closely regulated by the FWS. Each skin had to be sealed with a metal tag by FWS personnel before it could be sold to a fur buyer. Lee brought Slim to my office to seal his beaver; after that Ham Island Slim considered me a friend.

Slim once said to me, "I don't want to be bothered by people. I just want to live alone in peace." I could understand this attitude and sometimes envied the sourdough's lifestyle.

I never knew much about the old recluse until my last year in Wrangell, when he got into a fight with a prospector who roamed the region in search of minerals. The explorer spotted Slim's cabin from a mountaintop and decided to pay him a visit. Slim had some cash buried behind his cabin and became suspicious of the prospector, convinced the man was trying to steal his money. They got into a fight. Slim managed to get the best of the stranger and tie him up in chains. He came into Wrangell to tell the local marshal what had happened. Jack, the marshal, was leery of the situation and asked me, as a fellow law enforcement officer, to accompany him to the cabin. I agreed, but Ham Island Slim did not go with us; he stayed with Lee Ellis to await our report.

Jack and I left the next day. We followed Slim's directions, boating up the Bradfield River, past the tidal flats, and then turned left into a narrow, unmarked channel. We followed the waterway for another two hundred yards before spotting the cabin partially hidden in the dense forest. The cabin was built of large spruce logs; the door consisted of heavy planking, bristling with six-inch-long sharpened spikes—a common practice for discouraging bears. The prospector had gotten loose before we arrived, but he had remained at the cabin. He told us a story about the dispute that was completely different from Slim's account.

Jack finished his investigation late in the day, and we decided to spend the night. The cabin was well equipped and had two bunks. Slim had lined the walls with pictures of women in brassieres he had torn from Sears Roebuck catalogs. Apparently this was Slim's version of pinups. But what attracted my attention was a portrait of Ham Island Slim's family. He came from a large, well-dressed Swedish family. As I studied the portrait, I wondered why he had left his family, what brought him to such a remote spot, and what had turned him into such a recluse. I never found out, however, as he was very evasive about his past.

Eventually the marshal settled the dispute without arresting anyone, and Ham Island Slim returned to his secluded lifestyle. I left Wrangell that fall and never saw or heard from him again.

Normally I did not work with any of these old characters, but there was one exception. He was hired by Elmer Copstead, who replaced Monte Clemmons in 1954 as the enforcement agent at Wrangell. Elmer thought we should substitute some of the college kids we had hired as stream guards with as many locals as possible.

The *Harlequin* was tied up at the dock in the small village of Point Baker, near the waters we were patrolling. When I returned to the vessel from visiting friends and stepped aboard, I was hit by an extremely pungent odor. As I walked into the galley, Elmer rose from his chair, greeted me, and then said, "I want you to meet our new stream guard, Dirty Yantzee."

Sitting at the galley table was a small, filthy, unkempt man. His beady eyes peered out from behind a tangled mop of oily hair and a rat's nest of a beard.

"Howdy, Will," he said, rising to shake my hand. Then he erupted into a high-pitched screech of a laugh that I would have expected from an insane person. Shivers shot down my spine.

The mystery of the pungent odor was solved. Yantzee's greasy, dirty clothes had obviously never been washed. His hands and face looked dark and grimy from an accumulation of weeks, months, and maybe even years of filth. I found out later he relished being called Dirty Yantzee and lived up to the name by never bathing. Dirty Yantzee and his friend Dirty George competed for the reputation of being the dirtiest man in Alaska. At that moment Yantzee led the contest because Dirty George had fallen into the ocean four years earlier. According to Dirty Yantzee, that amounted to taking a bath even if Dirty George's body had never been grazed by a cake of soap.

Later I asked Elmer, "Are you sure you want to hire this guy?"

"Yes. He'll be self-sufficient and keep the fishermen honest!" Elmer said. I doubted his judgment but did not argue the point.

About ten days later Thurston Orcutt and I made our rounds in the *Harlequin*, checking on the stream guards. Dirty Yantzee was stationed near the entrance to Rocky Pass, adjacent to several good salmon streams. I grabbed a few groceries, jumped in the skiff, and motored through the shallow water to where his small craft was anchored. Yantzee sat on a beach log with a rifle in his lap. I pulled up to the boat and greeted him cordially. He did not reply, his beady eyes staring at me through that mop of hair.

"I could have stopped you way out there!" he finally said in his high-pitched but matter-of-fact voice.

I was sure he did not recognize me, so I introduced myself again and asked if he needed any groceries. Yantzee then erupted in screechy laughter before stating he could use a little coffee and tea. He then invited me to his camp. He had no tent or cookstove, choosing to pitch his gear in a small cave just above the high-tide line and to cook over an open fire. I had to stoop to enter his cave. The camp was filthy. His smelly sleeping bag lay on the gravel, a few cooking utensils were strewn about on the ground, and an array of garbage littered the camp. I declined the coffee he offered in a dirty cup and soon departed.

Later someone told me that Dirty Yantzee had been a beaver poacher in Montana and had left for Alaska one step ahead of the law. Yantzee had the local fishermen buffaloed. He not only kept them from poaching fish, but he refused to let them anchor near his camp. As Elmer had predicted, he protected the salmon.

I never met the sourdough who had the biggest impact on my life. As a teenager on a farm in Indiana, I had read *The Wild Grizzlies of Alaska* by John M. Holzworth. The author described the life of Allen Hasselborg, a recluse who lived in Mole Harbor on Admiralty Island. Hasselborg inhabited this remote spot, populated by brown bears, for many years. He watched the huge bears pass by his cabin and followed their well-worn trails as he hiked through the forest. I was fascinated with the book, its description of the huge bears, and the life of the old sourdough. I vowed that someday I would go to Admiralty Island.

In early 1955 we anchored our patrol boat in Mole Harbor. I stood on the bow and gazed at Hasselborg's homestead, tucked into the edge of the rain forest. The bears were in hibernation, and I knew Hasselborg was no longer there; he had left a few years before, due to old age. I went ashore that evening to take a closer look at the old cabin. Some of his cooking utensils hung on the wall, and the stove was still present. I looked out the window, just as the old sourdough had done to watch brown bears pass by on his beach. I wondered if I would be standing in this remote spot in Alaska if I had not read the book. I walked about the homestead in awe, recalling Hasselborg's adventures. How I wished I could have met him!

Later in my Alaska travels I met other old sourdoughs, but these first acquaintances are still fresh in my mind. They were my introduction to a group of independent individuals whose different paths led to Alaska. In these remote forests they could live a life free from the responsibilities and social restraints of a more civilized life. I had to admire many of them. They were and are a breed of men that is gradually disappearing from Alaska.

Chapter 8

Romance in Juneau

My life changed dramatically in 1955. In early January the enforcement agent for the Juneau district, Sandy Matson, decided to retire. Dan Ralston, head of the FWS enforcement branch in Alaska, requested that I take over Sandy's duties for two or three months until a replacement could be found. This I agreed to do.

While in Juneau I shared an office near the boat harbor with Gomer Hilsinger, the fishery management agent. When I arrived, Gomer introduced me to his secretary, LuRue Quein, an attractive young lady who immediately caught my eye. I soon found out she was single. It took me a while to get to know LuRue, however; I was a little shy, as I had met so few young, single women since coming to Alaska. I was also in the field a lot during my first few months on the new job.

Juneau, the largest enforcement district in Southeast Alaska, was bounded by Cape Fanshaw on the south, Skagway on the northeast, and Yakutat on the north. It included all of Admiralty Island, the eastern portions of Chichagof and Baranof Islands, and numerous smaller islands, bays, and inlets.

The sixty-foot-long *Grizzly Bear* was our patrol vessel. Cletus Groves, who had been the deckhand and engineer under Sandy Matson, could pilot the vessel, so he became skipper while I was the acting enforcement agent.

A few days after I arrived in Juneau, Groves (he did not like to be called Cletus) and I made a patrol around Admiralty Island, checking for late trappers. I enjoyed exploring this island, and I walked many of its beaches checking for signs of trapping and wildlife activity. About halfway around the island I arrested one late trapper, seized some evidence, and directed him to appear in the Juneau court on

The FWS Grizzly Bear *was our patrol vessel in the Juneau district.*

a certain date. Though I hated to cut my field patrol short to handle the court case, I did look forward to seeing LuRue again. When we arrived back in town, however, I discovered that LuRue was in Whitehorse on a skiing trip. I left Juneau without seeing her.

During the next two months Groves and I were on almost constant game patrol with the *Grizzly Bear*, and I spent little time in Juneau. We patrolled the numerous bays of Chichagof and Baranof Islands and traveled to Haynes and Skagway. I enjoyed exploring all this new country, but my mind was often on LuRue in Juneau.

In early April we found that the *Grizzly Bear* needed some major repairs and would be out of commission for more than a month. I would need to spend most of my time in the office during this period. Normally, I would not have liked being stuck doing paperwork, but it gave me a chance to get to know LuRue. She liked the outdoors, and on weekends we hiked many of the trails around Juneau. I also took her to a few movies. I really enjoyed the time with her and began hoping for more than a friendship. I escorted her home one evening after a movie, and when we got to her apartment door, she turned around and looked into my eyes. I felt romance in the air and was about to try for a kiss—our first—when she blurted out, "Will, there is something I have to tell you."

The tone of her voice told me I was not going to like what came next.

"Chuck and I are dating. I'm not sure how serious it is, but for now I'm loyal to our relationship."

LuRue above Mendenhall Glacier in 1955 on one of our first hiking trips.

Wow! That sort of trimmed my sails. I knew Chuck, a fishery management agent, who was out on a long field assignment. I also knew they had previously dated, but I had no idea they were still romantically involved. I do not remember much of our conversation after that, but before I left, we agreed to continue taking hikes together—strictly as friends. I did not sleep well that night. I had been assuming a lot, and my bubble had been burst.

At about this time I decided not to continue my law enforcement career. I liked the fieldwork, but I did not like arresting people. I wanted to work directly with wildlife, so I decided to return to college for an advanced degree in wildlife biology. I discussed my plans with Dr. John Buckley, the leader of the Alaska Cooperative Wildlife Research Unit at the University of Alaska in Fairbanks. He granted me a fellowship at the unit with a stipend of $2,500 for the coming winter.

A few weeks later Dan Ralston requested I come to his office. Dan was rather gruff and did not engage in much chitchat. He motioned me to a chair next to his desk.

"I've been watching your performance, and as far as I'm concerned you are next in line to become a district enforcement agent," he said. "However, I've heard you want to become a biologist, and if that's the case, I can't see appointing you to a district."

LuRue with a string of trout caught in Young's Lake while on one of our first dates.

I was speechless for a minute, surprised and flattered that he would offer me a district. The job would mean more money and an advancement in my law enforcement career, but I had to level with him. I told him I loved enforcement fieldwork but preferred working directly with wildlife. I said that I intended to return to college for an advanced degree in biology even though I knew finding a wildlife position in Alaska would be a long shot. I thanked him for the opportunity to work in the enforcement branch the previous three years and said I would be glad to remain in Juneau as the acting agent until he could find a replacement.

He thanked me for my honest comments and told me that he respected my decision. We parted on good terms.

My two- to three-month assignment had already lengthened to four, and it was apparently going to continue for another month or more. I spent all my time in Juneau now, preparing for the commercial fishing season—buying supplies, hiring stream guards, overseeing the repair of the *Grizzly Bear*, and conducting a few patrols along the road system.

I saw LuRue on a daily basis, and we continued our friendship, chitchatting in the office, occasionally going out to lunch, and hiking together on weekends. I could tell she enjoyed my company, but she never gave any clues about her relationship with Chuck. I, of course, was hoping she might change her mind.

In early spring we went on an outing to Young Lake on Admiralty Island. I anchored the skiff near the mouth of the creek, and we hiked several miles to the lake. The Forest Service had a leaky rowboat in the lake. We used it, alternating our time between bailing out the water and fishing for cutthroat trout. We both got wet, but we had a lot of fun together.

We got a big surprise when we hiked back to the beach where I had anchored the skiff. The high tide had come in, and the skiff was now anchored far offshore. We could wait for the tide to recede in a few hours, or I could swim to the skiff. I decided to swim and told LuRue to turn her back while I stripped off my clothes and got the boat. Boy, that water was cold! I made the swim in record time. I could not tell if LuRue peeked while I was bringing the boat back, stark naked, but she was still standing with her back to the water when I landed.

I dressed quickly, and we both got into the skiff. On the way back to Juneau she teased me about my skinny-dipping abilities, and I accused her of peeking. We laughed about this episode for days, and she told me several times at the office how she had enjoyed the trip. I certainly had. Secretly I hoped things were not going well between her and Chuck, but I avoided this sensitive subject as I feared it might end our friendship.

About a week later LuRue told me that she needed to talk to me privately. We met that evening, and LuRue informed me she was breaking up with Chuck. I was elated inside, but I told her I was sorry things had not worked out between them. LuRue said she hoped we could continue our friendship and reiterated how she enjoyed hiking and talking with me. I could tell by the way she related this information that she now hoped that we could become more than friends.

Suddenly I saw where this thing was going, and I got cold feet. I told her I wanted a few days to think things over. I knew if we continued seeing each other, our friendship would turn into a serious relationship in a hurry, and I suspected she did, too.

I did not sleep much that night. My life seemed to be changing rapidly. Was I willing to commit to a serious relationship with LuRue at the same time I was quitting my job to return to college? Would this be fair to her? I was in turmoil, and it would take a few days to make a decision.

A week later I drove her to a remote beach overlooking the ocean and parked the car. The moon had just risen over a nearby mountain, and the surf swished on the beach in front of us. For an hour or so we both talked about our future plans and what we wanted out of life. There was no doubt we were falling in love.

Later that evening before we separated, I got that first kiss.

We saw each other daily at work and usually got together in the evening, talking about anything and everything. I loved how natural and easy it was to spend time with LuRue. We took hikes on weekends and swam in a pothole lake near Mendenhall Glacier. May came and our romance was blooming along with the wildflowers. Our coworkers noticed the romance and gave us some good-hearted razzing about it.

In June Fred Robards became the new Juneau enforcement agent, but I remained as his assistant until mid-July. I then transferred back to Wrangell until my resignation would become effective the first of September. Before I left, LuRue told me that she also wanted a change in life and was going to quit her job. She either wanted to move back to the States or to Anchorage. I told her I hoped it would be the latter so we could occasionally have a weekend together while I was in college. She smiled and said, "Yes, maybe that would be the best move. I'll think about it." She reached over and squeezed my hand.

I had been in Wrangell a few weeks when Dan Ralston called and said he and Regional Director Clarence Rhode were flying down to see me. I had no idea what they wanted, but I knew it must be big for Clarence to come. I happened to be in Petersburg, so they arranged to meet me there. Clarence told me that Russell Hoffman, the refuge manager for Kodiak, had decided to transfer to the States. Would I consider taking his position since I wanted to get into wildlife work? Man! I was stunned! It was exactly the type of position I wanted. As refuge manager I would finally be working directly with wildlife, especially with the big brown bears that the refuge was famous for. I had to tell Clarence, however, that I was already committed to Dr. Buckley's fellowship.

"You call Dr. Buckley," Clarence said. "I think he will understand and let you off the hook."

I promised him I would. I found out later that Clarence had already talked to Dr. Buckley and also to Dave Spencer, the refuge supervisor. We shook hands, and as we parted, Dan Ralston gave me a big wink. I realized then that he was one of my backers for the Kodiak job.

I called Dr. Buckley the next day and told him about the offer, but I assured him I was committed to accepting the fellowship and would keep my word.

"Listen, Will, you know how few wildlife jobs there are in Alaska," he said. "Even if you complete your master's, there is no guarantee you can get a job up here. This is an opportunity of a lifetime for you, and I recommend you take it."

I thanked him profusely. I was absolutely elated at the turn of events. As soon as I hung up the phone with Dr. Buckley, I called Clarence Rhode to accept the Kodiak position. He informed me I was to report to Dave Spencer in Kenai by mid-August. That was only two weeks away!

I tried to call LuRue that evening without success, but I reached her the next day and told her about my sudden change of plans. She was excited for me, but

LuRue with a dead sea lion we found on the beach.

I could tell she was wondering where it would leave our relationship. We talked a long time. I promised her I would spend the weekend in Juneau en route to Kodiak and we could discuss our future.

The next two weeks seemed to pass slowly. I said goodbye to my many friends and started preparing for my new job. I also wrote LuRue numerous letters, but I could hardly wait to see her in person.

The weekend I was to leave was also opening weekend of deer hunting season. Dave Klein, Doyle Cissney, and I had planned a hunt, but I canceled to visit LuRue. Boy, did I get razzed! "That Troyer sure is changing! He's actually flying to Juneau to see a girl instead of going deer hunting. I've never seen him turn down a deer hunt before."

LuRue and I spent the weekend together in Juneau. The time seemed even more special than before since it would be a while before we saw each other again. We talked about a lot of things, and LuRue told me she had definitely planned to move to Anchorage. I encouraged her to do so. I was becoming smitten with the love bug, and I could tell she was, too. We promised each other we would get together for weekends as often as possible.

We had many long talks that weekend. LuRue was so easy to talk to, and the more I saw of her the more I wanted to share my life with her. Somehow the word "marriage" slipped into the conversation, and we started planning a wedding. LuRue thought around Christmas would be a nice time to get married. I agreed.

That evening when I was alone, I thought, "Whoa! Are things moving too fast?" But by morning I had convinced myself that I was making the right decision.

The next day I left Juneau for Kenai, where I would meet my new boss, Dave Spencer. LuRue took me to the airport. She had tears in her eyes when we parted, and I had a big lump in my throat. She stood outside and waved as my plane started taxiing down the runway.

Man! Things were moving awfully fast. I now had the job of my dreams and, it appeared, also the girl of my dreams!

Chapter 9

Kodiak Refuge Manager

D ave Spencer, supervisor of Alaska's federal wildlife refuges, gave me an aerial tour of the two-million-acre Kodiak National Wildlife Refuge in late August 1955. I gazed down at this huge piece of real estate and saw bear trails crisscrossing the open grassy landscape that was interspersed with patches of alder, willow, and elderberry thickets. I was watching several bears walking the trails when Dave said, "Look at this." He made a sharp turn with the twin-engine Widgeon to show me a sow with three cubs entering a salmon stream. We continued down the river and saw another ten or twelve bears fishing. It certainly was excellent bear country, and I speculated that those bear trails below me would be easy to walk compared to the thick, devil's-club-infested forests of Southeast Alaska that I had just left. I later discovered the grassy meadows had vegetation higher than my head and the alder thickets were almost impenetrable jungles.

Dave, my new boss, was a rather quiet man, but he was well respected by his peers. When he had something to say, it was usually important, and he had an excellent knowledge of the Kodiak refuge. The day after our aerial tour he briefed me on the wildlife resources of Kodiak Island and on some of the controversial issues that surrounded the Kodiak brown bear.

The bear-cattle and bear-salmon conflicts were at their peak in 1955. The Russians had introduced cattle to the island in the late 1700s, but they remained in relatively low numbers during the Russian era. In the 1930s and 1940s ranchers increased their herds and moved them to outlying areas, where they were more vulnerable to bears. The ranchers started losing cattle to bear predation. The

I used the small twenty-three-foot Kodiak Bear for my coastal work around Kodiak and Afognak Islands.

cattlemen and other businessmen in Kodiak believed the cattle industry had a great future, and they saw the brown bear as a serious impediment to its success. They advocated reducing or eliminating bears on the island. The Alaska Territorial Legislature sided with the ranchers and in 1951 passed a resolution advocating removal of all protections for bears on Kodiak Island, including the Kodiak National Wildlife Refuge. This irritated various national conservation organizations, and thus a battle ensued.

At about this same time Dick Schuman, a fishery biologist, did some studies on bear-salmon predation in Karluk Lake and concluded that bears were a major reason for the decline of salmon in the lake. He also advocated reduction of bear numbers. The bear-cattle and bear-salmon controversies gave the bears a bad reputation.

Before Dave left, he said, "Well, Will, you're going to have your hands full dealing with these controversies, but...good luck." His warning proved to be an understatement.

The refuge headquarters were in Kodiak, the largest town on the island. In 1955 it was a commercial fishing town of approximately three thousand people. Like many fishing towns, it had some rough edges. The first time I walked downtown, a bar seemed to anchor every corner, and a few drunks stumbled along the streets. But Kodiak also had hints of its long history, which seemed to give it some stability. Our office, which we shared with the commercial fishery division, was located across the street from the Russian Orthodox church and near the historic governor's mansion, a reminder that Kodiak was once the capital of Russian Alaska. The office site is now in a city park.

The old Belmont Bar and Café was just a block from the office. The café occupied one side of the business, which was a large open room. It served excellent coffee, brewed with an ample supply of eggshells in the pot, which the cooks believed cut the acidity and settled the coffee grounds. The café was a popular gathering place for morning coffee, but at times patrons had to contend with drunks on the other side of the room who had imbibed too heavily the night before.

A few blocks up the street from the Belmont the FWS owned a house for use by the refuge manager. The two-story dwelling, built in about 1940, sat on a hill with a grand view of the sea and offshore islands. Heavy winter winds, with gusts exceeding eighty miles per hour, sometimes buffeted the house, causing it to shake and tremble. Occasionally the gusts blew out the furnace. The basement was unfinished and a haven for large rats. I frequently heard them crawling up the inside of the kitchen walls at night and gnawing on the wood. I constantly trapped and poisoned the rats, but it was a losing proposition; others moved in as soon as I eradicated the current residents.

As refuge manager, I was responsible for the well-being of all wildlife in the Kodiak archipelago, which included Kodiak Island, Afognak Island, and dozens of smaller islands. In the fall I spent a lot of time managing the deer on Kodiak and the elk on Afognak. Both species had been introduced in the late 1920s and early 1930s. The populations had grown enough so that the first hunting seasons had been held a few years before I arrived. Deer hunting was still confined to the short road system, and during my first fall the month-long season resulted in a take of less than sixty deer. By contrast, several thousand deer are now taken annually over the entire archipelago.

When I arrived to work in Kodiak, the refuge staff was small. A biologist and a boat operator were the refuge's only other full-time employees. The large Kodiak Naval Base, constructed near the town of Kodiak during World War II, had many personnel who fished the numerous streams and hunted deer, bear, and small game. As a result the navy had assigned a military game warden to assist the FWS in enforcing game and fish regulations along the road system. A man named Ray Mullins was the navy warden when I arrived. He was later replaced by Benny Ballenger, followed by Herb Downing. In addition to providing enforcement, they helped me by collecting hunting data.

A small refuge vessel provided transportation while I carried out management and enforcement duties around the perimeter of the island. If I needed aerial assistance, I chartered small planes from Kodiak Airways or Harvey's Flying Service.

Kim Clark was the refuge biologist. Soon after I arrived in Kodiak, I heard stories that Kim was controversial, something Dave had not mentioned. I did not get to meet him right away. Kim was living and working in the middle of the island while conducting bear-salmon studies. That fall, after the deer and elk hunting seasons ended, I decided to fly out to meet the man. Kim worked out of a small cabin on Camp Island in the middle of Karluk Lake. I arrived late in the evening and had a cup of tea with Kim and his wife, Shirley, before retiring to a primitive shed a hundred yards from the cabin. I noted Kim was dressed in rather dirty clothes, but I had heard of his unkempt appearance so I never gave it much thought.

The next morning, a little after seven o'clock, I walked down to the cabin, which was built from used weir pickets scrounged from commercial fishery research. The cabin had limited space, consisting of a small kitchen/dining room and an even smaller bedroom. Shirley was up and had brewed a fresh pot of coffee. I sat down at the kitchen table, which was positioned in front of a large window that offered an excellent view of the lake. I soon discovered that the Clarks had many pets, which had the run of the cabin. Their six dogs, fortunately, were not much larger than their seven cats. A pet magpie flew in and out of the cabin whenever the door was open, and two canaries lived in a cage that hung above the kitchen table. Shirley poured me a cup of coffee, and I immediately covered it with my hand to shield it from seeds being flicked down by the canaries.

Kim was not an early bird, so Shirley and I talked and drank coffee for nearly an hour before he got up. She was easy to talk to and obviously devoted to her eccentric husband and all their pets. Eventually, Kim emerged from the bedroom wearing only a sweater, which was so short it did not quite cover his private parts. He gave Shirley a big kiss and stretched, revealing himself even more. Then he announced, "I think I'll take a dip."

It was early October, and a little ice had formed along the edge of the lake. Kim took off the sweater when he got outside, rubbed soap on his body, and dove into the icy water, which was about twenty feet from where I sat. I tried to ignore the naked man outside and continued talking to Shirley. He slipped on his sweater a few minutes later and returned to the cabin, dripping wet. He gave Shirley a hug and kiss; I looked out the window pretending I did not notice. Having met the couple only the night before, I was quite embarrassed at this half-naked man smooching with his wife less than three feet from me.

Kim finally got dressed; Shirley started cooking and served some pancakes and bacon. I had taken only a few bites when a cat jumped on the table and tried to take some food off my plate. I was about to clobber it, but Kim reached over,

The majority of the FWS field personnel in 1957. Front row, left to right: John Buckley, George Warner, Orton, Lee Ellis, Joe Miner, Bob Burkholder, Ron Skoog, Clarence Rhode, Dan Ralston, John Findlay, Roger Allin, Stan Fredericksen, Bob Scott, Ray Woolford. Center, left to right: Holger Larsen, Chuck Graham, Dave Klein, Switzer, Ed Whitesel, Harry Pinkham, Bill Ackerknecht, Maurice Kelly, Presnell, Bob Jones, Theron Smith, Bob Baade, Jim Branson, Sig Olson, Ron Zigler, Ray Tremblay, Hank Hansen. Back, left to right: Sam Harbo, Will Troyer, Dave Spencer, Doug Swanson, Urban "Pete" Nelson, Virgil Crosby, Johnny Wendler, Smith, Neil Argy, Fred Robards.

put his hand on the cat, and said, "Now, Butter, be nice to our guest and get back on the floor. We'll feed you later."

Before he completed his sentence, another cat jumped on the table and headed for my plate. Kim must have sensed I was not too happy with the cats, so he gently put them on the floor. While all this was happening atop the table, below it I felt several dogs running over my feet; obviously they were hoping for a handout. One of them tried to hump my leg until I stomped on its hind foot. It yelped, so I quickly said, "Oh, I'm sorry. I must have accidentally stepped on its foot."

While I was fending off cats and dogs, seeds from the canary cage began dropping into the syrup pitcher. "Man!" I thought. "What have I gotten myself into here?"

After breakfast Kim and I boated up to a small stream where he was conducting bear-salmon predation studies. We returned at noon, and Shirley served us each a bowl of soup and a sandwich for lunch. While we were eating, the pet magpie flew into the cabin, landed on the table, and walked through Kim's bowl of soup. Kim did not even blink. Then the bird sat on the table, watching us. I guarded my bowl of soup with both hands, fearing it would be the bird's next wading pool. Kim continued eating, seemingly oblivious to the magpie's presence.

Later that day I caught a plane back to Kodiak, relieved that I did not have to eat dinner in that zoo!

Kim was a hippie before the term was even coined. He had a scraggly beard, wore tattered clothes, and often went barefoot. He sometimes disappeared from camp for a week or more. On these excursions he took along some of his dogs, carried a few cans of dog food, and subsisted on dog vittles, spawned-out salmon, and whatever edible vegetation and berries he could find. His odd behavior and dress could be ignored in the field, but not in the Kodiak office. On one occasion he arrived at the office reeking with the odor of a dead bear he had dissected. When the commercial fishery secretary said, "Kim, you stink!" he only smiled, relishing the reputation of smelling like a bear.

A year later, when Kim returned to town in the fall, he bought a taxicab and started a business to supplement his income. I told him I was concerned the business would conflict with his job. He assured me that he would run the cab business only on weekends and at night, when he was off duty. I was leery of this arrangement but decided I would wait and see. It was not long, however, before he parked the taxi by the office and made runs during the lunch hour. This made me even more uncomfortable, but it was still his personal time. When he started continuing the taxi business well into the afternoon on some days, I confronted him. Still, he defended his actions.

"I put in a lot of extra hours in the summertime," he said, "and I see no reason why I can't drive my cab on the job to compensate for those extra hours." I informed him that he could not drive the cab during working hours if he wanted to hold his job. He was unhappy at my orders.

My problems with Kim extended beyond his cab business. One time, upon returning to Kodiak after a short trip, I was unable to find our government pickup. I searched the town without success. On a tip, I drove to Kim's house and found the truck parked in his yard. Kim was using the cab of the truck as a dog kennel. Shirley told me two of his female dogs were in heat, and he wanted to keep them separated from the rest of the pack. The truck cab reeked with dog odor and was covered with dog hair and grime. I was livid! When I finally found Kim, I informed him that this was a misuse of government equipment, and I would not tolerate it. He protested, but I told him he either had to live by government rules or quit the job. He reluctantly complied for a while.

I gave Kim an unsatisfactory rating and recommended that he be terminated, but I learned how difficult it was to fire a government employee.

I also discovered that Kim was politically savvy. He had many supporters in town. He frequently talked to school groups and was an entertaining speaker; the students loved him. He persuaded some pupils to write a letter of support with the slogan "Keep Kim Clark in Kodiak." Kim even managed to get a letter of support from Senator Bob Bartlett. My employee had lined up some big guns to defend his job. It was obvious I was going to have trouble getting rid of him.

I was not surprised when, a month or two later, my recommendation to fire him was overturned by our Washington, D.C., office. Still, the news really got me down. It appeared I was permanently stuck with my eccentric biologist. About a year later, however, Kim decided to run for a house seat in the Alaska Territorial Legislature. The Hatch Act, passed in 1939, prohibited government employees from running for political office. I was sure Kim was aware of this law, so I wondered why he decided to defy the act. Perhaps he wanted a career change. Regardless of his motives, he was forced to resign his position, and I was finally relieved of a major personnel problem.

While the predicament with Kim and other controversies were causing turmoil in my professional life, my personal life was moving rapidly forward. Shortly after I arrived in Kodiak, LuRue told me she had changed her mind and decided to move to Kodiak instead of Anchorage. She felt we needed to know each other better if we were going to get married. She did not think an occasional weekend together would be adequate. I thought it would be difficult for her to find a job in town, but she was convinced otherwise. She arrived in Kodiak in late September, and we officially became engaged on October 2, 1955—my thirtieth birthday.

The refuge division in Kodiak did not have a secretary, and I decided we needed one since the files were a mess. I called Ray Nevin in the regional personnel office in Juneau and told him I needed a secretary. He agreed and then asked, "Do you know anyone in Kodiak who is qualified for the job?"

"Well, yes," I said, trying to sound as casual as possible. "LuRue Quein just moved to town and because of her previous experience with the FWS, I think she is highly qualified."

Ray knew we were romantically involved. He coughed a couple of times and then answered, "Well, yes, she certainly is." Within a week of arriving in Kodiak, LuRue was again working in my office as a secretary.

A few weeks later I went to Juneau on a business trip. The regional office in Juneau was small, and everyone was following our romance. Several people in the office reminded me that performance ratings would soon be due, and with grins on their faces they asked if I intended to give my secretary a satisfactory rating. I took the good-natured ribbing with a smile and answered, "I will evaluate her very thoroughly." This brought more smiles.

LuRue and I now saw each other every day except when I was in the field. We set the wedding date for a week before Christmas. The wedding was to take place in LuRue's hometown of Everett, Washington, where her parents still lived. She quit her job a couple of weeks before the wedding and flew to Everett. Just before leaving, she moved all her clothes from her apartment into my closet in the refuge house. I had been a bachelor a long time; when I came home that evening and spotted all those women things in my closet, I was a bit shaken.

"Boy, Troyer," I thought to myself. "You have really done it now!"

LuRue and I were married on December 17, 1955. After a brief honeymoon along the Oregon coast, we returned to Kodiak, where I began to get used to all those women things in my closet.

Chapter 10

Wrangling Kodiak Bears

The misconceptions and controversies that surrounded the Kodiak bears demanded some answers. The previous refuge staff had initiated studies that were primarily defensive in nature. They experimented with stringing electric fences around streams to keep bears from catching salmon; they also conducted additional studies on bear-salmon predation to prove that Dick Schuman's studies were flawed and exaggerated. They investigated cattle kills that ranchers attributed to bear predation and concluded that some of the livestock had died from natural causes.

When I arrived on the island, I came to the conclusion that we needed to conduct more positive studies to help improve the image of the bears. The fledgling guiding industry was expanding. The guides were bringing an increasing number of hunters to the island and taking more bears each year. I wondered how many bears were on the island and how many could be taken annually without reducing the bear population. How long did it take to grow a trophy bear? How many cubs could a female produce in her lifetime? How far did bears move?

The questions were endless, but I knew that in order to get some of this information we would need to perfect a method to live-trap, physically examine, and then mark some animals. That was a dilemma; no one in Alaska had done this. I did know that rangers in Yellowstone National Park sometimes captured nuisance grizzlies in culvert traps to move them, and biologists in a few eastern states had devised methods for capturing black bears. I reasoned that I could use the same techniques on Kodiak Island. I had limited funds for such a project, so I solicited help from personnel of the nearby naval base. In 1956 we constructed two portable steel culverts that were eight feet long and four feet in diameter. We installed a heavy steel gate on one end of each culvert. If a bear grabbed some bait attached to a wire on the inside end of the trap, the raised gate would drop, trapping the bear.

In the spring of 1957 the navy flew the two traps to Karluk Lake. We placed them at Thumb and O'Malley Rivers, two areas heavily used by bears during the salmon spawning season. I had two seasonal assistants that summer, Earl Fleming and Ken Durley. Earl had spent a number of winters in Alaska trapping fur animals, so I asked him to find a type of bait that would draw brown bears into the traps.

Earl experimented with various meats and concoctions along a well-used bear trail. He concluded that bears were easily attracted to bacon, so we baited the two traps with fresh bacon. We checked them each morning for a week without success. A few days later as we approached the Thumb trap, I said, "Hey look, guys, the gate is down."

Excited, I rushed to the trap and peeked through a small hole. "It's a fox," I said, discouraged.

"A fox!" Earl replied. "Damn! We don't want that little bugger!"

A few more days went by before we again found the gate down. I was looking into the peephole in the side of the trap when a bear's paw smacked against it. I jumped back. "Wow, we sure got one this time!" I said.

Both Earl and Ken looked in with the same results. We were excited. "Now, what are we going to do?" Earl asked.

"We're going to spray ether in that hole until the bear goes to sleep," I said.

We were all laughing and excited at catching our first bear. Earl looked in again. "It's a small one—no more than three hundred pounds," he predicted.

"We can manhandle that little critter," Ken boasted.

We got the gear ready and stuffed the holes in the side of the trap with rags. I started pumping ether into the trap with an ordinary fly sprayer. After we emptied the sprayer, Earl peeked in again. "I think it's about out, Will."

"Are you sure?" I asked. "You'd better poke it with a stick."

Earl got a small, thin alder, shoved it through the peephole, and jabbed the bear in the rear leg. Wham! Scrape! The bear jumped up and raked the side of the trap with its claws. "Let's give it some more," I said.

We filled the sprayer several times and continued to spray the bear with ether for another fifteen minutes. "Check it again," I said. This time when Earl poked the bear with the stick, it did not move. "We better punch him again, just to make sure," I said. I picked up the stick and prodded the bear several times, but it did not respond.

We used culvert traps in our early attempts to capture bears.

"Okay, let's hurry. Raise the gate and drag it out," I said.

Both Ken and Earl looked at me with big, wondering eyes, but there was no time to waste. We quickly raised the gate. The bear was lying with its tail toward us, so they each grabbed a rear leg and pulled it out. "Wow! It's a little one," Earl said.

When the bear moved its front feet, we jumped back. "Quick, Ken, put some cotton in that bucket and pour in ether," I instructed.

I straddled the bear and slipped the bucket over the bear's snout. Earl grabbed a pair of ear tags and clamped a numbered tag in each ear, while Ken started taking measurements. I did not want to overdose the bear, so I removed the bucket after a few minutes. I could not help but breathe in some ether fumes during the process, and they were making me a bit groggy. "Hurry, hurry, guys. It might come to."

About then, the bear raised its head. "It's getting up!" Earl yelled.

"Led it," I replied, still astraddle the bear.

"But we haven't weighed it yet," Earl protested.

"For-ged-it," I stammered, slightly woozy from the ether fumes, as I slid off the bear's back. The bear got slowly to its feet and staggered into the alders.

Excited that we had finally caught and marked a bear, we slapped each other on the back to celebrate. We speculated about how many more we might capture that summer. Then I remembered something. "Hey, we forgot to check its sex."

Ken started saying he thought it was a small female. "Naw," Earl interrupted emphatically. "I felt his balls."

"Baalls," I said, still a bit giddy from the fumes. "Earl, you're just a boar biologist." Everyone laughed at my attempted joke.

We eventually learned, however, that while bears liked the smell and taste of bacon, they were reluctant to enter the culvert traps to get it. We caught only two more bears that summer; both were juveniles. The abundance of salmon in nearby streams, an easy food source for the bears, probably contributed to our failure.

The following winter I corresponded with black bear biologists in Michigan and New York. They were capturing bears with steel leg traps, then lassoing and hog-tying the animals before anesthetizing them with ether. I concluded that we might be able to use the same technique on brown bears even though they were larger. I ordered a dozen No. 150 double-spring steel traps with offset jaws. They had a jaw spread of a little over eight inches when set. We wrapped the jaws with electrical tape to soften the edges and attached a ten-foot chain with a large, three-pronged steel drag to each trap. We hoped the drag would catch in bushes and hold the bear.

That summer we set the traps in well-worn bear trails that led to salmon streams around Karluk Lake. We covered each one with leaves, moss, and dirt, and then placed a series of sticks across the trail to try to trick the bears into stepping into the traps.

The first morning after we had made our sets, I got up early in anticipation of catching a bear. Earl was already in the kitchen, cooking up a batch of buckwheat cakes—his favorite breakfast. "Mornin', Will. Boy, I feel it in my bones. We're gonna catch a bear today."

"I sure hope you're right," I answered.

We finished breakfast, jumped in the skiff, and headed toward Thumb River, where we had set four traps. The first trail set was undisturbed, as was the next. The last two traps were both sprung, but no bears. "Damn!" Earl cursed. "Those bears are sure smart."

Ken and I both disagreed. We had reasoned that a bear would have to put its foot in the middle of the trap to get caught, so we were naturally going to get a lot of misses.

We found two more snapped traps that morning but no bears. We were a rather dejected crew as we returned to the cabin at noon.

We used primitive methods to weigh the first bears we captured.

The next morning we found another snapped trap, but when we checked the fourth set at Thumb, it was missing. We followed the drag trail through a patch of alders. About a hundred yards ahead I could see bushes shaking. I looked at Earl and Ken. "Boy, I think we got one!" I said, nervous and excited.

A small cottonwood tree stood nearby. "Ken, why don't you climb that tree and have a look," I said. Earl and I stationed ourselves in strategic locations on guard with our rifles. My heart was pounding as I still did not know if we had a single bear or possibly a cub that was being guarded by its mother.

I could occasionally see the leaves quaking. Ken called down, "We got one. It looks like a small single."

After Ken came down, the three of us cautiously approached the bear. It had torn down numerous bushes. When it saw us approach, the bear started thrashing around wildly, trying to get away. It was caught by a front foot, and the chain was well entangled in the bushes. Earl and I got out ropes and started throwing lassoes. Earl finally yelled, "I got one over its head!"

I hollered for him to pull hard as I made two more attempts before my own rope encircled the bear's head. We then both looped our ropes around several alder trees and cinched them tight. The bear could barely move its head, and Ken placed ropes around its feet. In a few minutes we had the bear on its back and hog-tied. In spite of my optimism that we could secure a bear caught in a trap, I was surprised at how quickly we did it.

Holding a bear with colored ear streamers.

"Gee, that went pretty smoothly," I said to Earl and Ken.

"Yeah, we showed that bugger who's boss," Earl replied. I put a bucket containing ether-soaked cotton over the bear's snout. It was not long before the bear was anesthetized and it quit struggling. We installed ear tags and six-inch colored plastic strips in each ear for future identification. We recorded the measurements and other data. Our last act was to weigh the animal. "Two hundred fifty-five pounds," Earl announced as he read the scales. It was a three-year-old female.

We moved away from the bear, watching her recover from the ether and slowly walk into the woods. "I think we got a system that will work," Earl said.

We all stood around, excitedly speculating about how many bears we might capture. In the next few weeks we did capture four more bears, all young single animals weighing between two hundred and three hundred fifty pounds. Handling the small animals became routine, and we gained confidence. I was exuber-

Holding a partially anesthetized brown bear cub.

ant and became convinced this new method of trapping bears would provide the information we were seeking.

Then one morning as we approached two trap sites at Salmon Creek, I heard a cub bawl. It was a high-pitched mournful call that sent shivers down my spine. It was obviously caught in a trap. I had theorized that cubs usually follow a mother down a trail so the chances of catching a cub were slim. Now it sounded like my theory was wrong. "What if the sow is nearby?" I whispered to Earl and Ken in alarm.

Neither answered, but Earl unslung his rifle and we quietly advanced through the brush and trees. "There it is," Earl hissed as we approached a small stream. He pointed toward the trapped yearling cub. "The sow and another cub are standing next to it," he whispered. Up to that point I had been hoping that we were wrong about the cub being trapped. But it had happened!

We stood quietly, pondering what to do next. Saliva dripped from the sow's lips as she paced back and forth with her other cub near her side. We knew she was intent on protecting her trapped cub. Fortunately, she had not seen us yet. "What are we going to do now?" I whispered to Earl. He did not answer but started walking toward a tree. Ken, who had no gun, was already climbing one. I started to look for my own tree when the sow spotted us and charged. I did not have time to think, only to react. I raised my rifle and fired into the small stream she was approaching, hoping it would stop her charge as I sure did not want to kill her. A geyser of water shot into the air. I wheeled and ran behind a nearby cottonwood tree. I frantically tried to climb it, but the tree had only two low branches. I tried to scratch and claw my way farther up the tree, but I was not making much progress. I expected to feel her teeth sink into my leg at any second. After a few frantic moments I realized I still had not been bitten, so I peeked around the tree and saw her running back to her trapped cub. Apparently the noise of the rifle shot and the spray of water had been enough to stop her.

After we all were safely in trees, we began firing rifles and shouting, hoping to scare her away from the trapped cub. The mother and her other cub left the scene after about five minutes of harassment. I was relieved but afraid she would return. We continued to shout and make noise to make sure she would not come back. Earl remembered he had a few firecrackers in his pack and now set them off periodically to add to the harassment.

Ten minutes passed and the sow did not return, so we finally came down from our perches and approached the trapped cub. While one of us stood guard with a rifle, the other two, working very quickly, subdued the animal, took the biological data, ear tagged the animal, and released it. The sow never returned while we were present. I was afraid she might abandon the cub, but two days later we saw the young cub with its mother and sibling. We were elated. We had now captured several single bears and successfully scared an angry sow away from her trapped cub.

We caught only eight bears that summer, but I felt we were making progress. We still had a lot to learn.

During the winter of 1958 I learned that black bear researchers had begun using two drugs to anesthetize bears instead of ether. The first drug, Sucostrin, a brand of succinylcholine, was a muscle relaxant. When injected into the large muscle tissue, it caused an animal to lose muscle control. It took effect within two minutes but lasted for only about ten minutes. While the animal was down, biologists administered another drug, phenobarbital sodium, into the intra-peritoneal cavity. The latter drug put the animal to sleep for an hour or more. Al Erickson, a newly hired biologist with the Alaska Territorial Fish and Game Department, had used the drugs on black bears in Michigan. He was able to give

Some of the equipment we used in drugging and capturing bears.

us some valuable information about how to administer the dosages. Al also told us what to expect from the bears as the drugs took effect.

This drug combination appeared to be a great advancement over ether. That winter I acquired a supply of each drug. I also purchased some newly developed foot snares. A steel spring fired a loop of airplane cable up around a bear's foot when it stepped on the trigger. I thought this device was safer to use than a trap and would be less likely to injure a bear's foot.

Things went pretty smoothly the next summer. After we captured a bear in a trap or snare, we administered Sucostrin by placing the proper dosage in a syringe attached to a ten-foot aluminum pole. While one of us attracted the bear's attention, another slipped behind the animal, jabbed the syringe in the rear leg muscle, and jumped out of reach before the bear could swing around. We still had to hog-tie the animal because the first drug often wore off before the second took effect, but this was much safer for us and less stressful for the bears than our old lasso-and-ether method.

We captured and processed thirty bears that summer, up from eight bears the summer before and three the first summer. I was pleased that we had finally established a successful method of capturing bears. During a six-year period we caught or recaptured more than two hundred bears using the new method. We were finally getting data on growth rates, movements, reproductive rates, and other biological information that we needed in managing the Kodiak bears.

Capturing bears became almost routine, but we continued to have many adventures. Angry mothers, whose cubs we caught, were our greatest challenge. We began carrying a shotgun with ShellCrackers to frighten the animals from the scene. A ShellCracker is a twelve-gauge shotgun shell with a firecracker inside. When fired, it travels about a hundred yards before it lands and the firecracker explodes with a loud bang. By shooting these near the sow, we were usually able to frighten her away.

But not always. Sometimes it took us several hours to scare away a protective female. These episodes often became a seesaw battle. We would fire ShellCrackers and shout as we advanced toward the sow. If she came in our direction or did not leave, we retreated to give her room to calm down. When she returned to her cub, we fired more ShellCrackers and advanced again. We were sometimes forced to climb trees when a sow was particularly protective. With enough harassment, she usually left the area long enough for us to collect our data and free the cub.

Usually...

One morning as we approached Meadow Creek, we heard the bawl of a yearling cub. We made a routine approach, shouting and firing ShellCrackers as we advanced. When the sow suddenly popped out of the brush, I yelled, "Back up, back up! Here she comes!" We retreated rapidly. As she returned to her cub, we again started forward. But she came back aggressively, forcing us to give ground. This seesaw continued for more than an hour, far longer than other similar encounters, which usually lasted ten minutes or less. Sometimes she retreated for fifty yards or so, but the persistent sow would not leave. I fought frustration and anxiety; I knew we were working on the edge. A miscalculation could end in one of us being mauled or the sow being killed.

Finally I got an idea born of desperation.

"The next time she moves back, let's anesthetize the cub," I said. "We'll have to be quick and do this in stages."

When the sow retreated again, we moved in and administered the first drug. "Here she comes again!" I yelled, and we jumped away. We stood, thirty yards apart, guns ready, as she moved back to her cub. We continued our harassment. When she retreated once more, we moved in to give her offspring the last drug and attach an ear tag. We began taking a measurement or two in the few moments we could keep her away. After another hour of back-and-forth action, we completed the process and released the cub from the snare. We backed off to watch the sow's reaction. She stayed by the cub until it recovered from the drugs, and then they disappeared into the brush.

Earl had said little during the entire operation, but as we watched them disappear, he said, "Let's go home. I've had enough excitement for one day."

I looked at him. He appeared exhausted. We all felt the same. Even though the day was cool, my shirt was soaked with perspiration.

Despite the tension and dangers involved in the process, humorous incidents were frequent while we were trapping, especially after Dick Hensel joined the crew in 1960. He later became refuge manager and was in charge of bear research after I left.

One morning soon after Dick's arrival we captured a fairly large bear. The drag was entangled in an alder bush in such a manner that it gave the bear a lot of room to move about. Each time I tried to approach the bear from the rear to jab it with the syringe, the bear whirled around and threatened me. This went on for some time and I could not get close to the animal. We needed to try something different. A willow tree stood about fifteen feet away from the bear.

"See that willow leaning in toward the bear?" I said to Dick. "Try climbing it, and then shake it as much as you can to attract its attention."

Dick crawled into the tree, yelling and shaking like a wild man. He either misjudged the strength of the young willow or his own weight, for the tree began to bend over, slowly uprooting, placing Dick directly above the bear. As the tree went down, the bear lunged toward it. I watched, horror stricken but unable to help. Amazingly, Dick somehow did a backward somersault off the tree and landed on his feet running. Once out of range of the bear, he turned toward me and said matter-of-factly, "Well, did I or did I not attract its attention?"

Another time we captured a yearling along Thumb River. But when we checked our gear, we found the syringe missing. Though the cub was bawling loudly, we had not seen the sow and assumed she had left, as sometimes happened.

"You stay here and watch the cub while I run back to the cabin and get a syringe," I told Dick.

As I shoved off in the skiff, I looked back and saw Dick squatted down, answering a call of nature. Just then the sow came out of a patch of willows. Dick had his bare butt toward the bear and did not see her. "Here comes the sow!" I yelled.

Dick turned and saw her. He grabbed his pants with one hand, the shotgun with the other, and tried to run. But his pants hobbled him and he tripped, sprawling on the ground. As he fell, he accidentally fired the gun, which contained a ShellCracker. The loud bang scared the female back into the brush. As I pulled away in the skiff, I could just barely hear Dick cursing above my laughter. That episode has made a good fireside tale ever since.

One time the joke was on me. I had always warned my assistants not to work alone because of the danger. One day, however, when the others were elsewhere and late in returning, I became impatient and decided to inspect the traps and snares at Halfway Creek, which I knew had not been attended to that day. I took a skiff to the mouth of the creek and hiked to the first trail set. The trap was gone. I followed the drag marks into a patch of alders, where I spotted the trapped bear. It appeared to be asleep, but I could not get a good look to determine its size and sex. A medium-sized birch tree about twenty feet from the bear offered a better view. Moving quietly, I climbed up about six feet and saw that the drag was caught on a root about halfway between me and the bear. If it awoke and came toward me, it could reach the tree I was in. As I watched, the bear suddenly got up and came to the base of my tree. I climbed as high as I could, which was not far since the trunk was only about seven inches in diameter. The bear began to chomp on the tree, and I worried that it might knock the tree down. I tried to shoot off the root that held the trap, in hopes the bear would leave, but that proved useless. After a while the bear quit trying to get me and bedded down beneath the tree. It had now turned the tables and trapped me!

I pondered my dilemma. No one in camp knew where I was, as I had failed to leave a note. "Troyer, how could you be so stupid?" I scolded myself. No one was likely to become alarmed until I failed to return that evening, and by then darkness would make a search impossible until the next day. I did not want to spend the night in the tree; neither did I want to shoot the bear. I was in a predicament and needed another solution.

A large cottonwood tree stood about five feet from where the bear lay. It had some branches that extended close to my tree. I reasoned that if I jumped and caught one of these limbs, I could climb down along the opposite side of the tree and be out of the bear's reach. The more I thought about it, the more convinced I became that jumping was the best way out of my plight.

To free up both hands, I hung my rifle on a limb of the tree I was in. Then I crouched and leaped for the nearest cottonwood branch. The limb looked strong, but cottonwoods are often partially rotten; unfortunately, this tree was one of the rotten ones. The first branch broke. So did the next one. I clawed with both hands for something solid to check my fall, but nothing held.

"You better land running!" I thought as I kept dropping.

I fell with a thud about three feet from the rear of the bear. I did not land running, but I scrambled on hands and knees. It was an impressive scramble. I was

Dick Hensel at the entrance of a bear den.

ten feet away before the bear realized what had happened. It raised its head but did not get up. I was relieved that I had gotten myself out of the predicament and swore I would never repeat such a dumb stunt.

On the way back to the cabin I decided to keep this little incident to myself.

Dick and Howard Chrest, a seasonal employee, returned to camp about an hour after I got back, and I told them we had a bear to process at Halfway. After a quick cup of coffee we jumped in the skiff and returned to Halfway Creek. We found the bear still lying under the tree. I was about to jab the bear with the syringe when Dick looked up and asked, "What's that rifle doing up in the tree?" The jig was up; now I had to confess. Dick has never let me forget that experience.

On another occasion Dick and I were checking our traps on Grassy Creek. Near one of the trail sets, I spotted the rear end of a bear. It was apparently sound asleep. "Hey, Dick," I whispered. "We got a bear. It's asleep."

Working as quietly as possible, we prepared a syringe with Sucostrin. I slipped up behind the bear and stuck the needle into its thigh. The bear jumped up and ran down the trail, its legs free of any traps. It had not been caught in a snare, but was just sleeping. I stood there dumbfounded while Dick howled with laughter as the animal disappeared into the woods. Dick and I followed and eventually found and processed the bear. It was the only free-roaming bear we ever captured at Karluk Lake.

During my time at Kodiak we lost three bears while processing a total of two hundred or so. Two were killed by other bears before we arrived to process the bears and free them from our traps. Another we accidentally overdosed with drugs. Incredibly, we never had to kill an animal in self-defense.

In retrospect I realize it must have been traumatic for a bear to be caught in a trap for hours or for a female to have her cub bawling and fighting to get out of a snare. At the time, though, we did not know of a less disturbing method of capturing bears, and we thought the information we gleaned was worth the disturbance we caused.

In hindsight I also realize we took a lot of chances and some of our close encounters could just as easily have ended in disaster. I knew we were often working on the edge, but we were so pumped up with adrenalin that we failed to consider the consequences if things had gone wrong. If I or one of my crew had been injured, these episodes would not have seemed so funny. We were extremely lucky to come through unscathed in our pioneering bear-capturing efforts.

Chapter 11

Life at Camp Island

L uRue gave birth to our first child, Janice, in May 1957. After that it became more difficult for LuRue to accompany me in the field, as she had occasionally done since we had married. By 1958 I was spending most of the summer months at Karluk Lake live-trapping and gathering other biological information on brown bears. I saw very little of my family during this period. That winter LuRue and I discussed these absences, and we decided that in the future she and Janice would accompany me to Karluk Lake during this very busy field season.

LuRue had visited our field camp in Karluk Lake and knew conditions were somewhat primitive. Our cabin at Camp Island was small, without electricity or indoor plumbing. LuRue, now a stay-at-home mom, was eager for a change of scenery after a long winter in Kodiak and was willing to face some hardships to be with me each summer. As the lake was accessible only by air from Kodiak and flights were infrequent, she and I had to do a lot of planning to get supplies to the lake for the family as well as the rest of the bear research crew.

Eventually I needed to increase the size of the living quarters, but we had no funds to construct new facilities. At the time, the Kodiak refuge budget was only $8,000—about $50,000 in today's dollars. From those funds I had to manage the refuge, conduct research, and pay the salaries of my summer seasonal employees, who earned about $1,000 each per season. I sometimes used innovative methods to accomplish these goals.

Prior to my arrival, the refuge manager had issued permits to three bear hunting guides for constructing small cabins on the lake to use in their hunting

This cabin on Camp Island in Karluk Lake served as headquarters for summer bear research. It also housed my family for a few months each summer.

businesses. Bill Pinnell and Morris Talifson had a cabin near the mouth of O'Malley River. Alf Madsen and Johnny Morton each owned a cabin near Camp Island. Morton did little guiding by 1957 and wanted to sell his camp. Alf did not want additional competition in his area, and he approached me about buying Morton's cabin. Refuge regulations permitted only one small cabin per guide in Karluk; if Alf purchased Morton's cabin, he would have to remove it from the lake, which would cost him time and money. I offered him an alternative. He could buy the cabin from Morton, give it to the refuge, and we would dispose of it. Alf agreed. Morton and Alf were both happy with this arrangement, and the refuge gained a cabin.

With some hard work but little cost, we disassembled the cabin, moved it to Camp Island, and attached it to one end of our existing cabin. At the back of the cabin we attached a shed that came with the structure; it served as a pantry and storage shed. In the end we had doubled the original housing space.

Commercial fishery employees had worked at Karluk Lake since the 1920s, but most of their efforts were conducted at the outlet of the lake, where they maintained a weir and a cabin. They had a small boat shed, which they no longer

LuRue did the family laundry by hand.

used, on Camp Island, about one hundred yards from our cabin. I had camped out in it during my initial trips to Karluk Lake. During the first summer season, we had converted this shed into a bunkhouse for my assistants. With the addition of the hunting cabin and shed, we now had ample living quarters at Karluk Lake to more comfortably house both my growing family and the larger summer bear-research crew, even if the facilities were lacking in architectural beauty.

I made additional improvements. We attached a water barrel to the outside of the cabin below the roof. Each morning we pumped the barrel full of lake water. A hose connected the barrel to the kitchen faucet inside, and gravity did the rest.

The room that served as a kitchen/living room/office for both our family and the assistants was extremely small by today's standards. My field crew and I usually ate breakfast and departed before the rest of my family got up each morning. In the evening, however, LuRue cooked dinner for everyone, and we sat at the table and ate family-style. After dinner we discussed the day's activities and wrote up our field notes. There was little privacy for the family until the assistants retired to the bunkhouse late in the evening.

When I first arrived in Kodiak, employees at Camp Island kept food cool for a few days by burying it underground in a five-gallon can. I eventually purchased a kerosene refrigerator and kept it in the pantry and storage shed. The refrigerator was a bit cantankerous, and every few weeks it quit operating. Through a series

Janice and Eric spent most of their time playing in the boats or in the shallow lake waters.

of experiments we learned to treat it as though we were doctors and it was an exhausted patient. We removed the food, laid the refrigerator on its side, let it rest for an hour or two, and then set it upright. This kept the refrigerator running for a while before we had to "treat" it again.

Our only toilet was an outhouse that sat on a rise above the cabin and was used by both men and women. To avoid awkward encounters, LuRue rigged up an occupied sign that a person raised when using the toilet. One evening LuRue needed to use it, but to avoid the long hike to the outhouse in the dark, she decided to go out the back door and step behind a bush. At about the same time, Dick Hensel came down the trail and spotted her. To relieve the embarrassment, he started singing "Tinkle, tinkle, little star."

During our summers at Karluk Lake we always had kids in diapers. Eric was born in 1960 and Teresa in the spring of 1963. The kids spent most of their time crawling around outside in the dirt. LuRue was constantly doing laundry, and she had to do it the old-fashioned way, scrubbing clothes on a washboard. Many days it rained before things dried, and she had to take them down to rehang in the cabin. Considering how much effort this took, I still find it hard to believe that LuRue actually looked forward to going to Camp Island each summer. In 1962 she bought a very small five-gallon electric washer that could be operated with

One way to pack a small child in the wilderness.

the generator we used to power our radio for communicating with the Kodiak office. That little washer saved her a lot of hand scrubbing.

Life at the lake gave our kids some unique opportunities for play. Eric and Janice spent hours on the boat ramp in front of the cabin catching stickleback and small salmon fry. They often waded out into the chilly water, patiently waiting for the fish to come near, oblivious to the temperatures. Their clothes became thoroughly soaked, but they loved the activity and amazingly never caught a cold while we were at the lake.

At first the social life of Camp Island was quiet, but then the commercial fishery people built a large complex on the other side of the island. Beginning in about 1960 Bob Raleigh, who was in charge of the Karluk fishery project, also moved his family to the island each summer. Bob's wife, Pauline, and their three daughters became good friends with LuRue. Later, Bob's assistant, Ben Drucker, and his wife, Sandy, stayed in camp each summer as well. To facilitate communications between the two camps, we strung telephone wires between them and installed a phone in each main cabin. The phones were old hand-crank models. You cranked so many shorts and longs to ring the opposite camp to talk. We also built a trail between the two camps, but the phone system saved a lot of steps.

Usually at least twenty people lived at the lake during the busy summer, and we occasionally got together for an evening of socializing. We would have an outdoor wiener roast when the weather permitted or an indoor popcorn party and songfest during Kodiak drizzles. Often Doss Jones, one of the young summer field assistants, brought his guitar, and we spent the evening trying to harmonize old songs.

The big social event of the summer was the Fourth of July celebration. We planned this well in advance with lots of food and games. A herd of wild reindeer thrived on the south end of the island; it was my duty to shoot one and bring it to camp for the holiday barbecue. No closed season existed on these feral reindeer, and in early July the bulls were unusually fat, which made for excellent eating.

We arose early on the Fourth, got our work done, and then spent the afternoon and evening celebrating. Everyone gathered around the outdoor fire, helping themselves to barbecued reindeer meat and other food brought to the feast. After the meal came a fireworks display, sack races, and swimming contests to see who could stay in the icy waters of Karluk Lake the longest.

One year Dick Hensel and Darrel Farmen acquired a pair of water skis. I had just purchased two new ten-horsepower Johnson motors for our skiff. Dick put one on a small skiff to pull a skier, but in his excitement he failed to fasten the engine on the transom properly and to put on a safety chain. When he revved up the engine to give the water skier a thrill, the engine flew off the transom and sank into thirty feet of water. That ended the water skiing for the day. Dick and Darrel spent several hours dragging the lake before they managed to snag the motor.

After dark we gathered around the campfire, told stories, and sang songs. This festive occasion was always appreciated by those of us who worked every day during the summer season.

A friendly rivalry existed between the refuge and fishery crews, and we often played tricks on each other, especially after Dick had joined our crew. He was a master at thinking up ways to harass our rivals. One evening we slipped over to their camp after dark, crawled under the cabin, and hid firecrackers with fuses cut to various lengths. A firecracker detonated every thirty minutes throughout the night. As soon as the first one went off, the fishery crew knew the refuge guys had got them again, but after each explosion, they thought it would be the last. The last one finally went off at five in the morning.

Another time we took advantage of some "work" to pull a prank on the fishery gang. An old collapsed cabin sat on our end of the island. One night, well after dark, Dick and I decided to burn it and get rid of the trashy eyesore. We purposely did not notify the fish people we intended to burn the cabin. We lit it afire, and the flames shot high in the sky. About ten minutes later the fishery crew came roaring around the corner in their skiff full of water buckets and fire-fighting equipment. We pretended to be surprised they had responded.

They accidentally got even with our fire prank. One afternoon the hand-cranked phone rang, and Pauline Raleigh shouted, "There's a fire at the other end of the lake by the weir!" I ran outside and saw plenty of smoke in that direction. I gathered up my crew. We threw our firefighting equipment in the skiff and sped six miles down to the other end of the lake. Several acres of brush and grass were burning near the camp. We worked like beavers for an hour or two before we put out the fire. I looked for the source of the fire, and it appeared to have started near the outhouse. Finally one of the fishery crew confessed. "Yeah, I was sitting on the hole and the mosquitoes were just fierce. They were biting my butt in swarms, so I wadded up some toilet paper, lit it with a match, and threw it down the hole. It worked. I was sitting and enjoying myself, when I heard the dry grass crackling outside. I ran outside and found a fire spreading through the brush. I took my pants off and tried to beat it out, but it got away from me."

Although this incident was an accident, Dick and I thought it was an excellent joke. We always referred to him thereafter as the "fire flusher."

Pauline never missed anything that happened out on the lake on their side of the island. One morning as we returned from checking our bear traps, we decided to check her alertness. As we passed in front of their camp, the three of us ducked down in the skiff so that we could not be seen. Pauline spotted the unmanned skiff and yelled to her husband, "Bob, there's an empty skiff running down the lake. I think the guys have fallen overboard! Do something quick!"

Peeking through a crack in the side of the skiff, Dick kept up a running commentary of their reactions. Bob and several of his assistants came running out of the cabin. Two fellows jumped in one skiff and followed back on our wake looking for people in the water. Bob jumped in the other skiff and headed toward us. "Here comes Bob," Dick whispered. "Stay down, he's coming fast. Now get ready...he's just about here."

We waited for Bob's face to appear just above the side of the skiff, then jumped up and yelled, "Gotcha!" Bob's face turned several colors. He did not think it was funny. "If you guys ever really fall overboard, I'm going to let you swim home!"

About a week later we tried a similar stunt. We were moving a nuisance bear by boat and decided to prop the bear up at the skiff's controls. We then ducked down and steered the skiff past the fishery camp. They immediately realized it was another prank and did not respond. They later told us, though, that it had looked funny to see the bear driving the boat; they regretted not photographing the caper.

One of our best pranks fell a bit short. One week the fish people told us a bear hanging around the weir on the outlet of the lake had broken into their cabin. They wanted us to move the bear. Our small crew set some traps, and the first morning we caught a young male bear in the three-hundred-pound class. Dick and I processed the animal and then dragged him to the skiff to move him to Thumb River.

About halfway down the lake the bear began to come out of the anesthesia. He flopped around the skiff groggily, but two of us jumped on him and gave him another shot of drugs, putting him back to sleep. We were approaching Thumb when Dick got a bright idea. "Let's put the bear in the fishery outhouse!"

His idea struck me as funny. I immediately steered toward the island and pulled to shore behind some bushes. The three of us dragged the bear to the outhouse, opened the door, and sat him on the hole. We propped the bear up to make him appear alert, shut the door, and then hid behind a bush to watch.

We laughed in anticipation of what was going to happen. "I'll bet there's going to be one big scream," Dick said, quietly mimicking the high-pitched sound Pauline would make when she opened the door.

We waited thirty minutes, but no one came. I was getting a bit antsy, knowing the bear's anesthesia was going to wear off soon. "Oh, let's give it a few more minutes," Dick said.

He and I both hated to lose out on this good joke, but I finally lost my nerve and decided we had better get that bear back into the skiff. As we were dragging it to the boat, a couple of women from the fishery camp spotted us and came running over. "What in the world are you doing with that bear on our island?" one of them demanded to know.

We tried to lie by telling them we had spotted the bear on the island, and since it might injure someone, we were removing it. But they saw the drag marks leading to the outhouse, opened the door, and saw bear hairs all over the toilet seat. We had been found out.

Our antics with the fishery crew were not one-sided. They often played pranks on us. One day, though, they outdid themselves. I got up one morning and turned on the faucet to fill the coffee pot. The water was green! I looked at it in horror, but then I got suspicious and tasted it. The green was obviously food coloring. When the rest of the guys showed up for breakfast, I told them about the prank. "Is that the best they can do?" asked Dick.

Watching bears with two of my young kids.

After breakfast we got our gear together, jumped into the skiff, and started the motor, but the boat didn't move out. The propeller shear pins had been removed. We chuckled at the joke, replaced the shear pins, and proceeded to Grassy Creek to check our traps.

The first trap was missing, and the nearby bushes were ripped asunder where the drag had caught while the bear had tried to escape. We followed the bear's path, which was clearly marked by ripped up bushes and bark torn from small trees. The bear was obviously angry with a trap on its foot and was biting and clawing everything in sight. We nervously steeled ourselves for a fight. We followed the drag marks for another hundred yards. They finally ended in a huge patch of elderberries. The drag was hooked to a root outside the patch, but the rest of the chain and trap disappeared into the thick brush. We cautiously worked our way around the edge of the elderberries, trying to get a glimpse of the bear, but it was too well hidden. I even climbed a nearby tree to get a better vantage point, but I was not able to see the bear. Dick shot off a ShellCracker, but it brought no reaction from the bushes.

"I think it got loose, and the trap is lying inside the bushes empty," I said. "You guys stand guard. I'll slip up, grab the drag, and give it a big jerk."

The guys stood behind me with guns ready, just in case there was a bear and I provoked it into a charge. I grabbed the drag and gave the chain a mighty yank. The chain and trap flew out of the bushes. In the trap jaws was a small teddy bear. "We've been had!" Dick groaned.

Upon closer examination, I found it was my own kids' teddy bear! LuRue was obviously in on the joke! And worse, attached to the toy bear was a nice little poem saying it must have taken a lot of brave men to catch this tiny bear who did not enjoy being abused by these he-men bear trappers. We stood looking at the note in disbelief, but we had to laugh. Those fishery guys had finally beaten us in the "gotcha" contest.

These practical jokes added to the experiences of our summers. The jokes and tricks our crews played on each other helped relieve the tension and stress that often developed from working long hours with rarely a day off.

Chapter 12

Disaster at Tonki Cape

One fall day in 1957 I chartered a Kodiak Airways Piper Super Cub to monitor elk populations and hunting on the northern end of Afognak Island. Before I left, I told LuRue of my plans.

"See you early this evening," I said.

I was often delayed by stormy weather when conducting wildlife studies around the islands, but today was one of those rare clear days at Kodiak. We were both sure I would get home as scheduled. LuRue said she would hold dinner until I got back. Little did she realize how long she would have to keep the food warm.

The Roosevelt elk of Afognak Island are a big success story. Eight animals had been introduced to the island in 1929. They thrived, and by the 1950s an estimated one thousand elk inhabited Afognak and nearby Raspberry Island. The first elk hunting season was held in 1950. They became a popular game animal for the local people; a large bull provides nearly five hundred pounds of meat.

Afognak Island was not part of the refuge, but prior to 1960 the Fish and Wildlife Service had been given responsibility for managing wildlife on the entire Kodiak archipelago. Soon after I arrived at Kodiak, I had a small cabin built at Raspberry Strait, a body of water separating Raspberry and Afognak Islands. Each fall during elk hunting season an assistant and I would work out of the cabin, checking hunters and gathering biological information.

On this sunny October day pilot Doug Haynes and I flew to Raspberry Strait, checking boats in the region; we also delivered supplies to the cabin for my assistant Earl Fleming. After leaving Earl, we crossed over to Paramanof Bay to survey a small herd of elk. We did not see any hunters in the bay, so we continued to Tonki Cape, an area on the northeast end of Afognak with a rugged coastline that is pounded by treacherous seas. Because the area lacked any safe boat harbors, I always used aircraft to conduct wildlife surveys and patrols in this remote region.

The wind was relatively calm, and we circled over some of the high terrain, spotting several groups of elk. I saw a large vessel with hunters anchored in nearby King Cove, but we decided against landing there because large sea swells were rolling into the bay.

We flew over more high ridges around Tonki Cape looking for elk and for hunters. I saw a herd of elk near a small lake and pointed them out to Doug. I shouted over the roar of the engine, "Is that lake large enough to land on?"

"Sure—plenty of room. Want to land?"

"Yeah, let's stop and stretch our legs," I said. "We have plenty of time."

Doug circled the lake and then throttled back, landed, and taxied to the far end of the lake. We enjoyed flexing our legs after several hours of flying. I walked over to a tree and was relieving myself when I heard an elk bugle. The long, shrill notes shattered the quiet wilderness. A few minutes later another bull answered.

"Wow, that sounds close," I said to Doug.

"It sure does. Let's take a look."

I always carried a rifle when flying patrols in remote areas. I returned to the plane and pulled out my .300-caliber Winchester.

"I'll take this along just in case," I said to Doug. I needed an elk for my freezer.

We climbed a ridge near the lake, and I glassed the small group of elk with my binoculars.

"Hey look, Doug, there's a large bull," I said, pointing out the elk and handing him the binoculars.

"Wow! That's a nice one. Why don't you make a try for him?"

I looked at my watch. It was only three o'clock. I had plenty of time, and the weather was nice. I could shoot the bull and dress it out today. The next day I could charter Doug's plane for personal use, to fly out the meat.

I slipped behind a grove of spruce and quietly walked through the trees to the other side. I was within 150 yards of the magnificent six-point bull, which was now standing in a small clearing. I steadied the rifle against a tree trunk, took aim, and fired. The bull dropped, shot through the neck. It was huge, and I knew it would take me many trips to pack the meat to the lake. I had the elk half gutted when Doug arrived.

"Boy, what a bull!" he said, admiring the rack and the size of the animal.

"It's a nice one," I answered. "It'll be my winter's supply of meat. I'll give you a chunk when we get it back to Kodiak." I worked as fast as I could because I knew Doug was anxious to get going. I finished dressing the animal and was putting the heart and liver in a plastic bag when Doug noticed something.

"Uh-oh, the fog is rolling in," he said, looking at the mist drifting through the trees.

I grabbed the rifle and the small bag of meat, and we ran for the plane. Doug started the engine and taxied toward the other end of the lake as wisps of fog drifted over the water. But before we could take off, thick fog engulfed the entire lake and cut visibility nearly to zero.

"Damn! We'll have to wait for it to clear," Doug said. He was frustrated, but not overly upset. This was a common occurrence in Kodiak.

We taxied back to the other end of the lake and tied up the plane. After waiting an hour we realized we would probably have to spend the night. Doug and I took stock of our survival gear. There was not much. We had one sleeping bag between us, but no tent or tarp. Doug had a sandwich, several candy bars, and matches. I also had a few candy bars and an apple. An ample supply of blueberries grew nearby and, of course, we had plenty of elk meat. Doug tried to raise his office on the plane's radio but could not make contact.

That evening we built a fire near a big spruce tree, and I spread the sleeping bag under it. During the night we took turns keeping the fire going in two-hour shifts while the other slept. Morning was a long time coming, and the fog was thicker than ever. I had lived in Kodiak long enough to know that fog often remained for several days, but I did not want to be pessimistic.

"Oh, the fog will lift by tonight," I said.

"Yeah, I'm sure it will. If not, then tomorrow. At least we have plenty of food," Doug replied, also trying to stay optimistic.

We spent the day skinning the elk and packing the meat to the lake. A light mist began to fall and dampened everything. I built a brush pile, laid the meat on top, and then covered it with the elk hide. Air circulating through the brush pile would keep the meat from spoiling for a long time. That evening we finished the candy bars and ate plenty of blueberries. I roasted a few slices of liver over the fire, but we did not have any salt, so it did not taste very good.

The big spruce tree had protected us the evening before, but the constant rain now soaked everything. That night we decided to share the sleeping bag. We placed our raincoats over the bag to keep it as dry as possible. The bag was narrow, forcing us both to sleep on our sides. Every time one of us moved, the other woke up. The hard ground was uncomfortable; when my side got sore, I would lightly punch Doug and say, "Hey, it's time to turn over." We would attempt to turn in unison in an effort to keep the bag dry, but it got damp in spite of our efforts. Rain also dripped on my face constantly. We got some rest, but not much sleep.

At dawn I crawled from the sleeping bag and got a fire going. Thick fog continued to envelop the trees, and the unrelenting drizzle dampened our spirits along with everything else.

"Oh, boy. What's for breakfast?" Doug asked, his voice dripping with sarcasm.

"Elk steak and blueberries are on the menu," I replied. "That's almost like steak and eggs."

Ignoring my attempt at humor, Doug glared into the fire. After a few minutes he broke the silence.

"Let's try some of that heart for a change."

He walked over to the pile of meat, fished out the heart, and sliced off a few chunks. We roasted them over the fire. The meat looked and smelled delicious, but it had the same bland taste.

"Boy, what I wouldn't give for a shaker full of salt," Doug said.

"Here, try some blueberries," I said, offering him a plastic sack I had filled that morning. We both liked blueberries, but after eating them constantly for two days, they also seemed tasteless.

We spent the day taking short hikes, but since neither of us had a compass, we did not travel far. By noon we knew that we would be spending another damp night in the woods—our third. That afternoon we cut some spruce poles and built a lean-to, covering it with spruce branches and a layer of moss a foot thick. It was a big improvement from the shelter of the spruce tree, and we slept better that night.

It poured rain most of the fourth day. We kept a fire going and spent the day drying our clothes and the sleeping bag. That evening we tried to be upbeat.

"Oh, it's bound to clear up. These storms usually last only three or four days," Doug said as we cooked dinner around the fire.

"Yeah, it'll clear tomorrow. I feel it in my bones," I answered. "Here, try this delicious steak." I thrust at him a forked stick with a piece of tenderloin that I had roasted in the coals for a few minutes. I tried one myself and decided it tasted a bit better than the heart and liver.

We discussed walking to the beach if the fog and rain continued, but we knew the chances of getting rescued by a boat in this remote area were slim. Doug tried to raise his office on the radio again but could not make contact. I wondered if LuRue was worried about me. It was not the first time I had been stormbound, so I assumed she knew why I had not returned yet.

Rain continued most of the night. All that water was too much for our little lean-to. It seemed to leak everywhere. The sleeping bag got soaked, and we did not get much sleep. Soon after daylight I heard something.

"Hey, Doug, I think I hear a plane!"

"Yeah, me too!"

We clambered out of our wet sleeping bag and the lean-to. The rain had quit, but fog still covered the treetops. Hearing an airplane circling, I shouted to Doug, "Maybe this is our lucky day."

We ran for the Cub. Doug jumped in, started the engine, turned on the radio, and contacted the plane. The plane above wanted to know if we were okay. They told us the fog was dissipating fast and it had already cleared in Kodiak. I looked up and saw a patch of blue sky through an opening in the fog.

"Whoopee! What a beautiful sight!" I yelled. After a few more minutes the fog cleared. We took off in the plane, climbing out of the little lake where we had been trapped for several days.

The town of Kodiak was a welcome sight, and as soon as we landed, I rushed home. LuRue met me at the door and gave me a big, long hug.

"Were you worried about me?" I asked.

"Yes, but I knew the weather was bad, and I was sure you'd be back as soon as the fog lifted," she said. Still, she was clearly relieved, and we savored the moment.

I got out of my dirty clothes and cleaned up, happy to be home. LuRue prepared several delicious venison sandwiches, which I salted twice. I finished off the meal with a big bowl of ice cream. What a treat! I told LuRue about the elk I had killed. I would need to go back, but I assured her that the trip would be the following day. I was looking forward to a good night's sleep in a soft bed.

The weather stayed clear and calm in Kodiak, quite a contrast to the rain and fog that had trapped us for four days. I told LuRue, "Maybe I had better go back and get a load of meat this afternoon, as long as the weather holds."

She made a face and said, "Okay, but go now to make sure you get home before dark."

I called Doug that afternoon. "What do you think about flying back out and getting a load of meat today?"

"Sounds good to me," he said. "I'll be ready as soon as you get down here."

I got my gear together, kissed LuRue goodbye, and headed down to the float-plane pond. While we had been missing, a search party had put together a package containing a sack of sandwiches and matches in a waterproof case, plus two sleeping bags in case they needed to make an airdrop. Just before we left, one of the employees gave the gear to Doug.

"Here, take these...just in case," the man said.

Doug thought the package was unnecessary, but he threw it into the back of the plane anyway.

We got to Tonki Cape at about five o'clock and landed at the little lake. To make room for more meat, Doug took out the sandwiches and sleeping bags and left them by our old campsite. Getting the meat back to Kodiak would take more than one flight, so we could bring the rescue gear back on the last flight. We loaded the plane with several hundred pounds of elk meat. To balance the load, Doug laid a hind leg on the rear seat. I crawled into the plane and sat atop the leg. Doug started the engine. "Are you ready?" he asked.

"Yep, let's go," I answered.

Doug gave the Cub full power, but it would not get on step. We were obviously overloaded, so he throttled back the engine. We taxied back to the other end of the lake and tried again, with the same result.

"Doug, let's unload some of this meat," I said.

"Let me give it one more try."

While we were taxiing back from the previous attempt, a breeze had sprung up. Doug again gave the Cub full power, and it climbed on step. My spirits rose. We were going to make it! We were well down the lake when the plane staggered off the water. I did not like how the plane felt, so I peeked around Doug's shoulder and saw nothing but trees ahead. We were gaining altitude, but not fast enough! I thought we might clear the trees, but it was going to be close. Awfully close! My heart was in my throat.

Doug lost his nerve and tried to make a tight turn. To this day, I do not know if our floats would have cleared the trees. The plane stalled as Doug tried to turn, and we dropped like a stone. The plane hit the lake nose first and flipped. Almost immediately the cabin filled with water. I knew we were sinking to the bottom of the lake. People have told me that their whole life flashed through their mind during a near-death experience. However, I had only two thoughts: "This is a heck of a way to go," and "I've got to get out of here."

I wrestled the door open, but as I attempted to get out, I realized my seat belt was still fastened. Submerged in cold water, I held my breath as I undid the belt. It seemed to take an eternity. I did not expect to survive, as I thought we were on the bottom of the lake, but I had to try. Once I cleared the cabin, I stroked my arms a couple of times and popped to the surface. I could not believe it! How did I get up so quickly? A quick look around showed that the plane was hanging upside down from its floats. Despite being somewhat disoriented, I thought, "I have to go down and get Doug." Before I could act, his head appeared. I was extremely relieved to see him, but we did not say anything to each other. We each crawled onto a float, breathing heavily. Neither of us was injured, although my back was really sore.

We sat for a few moments, shivering from shock and cold. Doug broke the silence. "I'm sure not going to try to swim in this cold water. Let's see if we can paddle the plane to shore," he said. Lying on the floats, we started paddling with our hands. It was slow going, but the lake was narrow. Eventually we reached shore and jumped off, glad to be on solid ground.

"What a dumb thing to do!" Doug said. "We should have unloaded some meat."

"I thought we were going to make it," I replied weakly.

As reality sank in, we realized we would be spending another night in the woods. No one in Kodiak would become alarmed until night fell and we failed to return. I wondered what LuRue would think when I did not return. I had promised her I would be right back. I was sure she would really be concerned this time, as weather was not a factor.

I was feeling pretty low about our plight. Tonki Cape seemed jinxed for us. I glumly walked over to our old campsite and saw the sack of sandwiches and sleeping bags.

"At least we've got something to eat tonight," I thought.

We got a fire going and began to dry our wet clothes. This was a far cry from the warm house and bed I had expected to enjoy that night. I was really depressed and blamed myself for getting into this jam. Why did I have to shoot that elk? Most of it was now underwater and probably spoiled. I also wondered what was going through LuRue's mind. If only I had just waited another day before returning for the meat, I would not be here tonight. If only...

Doug broke my train of thought when he offered me a sandwich. I did not have much of an appetite, but I ate the sandwich anyway and had to admit that it tasted good. After our clothes were fairly dry, we each grabbed a sleeping bag and laid it under the spruce tree. The sun had dried things out, and I should have slept well, but I woke periodically, thinking about our predicament. I should have felt better knowing we were lucky to be alive. I tried to console myself with that thought.

The next morning we got a big brush pile ready to burn. Doug and I feared that when a search plane arrived, the pilot would spot our plane upside down in the lake and think we were dead.

Before long we heard the drone of an airplane. I immediately lit the brush pile, and we stood beside the flames waving our arms. The plane circled, and the pilot dipped his wings several times to acknowledge that he and his passenger had seen us. He radioed Kodiak Airways about the accident and told them we appeared to be okay.

After the plane landed, Doug explained the accident to the pilot. We talked a bit more about the incident and then discussed arrangements for getting us back to town. The rescue plane could hold only one other person besides the pilot.

"One of you guys get in. I can wait," said the passenger of the rescue plane. I told Doug to go first, since he would have to explain the accident to his boss.

The plane finally returned for me, and I arrived in Kodiak at about noon. When I got out of the plane, LuRue was waiting for me with baby Janice in her arms. We hugged for a long time. I could tell by the look on her face that she had been through a lot of stress. I had nearly made her a widow at the young age of twenty-five. I vowed to be more careful in the future.

During the next two years I found out just how lucky we had been. Two planes crashed in the Tonki Cape area during elk hunting trips, and three of four hunters drowned while trying to swim ashore.

Chapter 13

Becoming a Bush Pilot

After the Tonki Cape incident I resolved to qualify as an official FWS pilot. I had acquired a private license in 1949, before coming to Alaska; I enjoyed flying and envied my colleagues stationed in interior Alaska who had become government pilots. In my early years, however, I worked in the coastal regions, where water-going vessels were the primary mode of transportation.

The FWS employed professionals to fly their larger twin-engine planes, but they encouraged biologists and enforcement agents to obtain a private pilot license and a minimum of one hundred hours of solo time. Once qualified, they could fly the smaller single-engine Pacers, Piper Super Cubs, and Cessna 180s that were used in interior Alaska.

In Kodiak I saw a need for a small plane to conduct bear surveys and patrol the refuge, and I wanted to be at the controls. I petitioned my superiors for an FWS single-engine plane, but without success. They believed that chartering small planes from the local airlines would be adequate and cheaper.

When Dick Hensel became my assistant in 1960, we frequently discussed this policy and debated strategies for changing it. One day over a cup of coffee I said to Dick, "The only way we will ever get the aircraft division to station a plane in Kodiak is for us to meet the pilot requirements and then petition them for a plane."

Dick agreed, but he reminded me that getting flight training would be very expensive as there were no flight schools in Kodiak. To get our training, we would have to go to Anchorage. But then he added, "Let's form a flying club so we can do our flight training here in Kodiak for less money."

Dick Hensel and I used this personal Tcraft for flight training and in our wildlife work.

I thought it was a great idea. We both became enthusiastic about a flying club and talked four other friends into joining us. In the spring of 1961 the club purchased an eighty-five-horsepower Taylorcraft with wheels and floats for $3,000. The Tcraft, a small plane with little cargo space, carried two passengers side by side. On wheels it performed fine, but Kodiak had few landing strips and a lot of water, so we kept it on floats.

The little plane was pushed to its limits when flown with a large pilot and a passenger, and it needed a lot of room to get airborne. The lake where we kept the plane in Kodiak was of marginal length when we had a heavy load, unless there was a good headwind to help provide lift. In addition, the engine had a habit of coughing, due to a misfiring piston, when you gave it full power. An aircraft mechanic inspected the engine several times but failed to find the source of the problem. "It just has a bad cold," Dick would say. "Don't worry about it." Eventually the engine did quit missing and hummed along beautifully, so maybe he was right. These difficulties encouraged flying club members to be cautious on takeoffs, however.

We discovered that getting flight instruction at Kodiak was difficult. The two licensed instructors in town, Gil Jarvela and John Warren, flew for Kodiak Airways; they worked long hours and were generally unavailable. In addition, the weather in Kodiak was often too nasty to fly.

I needed less flight time than the others because I already had my license; I needed only to become proficient on floats. I received a float rating in early September 1961, which authorized me to carry passengers. Because club members often could not hire the busy flight instructors, they offered to pay my flying expenses if they could accompany me and gain some flight experience. I agreed and gladly accepted their offers; however, it was a case of the near-blind leading the blind. With fewer than a hundred hours of solo flight time, I had limited skills.

I primarily taught takeoff and landing procedures to the club members. We practiced these in the saltwater channels around Near Island, which provided unlimited landing space. I worked especially with Dick, because I wanted him to get his private license as soon as possible. Dick was eager, but during the first few flights he sometimes tensed up when we were about to touch down. He would clutch the controls fiercely and stare ahead with glazed eyes. I had to wrest the controls from him before we landed.

"Let go of the wheel!" I would yell as he sat transfixed.

"I have, I have!" he yelled in return while his knuckles turned white from gripping the wheel.

I then had to give the engine full power and fly around again while Dick's nerves calmed. Eventually he learned to relax, and he became a good student.

Dick and I had many adventures together while learning to fly. One evening after work I agreed to give him a flight lesson. I opted to fly the plane to the saltwater channel in town and pick him up. After landing in the bay and taxiing into the boat harbor, I pulled the plane tail first onto a floating ramp to get Dick. The Tcraft did not have a starter and had to be hand cranked. I briefed Dick on how to pull the propeller. I got inside, set the switch and throttle, and motioned for Dick to start cranking. But every time he walked forward on the floats to pull the prop, the plane slid down the slippery ramp, and Dick had to run back on the floats to pull the plane back up. After about four attempts I yelled at Dick, "This isn't gonna work. Let me try."

Dick got into the plane, and I instructed him on how to turn on the switch and set the throttle. I got out on the float and yelled, "Are you ready?" He nodded, and I gave the prop a mighty heave. The engine caught on the first pull, but I lost my balance, slipped off the float, and fell into the water. The plane slid from the ramp and started taxiing out into the boat harbor with Dick in the passenger seat. At that point he did not know much about the control panel. I was trying to crawl back onto the ramp with two hip boots full of water when Dick stuck his head out the plane door and yelled, "Will! Will! What should I do?"

The plane was taxiing toward a boat. I saw a catastrophe in the making!

"Pull back on the throttle and cut the switch!" I yelled.

In a few seconds Dick came to his senses and almost jerked the throttle out of the panel. The engine stopped. Dick climbed out on the floats, grabbed the canoe paddle we always carried, and began to paddle the plane toward the dock.

I was sheepishly walking around to where Dick was docking the plane when an amused fisherman stuck his head out his wheelhouse window and yelled, "Maybe you need a boat operator's license instead of a pilot's."

I gave him the finger. He just laughed and yelled something back.

On a ptarmigan hunting trip that fall Dick and I loaded our two black Labs into the Tcraft and flew to Bear Lake, on the south end of the island. When we returned to the small, round lake after the hunt, it was completely calm. I was nervous about taking off. A floatplane needs to break free of the water tension, climb onto the surface, and hydroplane like a boat in order to gain enough speed for takeoff. Besides helping with lift, wind creates waves that break that surface tension. With no other good options, I decided to try it. We loaded our dogs and our gear and climbed in. I gave the engine full throttle down the length of the lake, but with the heavy load and no wind I was unable to get it on step. I made several attempts without success.

"Looks like I'm gonna have to leave you here," I said to Dick.

"No way! This airplane is staying here until the wind comes up," Dick replied, a worried look on his face. I was only joking, but Dick had taken me seriously.

During our several takeoff attempts I noticed we were creating waves that broke up the smooth surface of the lake. It was then that I discovered a trick most bush pilots eventually learn. I circled the lake several times at full throttle until the floats created a series of rolling waves. When I turned into the wake, the choppy water broke the suction under the floats. The plane climbed on step, gained speed, and became airborne. I glanced over at Dick and saw a big look of relief on his face.

On another ptarmigan hunting trip Dick and I landed in a small lake southwest of Karluk Lake. The moment we touched down I realized the lake was too short; before we came to a stop, the floats slid up onto the tundra shoreline. Dick and I managed to push and pull the light plane back to the water. We went ahead with our hunt.

After we returned to the lake, I said to Dick, "There is no way the two of us can take off in this small lake. You're going to have to walk back."

"Are you sure?" he asked dejectedly.

"I'm sure. There isn't any use in even trying."

I got into the plane and flew it back to Karluk Lake in ten minutes while Dick spent two hours slogging through wet marshes to reach our rendezvous point.

The little Tcraft in Kodiak finally met its fate in Karluk Lake in April 1963. I had planned to fly Dick to the lake to start some early bald eagle–nesting studies. On the evening before the flight Dick called and suggested he take a load of supplies to the lake with the Tcraft to gain some cross-country flying experience. The weather forecast was good, so I gave him the go-ahead.

A few hours after I watched him take off, I got a message from the Kodiak Airways office. They told me they had received a call from Dick. He was at Karluk Lake and wanted to talk to me on their radio; our office radio was not working at the time. I radioed the camp and in a few moments I heard Dick's voice crackling over the airwaves.

"This is Dick. Will, I wonder if you could fly down and pick me up. I can't seem to get the plane started."

"Roger, roger, Dick, but are you sure you can't get it started?"

Dick assured me he could not start the plane, but I knew that the Tcraft's carburetor often flooded while I was trying to start it. I had learned to turn off the main switch and crank the prop backward a few turns to solve the problem.

"Dick, the plane drowns real easy. Just crank it backward a few turns and I'm sure it will start."

There was silence for a few moments, and then Dick's voice crackled again. "Yes, Will, I hear what you're saying, but I don't think it will start this time. It's really drowned!"

I informed him I would come out that afternoon to either pick him up or help him start the Tcraft. He said, "Okay," but I sensed some distress in his voice.

Before I could leave, he arrived at the office, having caught a ride to town with Kodiak Airways. He had some cuts on his upper lip and seemed in shock.

"What in the world happened to you?" I asked.

"I had a wreck!"

"A wreck?" I said in disbelief. "You mean you crashed the plane?"

I then got the full story from Dick. Karluk Lake had been like a mirror when Dick arrived in the Tcraft. He decided to buzz the fishery camp before landing. Several of the biologists stepped out of the cabin and waved to acknowledge his arrival. He made a huge turn to land. Dick's flying experience was still limited, and he made the mistake of looking directly down into the glassy, calm water while making his turn. An experienced floatplane pilot knows you cannot judge your elevation by looking directly down into water with no ripples. The transparency of the water prevents a pilot from judging elevation; you need to look at the shoreline or the far horizon. Dick thought he was still a hundred feet in the air when one wingtip hit the water. The plane spun in sideways, the force ripping the floats from the fuselage.

Dick was dazed by the crash, but he snapped back to reality when water poured over his lap. Fortunately, he was able to climb out of the plane before it sank. The water was bitterly cold, but Dick had wisely worn his life jacket. The fishery crew saw the crash, jumped into a skiff, and rushed over to fish him out of the water. They expected to find a severely injured pilot, but Dick was bobbing around with only a few bloody facial scratches and an undamaged sense of humor.

"Hey, I thought I'd just drop in to say howdy," he greeted them.

The Tcraft remained at the bottom of the deep lake, and that was the end of the flying club. Dick eventually got his private pilot license and became a qualified FWS pilot. Like many other bush pilots, he had learned a lesson the hard way.

But before its demise, the Tcraft became a stepping-stone to my goal of getting a government plane for my job. After I received my float rating and had accumulated more than a hundred hours of flying time, I used the club's Tcraft to conduct wildlife surveys for the refuge, even though I had to pay for the flight time out of my own pocket. I gained a lot of experience, but I resented having to shoulder the costs. I called Theron Smith, head of the FWS aircraft division, to see if there was any way I could get the agency to share some of my flying costs. Theron considered my situation and agreed to help me.

"Come to Anchorage," he said. "I'll give you some training and a check ride to see if you can become a qualified FWS pilot."

In early June 1962 I flew to Anchorage. Theron spent many hours teaching me various low-level flight maneuvers and how to taxi on the water in a Super Cub in adverse wind conditions. At the end of the week's training I passed his stringent tests. I had finally reached my goal of becoming an authorized FWS pilot. It was a big achievement, but I had not reached my ultimate goal. I still did not have a government plane to fly at Kodiak.

Dick and I schemed some more. We encouraged Herb Downing, an eager flying club member who had some extra money, to purchase a surplus FWS Super Cub that was for sale. I told him that if he purchased the plane, I would lease it for my refuge wildlife work and he could make some money. Herb bought the plane, overhauled the engine, recovered the wings, and painted the body. It looked and flew like a new plane. With the approval of my superiors, I leased the surplus Cub from Herb. During my last two years in Kodiak I gained a lot of experience in flying and in caring for a small plane.

A longtime pilot told me early in my flying career, "Becoming a good bush pilot requires a variety of flying experiences. Either you learn from your mistakes and near accidents or you don't survive very long."

Kodiak was a good place to get that experience. The weather conditions were often atrocious; storms moved in rapidly and strong winds buffeted the area. I learned how to judge good and bad flying conditions and how to land in choppy water. Fog frequently settled over all or various parts of the island. On several occasions I left town under clear blue skies to make a short flight, only to find when I returned a few hours later that Kodiak was totally obscured by fog. Sometimes I was able to find my way into town by hugging the shoreline. Other times the visibility was just too poor, so I had to turn around and land in some bay and wait for the weather to improve.

One day I was returning from Karluk Lake in bad weather with Darrel Farmen. The closer we got to Kodiak, the worse the visibility became. I throttled the engine back to slow the plane's speed and flew just above the water, keeping an eye on the shore. Near Monashka Mountain I crossed a small bight and lost sight of the shoreline. I knew I was in trouble and tried to make a 180-degree turn, but I overcompensated in the fog.

"There's a mountain!" Darrel yelled, pointing straight ahead.

Through the foggy mist I saw the trees. I stomped on the right rudder and banked sharply. As we turned away from the mountain, I spotted the shoreline again. Relieved, I followed it back out of the bay, and my pulse slowly returned to normal. I had made a mistake that nearly killed us.

The ceiling remained low, but visibility improved as we flew away from town. I managed to find my way into Anton Larsen Bay at the end of the road system and land the plane. I was shaken up by the close call and needed several minutes to calm my nerves. I could not raise anyone on the plane's radio, so Darrel volunteered to walk the six miles into town. He seemed awfully eager to get back to town on foot rather than in the plane.

About thirty minutes after Darrel left, I saw a little light through the pass. The fog lay just above the treetops. I felt confident I could navigate back to town by following the road and flying just above the treetops and below the fog. I took off and passed Darrel.

"You almost knocked my hat off when you flew over," Darrel told me later.

Once I got to town, I managed to find the floatplane lake. When the floats touched the water, relief washed over me. I vowed never again to fly in such poor weather conditions. But of course I did get caught in bad weather again, as all longtime Alaska pilots do.

The Super Cub is an ideal plane for conducting wildlife surveys. Tandem seating in the narrow cabin permits excellent visibility on either side of the aircraft for both pilot and passenger. It can be flown at slow speeds and has a tight turning radius. The Cub is also capable of landing and taking off from very short airstrips or small lakes. The small, light craft is easily tossed about by strong winds, however. I gradually learned its wind limitations, both in the air and on the ground. Over the years I spent many hours flying Super Cubs. Piloting the Cub became almost automatic; I always felt I wore the Cub rather than flew it.

I kept Herb's Cub at Karluk Lake during the summer field seasons of 1962 and 1963. Dick and I built a wooden airplane ramp with good tie-downs near our cabin on Camp Island. The gale-force winds that sometimes buffeted Karluk Lake made it challenging to keep the small plane safely moored during storms. Sometimes I filled the floats with water; the extra weight helped keep the plane from blowing away. I often got out of bed at night during windstorms to check the Cub and retie the ropes. I learned that it was a lot of work to be a pilot, but I preferred having control of the plane while conducting wildlife surveys.

Later, after moving to Kenai, I was pleasantly surprised to find that the Kenai Peninsula had much better flying conditions. Foggy days and windy weather were less frequent. Numerous lakes provided many landing sites for floatplanes during summer and ski-equipped planes during winter.

The colder winter days required a lot more work to prepare an airplane for flight. During those early days we did not have insulated engine covers and electric heaters to keep the plane's engine warm at night. At the end of a flying day I tied down the plane and slipped canvas covers over the wings and the windshield to keep them free of frost and snow. I drained the engine oil into a large enclosed pan and took it inside the house to keep warm.

In the morning I used an old Herman Nelson gas heater with large air hoses to heat the cold engine. Once the engine was warm, I removed the wing covers, poured in the oil, and started the plane. During winter I spent about an hour getting the plane ready each day I flew.

The Cub's cabin was not insulated. It leaked cold air and had a poor heater. When flying in temperatures near or below zero, I usually bundled up in bunny boots, heavy coveralls, and a parka.

I flew twenty years in my career as a wildlife biologist in Alaska and logged several thousand hours. This is not a lot of flying time for a career pilot; however, 90 percent of my flying hours were spent conducting low-level wildlife surveys with the small Super Cub. I flew many hours observing moose, caribou, brown bear, bald eagles, and other species in the lowlands. Other days I circled Alaska's rugged mountains to count Dall sheep and mountain goats. Flying itself was not an obsession for me, but low-level flights to observe wildlife at close range were. Being an FWS pilot required a lot of extra work, but to me it was well worth the effort.

Chapter 14

Bear Surveys

T he sun had not yet risen over the mountains as I approached the headwaters of Dog Salmon Creek in the Super Cub. About three hundred yards ahead I spotted a sow with two yearling cubs chasing salmon in a shallow riffle. Just downstream of the family, a small single sat on the bank. I turned the Cub sharply, circling to get a better look at the four bears. I recorded my observations into a tape recorder, talking loudly above the drone of the plane's engine. I continued downstream, dipping the Cub's wings from side to side to view any animals that might be directly under the plane. A minute later I spotted a large sow chasing salmon in the middle of the river while her cubs sat on the bank. I circled to get a better look and shouted information into my tape recorder. "She has three small cubs—two with white neck collars."

Several hundred yards farther two large males caught my eye, and I spotted a small single running along the bank. Then there was a short lull in bear activity until I observed a sow with a small yearling fishing; another sow with two yearlings also came into view. I occasionally made 360-degree turns to verify dark objects that I thought were bears in the brush. By the time I reached the mouth of Dog Salmon Creek, I had seen thirty-four bears.

I then flew northwest to census Connecticut Creek and the upper part of the Red River. After three hours of flying I was tired, and I returned to Camp Island, hungry for breakfast.

While I was having a cup of coffee, I turned on the tape recorder and tabulated the results of my surveys. I had counted seventy-five bears that morning, and 60 percent of those recorded were cubs or yearlings. I was elated.

The Super Cub I used to fly aerial bear surveys after I became a qualified FWS pilot.

The aerial surveys that I conducted each year on Kodiak provided information on the minimum number of bears using each drainage and the ratio of young to adults in the population; large numbers of juveniles indicated a healthy population. I knew, however, that I was seeing only a small portion of the total bears in any given drainage; many animals were hidden in the dense vegetation.

To augment these aerial counts, I also conducted ground counts. I hiked into selected drainages, spent a day or two camped on ridges overlooking the salmon streams, and tabulated the bears with the aid of binoculars and a spotting scope. While the flights allowed me to cover numerous drainages quickly, the ground counts were more comprehensive as I saw a larger percentage of the bear population using a specific area.

I usually did the foot surveys by myself, but occasionally one of my colleagues would come along. One day in late July 1958 Earl Fleming accompanied me into the Sturgeon River drainage, which does not have any suitable airplane landing sites. The only way to reach its headwaters is by a long, arduous hike.

Earl and I carried a minimum of food and camping gear to lighten our load during the lengthy hike. The first leg of the trip traversed a wet, marshy area. Hiking through these bogs was tough walking as our feet sank deep into the spongy ground at each step. By the time we reached the headwaters a few hours later, we were both exhausted. We sat down for a rest.

"Do you think we need all this gear?" I asked Earl.

"Naw—the weather looks good," he answered. "We don't really need a tent; a light plastic tarp will do. Nor do we need this much food. There are plenty of fish and berries to eat."

We shed about twenty pounds of weight and stashed the supplies on a rock ledge at the base of a mountain. We were glad we had, because by the time we intercepted a small fork of the headwaters of the Sturgeon River, we still faced many more hours of hiking to reach our survey site on the lower river.

The shallow stream was only about two feet wide, but several dog salmon were already spawning in a riffle. As we approached, they skittered into a deep pool. We could tell by the many salmon carcasses, along with fresh bear tracks and scat, that the bruins were having an easy time fishing this remote stream.

"This is real bear country," I said, pointing at several dead salmon.

"We should be running into one before long," Earl replied.

About a quarter mile farther downstream I heard the splashing of a bear chasing salmon. I stopped and raised my hand to signal Earl to halt.

"I hear one coming," I whispered to Earl.

"I hear it, too," he whispered back. "Let's stay here and watch the bear's reaction when it comes around that corner."

We waited, listening to the animal approach. We finally saw its back through gaps in the brush. It rounded the bend about sixty yards downstream. I wanted to make sure it knew we were there; surprising a bear can be deadly. I raised my arms and yelled, "Hey, bear—watch where you're going!"

Earl removed the rifle from his shoulder, and we waited for its reaction. The bear stopped and rose to its hind feet.

"Watch it, bear. We're not going to hurt you," I said in a loud but calm voice. "Now, just run over into that brush while we pass through your fishing grounds."

The bear continued to stand, its dark eyes focused on us. It dropped to all fours, moved forward another fifty feet, and stood on its hind legs again. I heard Earl click off the rifle safety. We stood there, eyeball to eyeball, for a full minute. Earl and I had dealt with a lot of bears before, but most of the time they ran off when they realized we were human. I was wondering what our next move should be when I felt a breeze hit the back of my neck. Our scent drifted down to the bear. It caught our scent, dropped to all four feet, and galloped away toward a brushy mountain slope.

"Whew!" Earl said. "I thought for a minute I was going to have to fire a warning shot."

"Maybe it's never seen a man before," I said. And perhaps it had not in this remote valley.

We continued downriver, occasionally flushing bald eagles or gulls feeding on salmon remains. We cautiously passed several bears sleeping on a knoll. In another mile we came to a slope that led up a mountain to a prominent overlook. I pointed it out to Earl.

"That knob has a great view of the upper Sturgeon. I was planning to camp there to make a morning and evening count of the bears."

"Sounds good to me," Earl answered.

"But," I continued, "see that high ridge downriver through that narrow gap? That overlooks the heart of the Sturgeon River, and it's where most of the bears live. It's still early. If you're not too tired, let's try to make it down there and do our first bear counts tonight."

"Okay with me, Will—lead the way."

As we entered the narrow valley, the river became wider and had many deep pools. Some were filled with masses of chum salmon; some were black with small Dolly Varden trout.

"They would sure make a tasty meal," Earl said.

"They're thick," I said, nodding in agreement. "Let's see if we can catch some by hand."

We tried several times to grab a fish, but they were too slippery...too quick. Then Earl took out his pocketknife, removed his bill cap, and punched it full of holes.

"Boy, you ruined a good hat," I said, seeing where this was going but skeptical of his plan.

"Yeah, but maybe it'll be worth it," he replied. Earl swept his makeshift seine through a shallow pool black with trout. His first few sweeps were unsuccessful, but on the third try he caught two seven-inchers. He waited a few minutes to let the fish in the pool settle down before trying again. After a few sweeps he caught a couple more. Within twenty minutes, Earl had caught ten trout from six to eight inches long.

"Now, what do you think of my little seine?" he said, looking at me with a grin.

"Not bad, Earl. We'll eat well tonight."

We cleaned the fish, slid them into plastic sacks, and tossed them into our packs. In another half mile downstream we left the river, cut across the valley, and started climbing the ridge that separated the two main forks of the Sturgeon River. On the way we passed a patch of ripe salmonberries.

"That'll be enough for dessert," I said, after picking a bunch.

Late that afternoon we crested the ridge, where we had a sweeping view of both forks of the Sturgeon. Ten miles downriver we could see Sturgeon Lagoon; beyond Shelikof Strait loomed the volcanic mountains of Katmai National Park.

Counting bears from a mountain ledge overlooking Canyon and O'Malley Rivers near Karluk Lake.

Like a huge spiderweb laid out below us, bear trails crisscrossed the broad valley floor, winding around patches of willows and through tundra heather. As I scanned the immense country with my binoculars, I could pick out many bears. Several were already fishing. Here, predator and prey were following their ancient rituals in a primitive scene unchanged for hundreds, perhaps thousands, of years. Tonight Earl and I would have grandstand seats in this ancient amphitheater.

I broke out of my reverie and looked at my watch. It was six o'clock, time to start the counts, as bears are more active in the late evening and early morning. Earl and I set up the tripod and attached the twenty-power spotting scope.

Using my binoculars, I scanned the mountainsides and valley floor. Here and there, bears were moving toward the river; others were already fishing. It was dinnertime in brown bear country, and everyone seemed to have a reservation. Directly below us, on the right-hand fork of the Sturgeon, two subadults were chasing salmon. I focused the powerful spotting scope on the pair.

"Earl, do you want to record the individuals or should I?" I asked.

"I'll do it," he said and grabbed a pencil and a pad of paper.

"Okay, mark down the subadult pair. One is a real blond and the other very dark," I said.

"Let me see." Earl leaned over and squinted into the scope. "Boy, what a beautiful, silky blond. That pair should be easy to remember."

I glassed down the river until I spotted two sows, each with cubs of the year (less than a year old). The cubs of the first sow were uniformly dark, but the second family had one cub with a very pronounced white neck collar. I called out descriptions as Earl recorded the details.

"Two medium-sized males at the junction," I said. "One is real dark with a big rubbed spot on his left front shoulder, and the medium brown has a scar on his left rear leg."

Earl recorded the information and then peered through the scope to verify my descriptions. As he looked out again over the valley, something caught his eye. He grabbed his binoculars.

"Wow! Look over to the right," he remarked.

A huge, dark male with a low-slung belly was approaching the river. He had an enormous, broad head; his neck was etched with scars from numerous past fights. A bear of stature, he walked slowly and deliberately through the river and sat down on a gravel bar in the middle. Like a gentleman going to dinner, he apparently wanted to eye the options. The main course was fresh chum salmon at the all-you-can-eat bar. Several fish moved through a shallow riffle, their backs out of the water. He saw one that was too tasty a morsel to ignore. The bear rose and pounced on it, pinning it down with his huge paw. He leaned down and clenched it between his teeth. Holding the struggling fish, the dark male walked to the other end of the gravel bar. There he lay down his prey, placed a foot on the head of the fish, and began ripping red flesh from his victim. In a few gulps he had consumed the entire fish.

The big boar continued walking downstream in quest of another salmon while several gulls swooped in to claim the remaining tidbits. He was soon chasing another salmon down the river. Meanwhile, just downstream and around the bend, a medium-sized male was pursuing another salmon upriver. From our vantage point on the ridge we could see that they were on a collision course. Both rounded the bend in the river, saw each other, and slammed to a halt only forty feet apart. They eyed each other briefly. Then the larger bear lowered his ears and charged. The drama was short; there was no fight. The smaller male turned, galloped from the stream, and disappeared into some willows.

While I was focused on the two bears, Earl spotted a sow with yearlings descending a mountain ridge. He pointed them out to me when I had finished watching the large bear's display of dominance. The mother moved steadily toward the river as her offspring romped and played. While we were watching the family group, three singles came out of the brush on the other fork of the river, directly below us. One was very light blond, and the other two were medium brown. One of the latter had a definite limp in his right foot. Earl recorded these distinguishing marks.

Bears were now spread out all along the river: singles, pairs, family groups. At one time we had thirty-five bears in view. But night was approaching, and light was fading rapidly. Distant bears appeared only as silhouettes. Some bears were leaving the river while others were still arriving for a late dinner, but the fading light made it difficult to see distinguishing marks.

"Let's call it a day; it's nearly ten," I said to Earl. "How many did we record?"

"That last family group made it sixty-two," he answered. "What a show! This is what I call real bear country."

"It's about the most peaceful and primitive scene that still exists on this earth," I replied, looking over the darkening valley.

"Yeah, this is bear heaven—the real happy hunting grounds," Earl said.

We were done with the bear count, but still we sat there enjoying the wildness of the scene. No winds stirred, and in the stillness we could hear bears splashing after salmon. Occasional deep growls revealed conflicts. A red fox yelped in the distance, and the flutelike notes of a hermit thrush reminded me of a trumpeter playing evening taps.

"Let's eat," I said, getting to my feet. I gathered a small bundle of dry willow branches from the surrounding bushes and started a fire on a patch of gravel. When the fire had burned down a bit, we each stuck a trout on the end of a willow pole and roasted it over the small bed of red-hot coals. The fish were delicious; we consumed all ten.

"It sure beats hot dogs," Earl said, reminding me of my typical camping dinner. I had to agree. After we finished the trout, we ate salmonberries for dessert. The wild meal seemed fitting in the wilderness setting.

The valley became darker, and the setting sun cast a colorful glow across the horizon. Yellows turned to pink, and hues of rose streaked the sky. Bears continued to move below us as ebony shadows. We sat by our small fire in silence, sipping tea, watching the fading colors, and listening to the night sounds. The primitive drama coming to a close had been staged in this outdoor theater for eons; tonight we were the audience. I was tired and finally broke the silence.

"I'm calling it a day."

I grabbed a sleeping bag, unrolled it between two crowberry hummocks, crawled in, and pulled a light tarp over me. The night sounds lulled me to sleep.

I awoke around five o'clock to the chiming song of a longspur. Earl and I arose, lit a small fire, and were soon sipping hot chocolate.

We started the morning count as bears began fishing the river. We identified many of the family groups and singles from the night before, but we were most interested in spotting any newcomers. They would add to our total number of bears using this section of the river. The parade continued for hours, gradually decreasing as the sun rose higher in the sky. By eight in the morning numerous bears had left the river and were now sleeping or resting on nearby knolls, no doubt content with bellies full of salmon. Others had chosen to bed down in willow patches, and many followed trails into the mountains. The decreasing bear activity signaled the end of our morning count.

"Well, Earl, time to eat and move on," I said.

"I could stay here forever," Earl replied. "This is what I call real wilderness."

But we had to travel up the valley and spend a night on another high point, counting bears closer to the headwaters of the Sturgeon. Only after that did we take the long hike back to Karluk Lake.

We often came in close contact with bears while conducting these ground surveys. Near encounters were sometimes a bit scary and always thrilling. I had only one incident, however, that I considered truly frightening.

Less than a week after I returned from the Sturgeon River, I decided to conduct one more count overlooking the O'Malley River near the south end of Karluk Lake. It was one of my favorite spots. The ledge from which I made my observations was relatively low, enabling me to be fairly close to many of the bears fishing in the river. I liked that intimate feel. In addition, the river was easily accessible from our Camp Island cabin. A six-mile skiff ride across Karluk Lake and a thirty- to forty-minute hike placed me on top of the ledge.

At about six in the evening I arrived at the survey site, where I had a sweeping view of the valley. Below me were streams and meadows; above me were three-thousand-foot mountain peaks rimming the valley. With the shorter streams at O'Malley River and Canyon Creek, bears were even more concentrated here than at the Sturgeon, and I knew from previous visits that anywhere from forty to fifty-five bears fished the valley's streams during the peak of the salmon spawning season.

The evening was calm and unusually quiet when I reached the ledge and began the count. I could hear bears splashing below me and bald eagles chortling or screaming as they fought over scraps of salmon. Several bears chased salmon while others approached the streams, following the numerous bear trails that crisscrossed the valley floor. Having walked many of these trails, I knew some were worn two feet deep from the thousands of bears that had trod the same routes for centuries. Eventually, I had twenty bears in view, including two sows with cubs of the year, one with yearlings, and some singles. Several subadults were having trouble catching salmon as they raced up and down the stream, chasing after fleeing fish. These young bears, now on their own, were still not very efficient, but they would improve with experience. Some huge males were feeding in the main channels, sometimes scattering smaller bears that did not want to challenge them. I had tabulated thirty-five individual bears by eight o'clock, including several new ones that I had not observed on my previous visit.

As the light began to fade, I knew it was time to return to camp, and I needed to reach my skiff on Karluk Lake before dark. As a precaution, I scanned my planned descent using binoculars. The route led through alders and then several small meadows. I noticed two subadults playing in the first meadow and made a mental note of their location.

I worked my way down through the thick alders and heard several bears fleeing in front of me as they smelled me or heard my noisy progress. When I arrived at the edge of the first meadow, where I had seen the two animals playing, I carefully looked around and saw a single animal, standing in the gloom. It had not yet detected me, and I assumed it was one of the two young bears. It was nearly dark. I was a little nervous but also in a hurry. I did not want to go around the bear or wait for it to leave. I was carrying a bolt-action rifle and decided to fire a shot in the air to frighten the animal away.

As soon as I fired, the bear dashed toward me. I was in total shock; I had expected it to run away. Instinctively, I jacked another shell into the chamber, raised the rifle to my shoulder, aimed, and fired. The animal dropped like a stone. Relief washed over me, while at the same time I felt distress at having killed a bear. If I had not acted, though, the bear would have been on top of me in another second.

I stood nervously in the deepening dusk, gathering my thoughts. Then I heard a snort and saw some movement behind a willow bush. I peered intently at the bush and saw two yearlings. With a terrible sinking feeling, I realized I had just shot their mother. The young bears were extremely agitated, running around nervously, huffing and snorting. I ran to the closest refuge—a tree that had broken off about seven feet above the ground. I scrambled up the leaning trunk to gain as much height as I could. From my precarious perch I turned to watch for the yearlings. I was uneasy and did not relish hiking through the brush that harbored the stressed bears. I looked around to scout a bypass route.

Then I saw the sow move. She had been lying motionless for a full minute or two. I had been certain she was dead. She started to rise but fell over. I had obviously wounded her, and a wounded bear is an extremely dangerous animal. I decided to finish her off. But before I could act, she struggled to her feet and ran into the brush, followed by her cubs. Considerably shaken, I climbed down from the tree and made a wide detour around the area where I had last seen the family.

I was jittery and scrutinized every dark shadow, afraid it might be the wounded bear. After I gained some distance, I ran back to the skiff.

As I pushed away from the shore, I could relax a bit, knowing that I was now out of harm's way. My mind was in turmoil as I crossed the lake, reviewing the events and trying to figure out how this could have happened...that I had wounded a bear.

I arrived back in camp well after dark. I contacted Earl, and he listened carefully as I related my bear encounter. We agreed that we should investigate the incident further to determine if the bear was dead or seriously wounded.

The next morning we hiked to the meadow to look for the bear. We found a few droplets of blood and followed the faint trail to the base of a mountain where the family had apparently scratched out a bed and rested. There was no blood beyond the bed, so we surmised that the wound had not been serious and that the bear had recovered. I had shot her head-on, so I suspected my bullet had probably just grazed her skull, momentarily stunning her. This raised my spirits; I had not wanted to kill a bear, especially a mother.

We returned to the shooting site in the meadow. I had been standing on a well-used bear trail near a large willow bush when I fired the two shots. The sow had been on the same trail about fifty yards away. When I shot the first time, she responded by running full-bore down the trail toward me. At the time I was convinced she was attacking me. Since it had been almost dark, however, and I had been standing next to the willow bush, it is possible that she had not seen me. Perhaps she had thought she was actually running away from the noise of the rifle shot.

Now that I had time to review the incident rationally, questions swirled through my mind: If I had quickly stepped off the trail, would she have run past me? What would have happened had I missed? The sow had collapsed ten steps from where I stood and fired. I would not have had time to shoot again.

I will never know the answers, of course. As Earl said to me later, "You were one lucky guy." Such close calls, though, were rare and did little to dampen my enthusiasm.

Conducting bear surveys was one of my favorite activities on Kodiak Island. Up-close-and-personal contact with the big brownies in remote mountain valleys never failed to stir my adventurous soul.

Chapter 15

Managing the Kenai Refuge

M oose were everywhere: big bulls with massive antlers, small bulls with spikes, single cows, and cows with calves. Dave Spencer circled the Piper Super Cub over the animals while I sat behind him and recorded the data. We were flying the annual winter moose census in the Caribou Hills, south of Tustumena Lake on the Kenai Peninsula. In the snowy landscape above timberline the dark moose stood out like black flies on a white wall.

As we flew each predetermined geographic section, Dave called out moose sightings on the left side of the plane; I tabulated his count and added the animals I was observing off our right side.

"There's a group of ten. Three large bulls, two spikes, a single cow, and two cows with calves," Dave yelled over the noise of the engine.

"Got it," I replied. "Take a look at this huge single bull right under us."

Dave made a steep turn and dropped down over the bull with the large rack.

"Yeah, that's a real trophy. Biggest one I've seen this year." He circled the animal several times before we continued the survey. Hour after hour we flew this high hill country observing and counting moose. I was pretty excited to see such large numbers of animals in such a beautiful Christmas-card scene.

During the late 1950s the moose population on the Kenai was at a peak due to the excellent browsing vegetation created by a large forest fire in 1947. Based on the November counts, Dave estimated that at least eight thousand moose lived in the Kenai National Moose Range.

After we had landed and secured the plane, I remarked to Dave, "Man, I never expected to see that many moose in a single day. They were all over the place."

"Yeah, they're concentrated in the high country this time of the year," Dave replied. "But when enough snow falls, they'll head for the lowlands." Then he asked, "Have you added up today's numbers?"

"Yep, I did, and according to my figures we saw 910 moose."

"Wow! That's impressive. It's one of the biggest counts I've ever made in a single day, and I've surveyed moose for years."

After I became refuge manager at Kodiak, Dave Spencer usually asked me to help each November with the Kenai moose count. The annual event involved two or three planes, each with a pilot and an observer. If conditions were good, it took about a week to complete the survey. Storms or low clouds could move in and delay any flying for several days, so we were grateful whenever we caught a break in the weather. I enjoyed helping with the census as it was a change from my Kodiak work.

During this period of moose abundance on the Kenai, long hunting seasons were authorized by the Alaska Game Commission and, after Alaska became a state in 1959, the Alaska Department of Fish and Game. The fall season occurred from August 20 until September 30, and the winter season lasted all of November, allowing people to hunt much longer than they can today. Many residents of the Kenai Peninsula depended on moose as their primary source of meat. October was closed to moose hunting mainly because the meat of bulls taken during the rutting period was considered to be less palatable.

The November season was called the homesteader's season, because by that month winter had arrived and the cold weather permitted rural residents to keep the meat for months without freezer facilities. There were plenty of animals for residents of other parts of Alaska as well. Sometimes I stayed after the survey and hunted during the November season.

I became quite familiar with the Kenai while helping on these temporary assignments. The Kenai National Moose Range had been established as a refuge in 1941*; oil was discovered in the Swanson River region of the range in 1957. As a result many roads and a major industrial complex had been built in this formerly isolated area in the middle of the refuge.

Alaska businesspeople and politicians believed that developing oil on the Kenai was necessary for Alaska's economy, but the industry created a lot of extra work

---

* The Kenai National Moose Range was renamed the Kenai National Wildlife Refuge by the Alaska National Interest Lands Conservation Act (ANILCA), signed into law by President Jimmy Carter on December 2, 1980.

Teresa and Eric help their mother dig clams on the shores of Cook Inlet.

and problems for refuge personnel. During my visits to the Kenai I saw the difficulties that oil development created. Roads supporting the oil field and drilling sites bisected former wild lands, and hundreds of miles of seismic trails crisscrossed the landscape, jeopardizing fish streams and other critical wildlife areas. All these activities had to be monitored and regulated by the refuge staff. I had no desire to become involved in the politics and controversies generated by oil development.

After being refuge manager at Kodiak for nearly eight years, however, I was looking for a new assignment. I loved studying the bears and hated to give up that aspect of the job, but I yearned for change and a new challenge. LuRue also wanted to leave Kodiak. She was getting "rock happy" as they called it in Kodiak. The road system was very limited, and the only other community you could drive to was the military base. Costs of leaving the island for a recreational break were prohibitive for a young family. I told her, "I don't plan to leave Alaska, and the possibilities of another job in the state are very limited. So don't get your hopes up of leaving here any time soon."

Not long after I began to look for a change, the Kenai job came open. John Hakala, the refuge manager at Kenai, decided to transfer to the Seney National Wildlife Refuge in Upper Michigan in the summer of 1963. Shortly after John's transfer became public, I received a phone call from Dave Spencer.

"You have probably heard that John Hakala is leaving. I'd like for you to consider taking the refuge manager's position here at Kenai."

"Oh, I don't know, Dave," I replied. "I'm ready to leave Kodiak all right, but I'm not sure I want to get involved with all that oil business in Kenai."

"Well, there's a lot more to the Kenai than oil. I hope you'll consider taking the job. The Kenai does have a bigger staff and we get more public use than at Kodiak, but I know you can handle the work. Why don't you come over and spend a few days looking around and talking to some of the other people? If you don't want the job, I'll understand."

I told Dave that was fair and that I would be over in a few days.

I visited Kenai in mid-August and looked into all aspects of the job. The larger staff would mean additional personnel responsibilities. However, the refuge headquarters was on a road system that connected the Kenai Peninsula with the city of Anchorage; the location would be an asset to our family. Ave Thayer, one of the assistant refuge managers whom I had known for many years, was particularly encouraging. He pointed out a lot of good things the job entailed, including the variety of wildlife found on the refuge and the outdoor recreational opportunities.

I found out that Hakala wanted to sell his house on Sports Lake, a few miles outside of Soldotna. I looked at the place, a beautiful Lincoln Log–type Pan Abode home. It was set on the shore with a grand view of the lake; in the distance the dormant volcano Mount Redoubt completed the postcard setting. I called LuRue; she encouraged me to take the job and buy the house. I thought about it for another day, and then I met with Dave again. I told him my concerns about the minimal amount of fieldwork that came with the job. I knew Hakala spent most of his time in the office, and I was not an office man.

"There's no reason why you can't do a lot of fieldwork on this job," Dave answered. "You have a couple of assistants here who are perfectly capable of handling some of the office work. It will be up to you to assign them some of the office duties so you can spend more time in the field."

"Okay, Dave, that's what I wanted to hear. In that case I'll accept the job."

After I made arrangements to buy Hakala's house on Sports Lake, I returned to Kodiak. LuRue was excited to move to a place with more possibilities, including attendance at some university classes. We had spent our entire married life at Kodiak and now had a family of three children: Janice, age six; Eric, three; and Teresa, an infant. Kodiak's incessant bad weather often confined LuRue to the house with the three kids, and she was looking forward to a friendlier climate.

Our 1966 Christmas card: Getting a Christmas tree for our home on Sports Lake.

We moved to the Kenai on September 15, 1963, and settled into our new home on Sports Lake, the only house on the lake at that time. A beautiful fall greeted us; the birch and aspen leaves shimmered in their gorgeous golden colors.

LuRue loved the house with its view of the lake and Mount Redoubt. Soon after we moved, I hauled a few loads of gravel and built a beach in front of the house. During our years there the kids spent a lot of time in the water, venturing in even before the ice was completely gone in the spring. LuRue kept an eye on them through the big living room windows.

I frequently put my canoe in the water and fished for rainbow trout during the long spring and summer evenings. Later I kept the FWS floatplane near the house. I often rose early in the morning to conduct wildlife surveys and then came home to eat breakfast before continuing to the office in Kenai. The weather on the Kenai Peninsula was a big improvement over the many rainy and windy days on Kodiak; it allowed for more outdoor activities.

I had one last Kodiak controversy to settle after I transferred to Kenai. Some residents of Kodiak had proposed introducing moose to Kodiak Island. Ron Batchelor of the Alaska Department of Fish and Game joined me in opposing the action. We feared that food competition with deer would lead to severe overgrazing. We were also concerned that if moose fed heavily on elderberry plants, they would have a negative impact on brown bears. Pete Deveau, the mayor of Kodiak and a former state representative, was a strong advocate of the transplant. He had threatened to use his political clout to eliminate our jobs if we continued to oppose the idea.

After I moved to Kenai, I decided to have one last word. I boxed up a number of moose pellets (droppings) and mailed Mayor Deveau a sample from the fictitious Animal Seed Company. Along with the box I included a letter with instructions. I thought this stunt might put the matter of the moose transplant to rest and my adversary would have to laugh at my joke.

Pete took the letter to the local newspaper, the *Kodiak Mirror*, hoping my attempt at humor would backfire and get me into trouble. The editor published it along with Pete's comments. Other newspapers in Alaska reprinted the article. Following is a copy of the news item as it appeared in the January 30, 1964, issue of the *Daily Alaska Empire* in Juneau:

Dramatic Discovery Makes Possible Moose from Seeds for Kodiak Area

(Reprinted from *Kodiak Mirror* of Jan. 17)

Moose WILL be planted on Kodiak Island! And we may even get apes on our capes!

Mayor Pete Deveau today told The Mirror that he had been advised by Will Troyer of a remarkable new development in the field of animal transplanting which will assure moose for Kodiak.

"It is nothing short of amazing what our government-sponsored and supported scientific technicians are able to develop these days," Deveau said.

"I have been so amazed and impressed with this new technique these wizards of biology and zoology have developed that I have forwarded the entire matter on to U.S. Senator Ernest Gruening who has been greatly interested in the transplanting of moose to Kodiak," Deveau said, adding, "I know he will be most interested in hearing about this technical triumph as it will enable him to take a proper stand when the budget of the wildlife agency comes under the scrutiny of Lyndon [Johnson]'s economy-minded administration."

Troyer's letter was accompanied by a small box of Moose Seeds as well as planting instructions. Following is the text of Troyer's letter and planting instructions:

Alaska Animal Seed Co.

Box 302

Soldotna, Alaska

It has come to my attention that you are interested in transplanting moose to Kodiak Island. As you know, this is quite an expensive operation. I believe I have a solution to this problem. My company (recently formed) has developed a method of producing animals from seeds, and at a very low cost. I'm enclosing a sample of moose seeds with directions for planting. I hope you will take advantage of our free offer and follow directions explicitly.

All our seeds are especially hand selected. Germination is guaranteed. We can presently supply seeds of every animal native to Alaska and in the near future hope to supply many African species including apes.

May we suggest an assortment of moose, caribou, sheep, and bison; or musk ox, moose, rabbits, polar bear, and sheep? Either of these samples will provide a nice mixed bag for the hunter.

Hoping to hear from you soon.

Respectfully,

Will Troyer, President

Alaska Animal Seed Co.

MOOSE SEED PLANTING INSTRUCTIONS

1.   Select a marshy site within shooting distance of road or airfield.
2.   Clear immediate area of all refuge managers, wildlife biologists, poachers, and other objectionable weeds.
3.   Spread seeds on soil at least 50 feet between would-be hunter-voters.
4.   Fertilize each seed well with political manure.
5.   Then cover seed bed at least two feet deep with moose transplant objectors.
6.   Now irrigate with democratic publicity.
7.   When plants sprout antlers, they are considered ripe for shooting.
8.   Invite any remaining refuge managers and biologists on first hunt—they can easily be eliminated on first shot.

Caution: Beware and not cross cow seeds with moose seeds, as the cross will result in a COOS—a non-huntable animal.

Nearly everyone thought the item was funny, and eventually Pete Deveau had to take it as a "gotcha" joke. About six months later I met him on the streets of Kodiak. He stopped me, grinned, and asked, "Have you got any more of those moose seeds?" We both laughed. It had helped heal the controversy. The plan to transplant moose to Kodiak eventually faded away when no one took up the cause with serious effort.

By the time I became refuge manager on the Kenai in 1963, the big battles between the oil companies and the refuge were almost over. The oil industry employees had learned to comply with the refuge regulations that were imposed on them, and the refuge staff had learned to operate around the oil industry. Many of the politicians, however, were not satisfied with our arrangement. They wanted to wrest control of part of the refuge from the Fish and Wildlife Service and place the potential oil lands under state jurisdiction. The two most vociferous individuals were U.S. Senator Ernest Gruening and Bob Atwood, owner and editor of the *Anchorage Times*, the largest newspaper in Alaska.

Atwood published numerous editorials and news articles about the importance of oil development in Alaska and, as he saw it, the obstructive effects the FWS had on the oil industry. I was not aware of Atwood's personal interest in oil on the Kenai until I became refuge manager and looked at the maps of the Kenai oil lease owners. Atwood's name was on many leases. He never mentioned this obvious conflict of interest to his readers.

Senator Gruening was also a big proponent of oil development and vociferously opposed the refuge policies that regulated the industry. Senator Gruening hated the FWS in general and made no bones about it. The FWS had led a successful fight against building the Rampart Dam on the Yukon River, a project the senator had promoted in the early 1960s. The dam would have flooded many Native villages and inundated one of the largest waterfowl nesting grounds in North America.

Soon after I became refuge manager, Senator Gruening introduced a proposal to remove a large portion of lowlands from the Kenai refuge so that the oil industry could develop the area with fewer restrictions. We at the refuge had to spend weeks in the office writing justifications for retaining this area. The senator's plan failed, but he immediately asked Congress to remove another section. Again it took a lot of time for my staff and me to counter these actions. Several state legislators also proposed removing parts of the refuge lands to promote cattle grazing and more homesteading.

In the meantime the local oil people and our refuge staff figured out a suitable working relationship; things were going fairly smoothly between us. They had to invest some additional work and money to meet our stipulations. We required them to reseed seismic trails that cut across steep hillsides and along the edges of streams to prevent erosion. They also had to clean up river crossings to remove obstructions that impeded fish migrations. They were required to build small dikes around each well to prevent any spilled oil from seeping into critical wildlife habitat areas. After meeting our criteria, they had a fairly neat oil field and were proud of this accomplishment. After Senator Gruening lost his seat in the U.S. Senate in 1968, our relationship with the political community became more congenial. Atwood continued to attack our policies in editorials; it was something I had to contend with the rest of my FWS career.

Monitoring the oil industry was sometimes demanding, but the variety and abundance of fish, wildlife, and scenic and recreational resources made the Kenai a great place to live and work. I enjoyed the challenges of managing this complex refuge. It provided opportunities to explore new country, to conduct studies on species of birds and other wildlife not found on Kodiak, and to develop new skills, such as planning and implementing recreational facilities. I never regretted my decision to become manager of the Kenai refuge.

Chapter 16

Building a Canoe System

T he canoe slid through the placid water. Only the dip of our paddles and the occasional splash of a leaping rainbow trout broke the quiet. The last rays of the setting sun cast an eerie glow across the lake. We moved silently along the edge of some water lilies and into a small bay. Just ahead of the canoe, the water surface rippled with rising fish. We stopped paddling and watched the trout feed for a few moments, our excitement building in anticipation.

"Okay, Cal, you make the first cast," I said, breaking the silence.

Cal Fair, my hunting and fishing companion, picked up his pole. Slowly, gracefully, he whipped the line back and forth and let the fly settle next to a ripple. Wham! The rainbow sucked in the fly and immediately raced toward shore. Cal's rod bent double as he fought to turn the fish away from the lily pads. It raced back and forth in front of the canoe, leaping out of the water several times. Though Cal had a fish on, I could not resist the temptation any longer. I cast a dry fly next to another rising fish on the other side of the canoe. The fly floated on the surface for a moment before it disappeared in a swirl of water. The fish leaped out of the water several times in an attempt to throw the hook and then raced under the canoe. My rod bent as I fought to bring the trout back to my side of the canoe. Slowly I regained line as the fish tired, and I led it next to the canoe. When it ceased struggling, I followed the line down with my finger and freed the fish from the barbless hook. The fish lay on its side for a moment; then, with a flick of its tail, it disappeared into the deep water.

That evening we caught and released many rainbows, most ranging from ten to fifteen inches long. As midnight approached, however, my bottom became sore from sitting on the hard metal seat for four hours.

"What do you think, Cal? Want to head in soon?" I asked, hoping he would agree.

"In a minute," he answered. "I hate to quit."

He hooked several more trout as I quietly put away my gear and listened thoughtfully to the night sounds. Cal finally reeled in, and we paddled back toward camp, content with the quality fishing experience on this remote lake.

"It's pretty hard to believe that we have this whole lake to ourselves," I remarked, as the paddles made small whirlpools in our wake.

"Just us and the loons," Cal answered.

As we were preparing to pull the canoe out of the water, a loon punctuated Cal's remark by sending a wild tremulous call rolling across the quiet lake. Another loon answered. Soon, others joined the chorus, filling the night with loon music.

"Man, this is the life. All that trail cutting was worth it," I said, as we sat around the campfire enjoying fresh fried trout and a cup of tea. Cal nodded and smiled in agreement.

Soon after becoming manager of the Kenai refuge I talked to Ave Thayer, one of my assistants, and Dave Spencer, my supervisor, about how to enhance the recreational opportunities on the refuge, especially along the Swanson River and Swan Lake Roads. These roads had been built for oil exploration and production, but they also provided access to many lowland lakes on the refuge. Before my arrival the refuge staff had built several campgrounds and trails to accessible lakes along the Swanson River Road. People were starting to use these sites for fishing and camping, but U.S. Senator Ernest Gruening considered this use insignificant and advocated removing portions of the lake area from the refuge. He felt the potential for oil development far outweighed any recreational use. Eventually, though, popularity of the area prevailed, and Senator Gruening moved on to other pursuits.

Ave and Dave had previously discussed linking some of the lakes by portage trails in order to develop a small canoe system. I had flown over the lakes many times and had also considered that potential. Dave said he was trying to get funding to develop the trail system.

His idea was great, but I was young and impatient. I did not want to wait years for special funds that might never arrive. I accepted Dave's approach at first, but the more I thought about the project, the more eager I became to get started. My patience lasted only a few weeks.

LuRue, Eric, and Janice canoeing on a stream in the Swan Lake canoe system.

"Unless you object, I plan to start cutting some portages myself this winter," I told Dave. He encouraged me to go ahead.

Ave and I studied maps of the lake system and laid out a route that started from what is now known as Canoe Lake, just off Swan Lake Road, looped through Swan Lake and other large lakes, and returned to the road about five miles north of the trail's beginning. During the fall I flew over the proposed route numerous times and mentally mapped the path for each portage. That winter, whenever I had a free day, I would fly to one of the lakes with one of my assistants and spend the day cutting a portage trail. Large portions of this region had been burned in 1947, so most of the trees were young and small. We cleared trail by cutting off the small saplings at ground level with a Pulaski, an axelike tool used by wilderness firefighting crews. We had to use a chainsaw to clear many of the downed and dead trees left from the fire. The work was hard and the progress slow, but over a period of several months we connected the lakes with a primitive trail system. By the end of April the first loop of the Swan Lake Canoe System was complete.

At the time only a few of the larger lakes in the area had names. I decided that each lake in the canoe system needed a name, as did many other undesignated ones on the refuge. A few locals were already naming lakes after themselves, their wives, or their girlfriends, such as Ruth, John, or Martha Lake. I did not think much of this practice. I thought these beautiful bodies of water in a wildlife refuge deserved better and should be called something more appropriate. My staff and I devoted nearly a week to poring over natural history terms in order to

Our campsite on Gavia Lake.

find appropriate labels for the several hundred lakes on the refuge. Thus we came up with names such as Canoe, Paddle, Birch, Mallard, Coyote, and Antler. We submitted our list to the U.S. Geological Survey, and all were accepted.

Despite all the work we did to create the canoe system, I was concerned that it might be too small to hold the interest of outdoor enthusiasts. I flew over the entire route several times that winter, but the trip took just a few minutes in an airplane. Would people find it boring? I wondered. To really get to know the canoe system, I had to wait for summer. That winter I bought a new seventeen-foot Grumman canoe and waited for the ice to melt.

On the first weekend in June 1964 we finally got to test out the new canoe system. Ave and I went in my new Grumman, and Dave and his family took their eighteen-foot canoe. With much excitement, we started on the east end at Portage Lake and began to follow our rough-hewn trails.

We had not yet marked the entrance to each portage, so our journey was a bit like a treasure hunt, looking for clues. When someone discovered a freshly cut trail, he yelled, "There it is!" and we excitedly raced to get to the portage.

As we reached each lake, a feeling of accomplishment rippled through our small group and we grinned at one another. We dropped our packs and got ready to paddle across to find the next portage point. The first few lakes were fairly small and devoid of fish, so we were not tempted to linger.

By early afternoon we arrived at Swan Lake, a large lake with numerous bays and peninsulas. Water lilies and other aquatic plants lined the shore and filled

Teresa, Janice, and Eric take a lunch break at the end of a long portage.

some small inlets. The Spencers headed out to explore a series of small lagoons on the far side. Very soon after Ave and I launched into the lake, we saw several trout rise along the edge of a group of water lilies. We eagerly prepared our gear and began casting to the feeding fish. On my third try a rainbow trout grabbed my lure, leaped out of the water repeatedly, and raced toward the lilies. Before I could check its run, the fish had wrapped the line around a lily stem. The line snapped. I reeled in the loose line, disappointed that the fish had gotten away but elated by the experience. Ave hooked and released several fish while I retrieved my line and tied on another lure. On the next cast I hooked another fish. This one swam straight toward the canoe, leaping high out of the water several times as I reeled frantically to take in the slack line. There was no need, however, as on its last jump the fish landed in the canoe!

"Wow! Did you see that?" I yelled to Ave. "I've never seen such hungry fish."

"Yeah, the fishing is good all right, but do you see what I see?" He pointed to a common loon sitting on a nest on a nearby island. We forgot the fish for a few minutes as we slowly paddled to within a hundred feet of the nest. The loon watched us quietly, the rays of the sun reflecting off its iridescent plumage.

"It's a beauty, all right, but let's back away before we scare it off the nest," I whispered. Ave nodded and we paddled out of the loon's sight.

We continued around another point and found a small bay filled with reeds, among which swam several red-necked grebes. Their shrill, cackling calls reverberated across the lake. Ave spotted one of their floating nests with two eggs in it. Beyond the reeds in a marsh along the shore a cow moose and calf were feeding. This place was something special, and we were ecstatic with so much wildlife in view.

"Well, Ave," I said as we paddled along the shoreline, "with all the wildlife and the great fishing, I'm convinced that this canoeing area is going to become a big public attraction after all. Maybe we did create something worthwhile."

"Absolutely," Ave replied. "I'm already thinking about making another trip out here."

After exploring Swan Lake we crossed several more portages and ended up at Gavia Lake for the night. The Spencer family, Ave, and I pitched our tents and enjoyed trout cooked over a campfire. That evening we discussed the merits of the canoe system.

"Boy, I've sure changed my view on the size of the canoe system. It seems so much bigger than when I flew over it last winter," I said.

Dave and Ave agreed.

"Yeah, I think your idea of not waiting for funds was the right move," said Dave. "We're already enjoying the fruits of your labor, and who knows, it might have been years before we received enough money to do it."

Ave felt the same way. We were all enthused about our canoeing experiences, and I was feeling particularly good that I had decided to tackle this project on a shoestring; the impatience of youth is sometimes rewarded with gratifying results.

The next day we continued to portage from lake to lake, enjoying the fishing and the wildlife we encountered.

"Well, what do you think? Was it worth it?" I asked Ave when we arrived at the last lake.

"No doubt about it! I'm going to come again in the near future," he replied emphatically.

"So will I. I can't wait to get LuRue and the kids out here for a few days," I said.

That week Ave and I talked to the rest of the staff about our canoe trip. We said that we would be adding other loops and connecting many more lakes during the following year or two. I showed them a wall map on which I had marked some of the additional routes I was considering.

"Eventually," I told the staff, "canoeists will have several route choices through the lakes and down the Moose River."

Our stories from the trip were received enthusiastically by many outdoor people, who were now eager to try out the canoe system for themselves.

*My staff and I planned and cut portages through some of the lowland lakes to create the first
canoe system in the Kenai National Wildlife Refuge.*

I was euphoric about what we had accomplished and eager to start on the
routes I planned to add. I also wanted to let the public know of this new outdoor
opportunity on the Kenai Peninsula. I called Loren Stewart, owner and editor of
the local *Cheechako News* in Soldotna, and invited him on a canoe trip.

The following week Loren and I spent three days traveling through the lakes.
I was pleasantly surprised to discover he was an enthusiastic fisherman and out-
doorsman. Sometimes we stayed out fishing until midnight, listening to loons
calling and watching moose and beaver. His enthusiasm was contagious, and he
raved about the great opportunities canoeists now had on the refuge.

A week later Loren published an article in his paper, illustrated with photographs, about our three-day canoe outing. News spread rapidly, and within a few
weeks many people were coming to check out the Swan Lake Canoe System.

The next winter Ave and I, along with Bob Richey, my new assistant in charge
of recreation, camped near Mink Lake for four days and cut trails that linked
Spruce Lake to Camp Island Lake, providing access to the headwaters of the
west fork of Moose River. Later that winter we also cut trails from Swan Lake
to Moosehorn Lake, at the headwaters of another branch of the Moose River.
Canoeists now had a variety of options in traveling the canoe system. They could
start at either of two entrances off Swan Lake Road, paddle through a variety of

lakes, and either loop back to Swan Lake Road or enter a branch of the Moose River and continue to the bridge at the Sterling Highway.

The public appreciated the various routes and the opportunity to paddle through thirty different lakes. I received many phone calls from enthusiastic users who had spent from a few days to a week traveling through the lakes, fishing, and watching wildlife. Our refuge staff was gratified to know that so many others were also enjoying our efforts.

My family eventually became avid canoeists. The kids loved these outings, though they had to learn to accept that carrying packs and equipment was part of the experience! Once we got to a camping spot and readied the camp, the kids could hardly wait to get into the canoe and catch fresh trout for dinner. Trout over a campfire was a lot better than the hot dogs I traditionally brought—just in case. As we sat around the coals, roasting marshmallows, I asked the kids to listen and identify various bird calls. They became quite skilled at identifying songs over the years and became enthusiastic birders.

After completing the Swan Lake Canoe System, my staff and I became keen to construct another canoeing area. We had studied topographic maps and had surveyed the area by plane. The new route would start at Paddle Lake, which was near the end of Swan Lake Road. It would connect a series of lakes and eventually enter the headwaters of the Swanson River. Before planning the exact route and cutting trails, however, I needed to know the fishing potential of each lake, a major attraction for many canoeists.

I worked with Larry Engel, a state fishery biologist, to gather this information. In the summer of 1966 seasonal assistants Dave Watsjold and Greg Olson surveyed the sport-fishing potential of the lakes east of the Swanson River. Using information from that study, Bob, Ave, and I planned a canoe route through some of the better fishing lakes that eventually included Gene and Pepper Lakes.

During the winter season some of my assistants and I cut a few of the portages, just as we had done to get the Swan Lake Canoe System started, but we did not complete all the routes I had planned. Due to the success of the Swan Lake Canoe System, Dave Spencer was able to secure some extra funds for the project, so I hired two more men to work on it that summer. Greg Erickson and Vaughn Phillips camped out each week and cut trails; I checked on them periodically and flew in needed supplies. They worked hard, and by the end of the summer the Swanson River Canoe System was complete.

Within this series of lakes were several commercial sportfishing camps owned by air taxi operators in Anchorage. I informed them that they were now within a canoe system where airplanes would be banned; they would either have to

My friend Cal Fair fishing in Pepper Lake.

close their camps or move them to other lakes in the Kenai refuge. Most of them chose the latter option without too much objection. Eventually we also banned outboard motors in the lakes.

I got a bit too enthusiastic about the project, however, and added some lakes I should not have. Early in the summer I gave Bob Richey the task of exploring these routes. Bob managed to get a canoe through all the channels, but he reported that some were so thick with vegetation they were very difficult to negotiate; he predicted that few people would use them. I eliminated several of the most arduous routes from our canoe maps. The Swanson River Canoe System eventually linked forty lakes and the upper part of the Swanson River.

Today many people use both canoe systems each summer. Some lakes close to the entrances can get a bit crowded on weekends, but canoeists willing to make additional portages can still find solitude on some of the more remote lakes.

I have passed my eightieth birthday, but I still put my canoe in the water each summer and travel to my favorite lakes. I enjoy fishing, sitting by a campfire at night, and listening to loon music. I get deep satisfaction knowing that many others also find pleasure and solitude on these lakes because of the work my staff and I did so many years ago.

Chapter 17

A Day in the Life
of a Refuge Manager

T he eastern sky was aglow from the rising sun as I left the house and walked to
the plane parked just down the hill on the shore of Sports Lake. The flutelike
call of a Swainson's thrush drifted down from the top of a tall spruce, and several
robins cheerily heralded the new day. I did a preflight check and then climbed into
the Super Cub, warmed up the engine, and roared down the lake. The plane lifted
off the water and climbed rapidly over the treetops. I leveled off at eight hundred
feet and followed my compass toward the Moose River. Moose calving had peaked
about May 25, and now, a week later, I wanted to determine the success of this
year's calf crop.

After about twenty minutes I intersected the Moose River and followed it
upstream to a diverse lowland of spruce forest, lakes, and muskegs, an area favored
by cows for calving. Before long I spotted several moose in an open glade. I cut
the throttle, dropped to four hundred feet, and circled the animals. I identified
two young bulls with stubby velvet antlers that protruded a few inches above their
skulls. A cow stood to their right, and as I circled, a small calf rose onto its wobbly
legs and began to suckle. Two hundred yards away another cow and her twin calves
stood feeding, partially hidden on the edge of the forest. I recorded the information
and continued upriver to another large muskeg. The rising sun cast long shadows
along the edge of a clump of trees. I scanned the muskeg and saw eight more animals ahead: two yearlings, a large bull, three single cows, and two other cows, each

with twin calves. A few hundred yards to my left another cow was trying to lead her calf across the Moose River. I was concerned for the calf's safety and circled until they were safely across.

I flew ten minutes without seeing any wildlife; then, as I turned toward another muskeg, my eye caught a flash of light brown. I flew closer, identifying a brown bear. I wondered what the animal was up to. I swooped down and circled the bear. It was feeding on a freshly killed moose calf—a nice breakfast for the bear at the expense of the calf and an unfortunate mother moose. It was probably the same bear I had seen a few days earlier with another dead calf. Some bears become proficient at capturing newborn calves and can take a heavy toll on the infant moose population. The predator-prey relationship can seem harsh, but it is the way of nature.

Ready to move to a new area, I shoved the throttle forward. The Cub responded like an exuberant bird, shooting upward several hundred feet before I leveled it off. The air was calm, and a rush of exhilaration washed over me as the plane responded so readily to a slight touch of the controls. I felt like an eagle soaring in the skies—turning, gliding, dipping, and diving over the lush green forests and lakes far below. Such freedom, mixed with an enormous sense of awe, was breathtaking as I looked down upon the Almighty's creation!

A little farther north, a thick clump in the top of a tall spruce tree caught my attention. I zipped over and circled the tree for a better look.

"Wow!" I said out loud. "That's an osprey nest!" An adult sat on a snag near the nest. Excited at finding one of these rare aeries, I got out a map and recorded its location.

More moose appeared on the horizon, and during the next five minutes I counted a yearling, two large single bulls, three single cows, and two cows, each trailing a single calf. On the edge of another marsh were two cows with twins. I was glad to see them because a high percentage of twin calves indicates a good calf crop.

As I was crossing a large lake with several small islands, I thought I saw movement on one of the islands. I made a steep turn and circled over it. Yes, there was a cow with a newborn calf. As I continued flying across the lake, a large black bear came into view on the far shore. While islands provide some protection to moose, bears can swim if they think there is a meal to be had. I hoped the animal had not scented the newborn. I watched the bear for a few minutes and then smiled when it moved north, away from the lakeshore. I realize, of course, that bears must eat, but I couldn't help but feel protective of very young calves.

I flew into the Chickaloon River drainage and followed the river toward Turnagain Arm. After I had found and tabulated a few more moose, I looked

A number of trumpeter swans nested on the Kenai National Wildlife Refuge.

at my watch. I had been in the air for nearly two hours. I decided to head for the Swanson River and begin working back toward Kenai. I saw and recorded several more moose. Most of the cows had dropped their calves, but a few still appeared pregnant.

I had classified about a hundred adult moose and thirty-five calves. My survey was complete for the day, but I needed to check three trumpeter swan nests in the vicinity. The first nesting swan stood up and spread her wings in defiance of the huge, noisy bird in the sky, revealing six eggs under her. The next nest, built on a beaver house, was empty. Scanning the area, I saw a pair of adults trailed by five fluffy cygnets. It is one of the prettiest sights I have seen in the bird world. As I circled, the family swam into some tall reeds, trying to hide. I let them be and flew to the next nest site. An adult was sitting on the raised mound. She swiveled her head to watch the intruder in the sky, but she did not flee her regal throne. I would return later to check the number of eggs she was incubating.

I was getting tired now; sitting in the small cockpit gave me very little wiggle room. I had been flying for more than three hours; it was time to head home. I followed my compass back toward Sports Lake. Twenty minutes later I cut the throttle and glided to a landing on the lake. I tied up the plane and hurried to the house. I was hungry, and the pancakes LuRue was cooking smelled delicious as I stepped in the door. I satisfied my appetite with several pancakes washed down with coffee and orange juice. It was now eight thirty in the morning. I said goodbye to my family and climbed into my car for the ten-mile commute to my office in Kenai.

As I walked in the door, my secretary handed me a note; the refuge office in Washington, D.C., had called. The end of the fiscal year was fast approaching, the person in Washington explained when I returned the call. "Can you use $10,000, and if so, what would you use it for?"

I always planned ahead for such windfalls. "Yes, I need some extra funds to complete a campground near Skilak Lake and construct several hiking trails in the same vicinity," I said. "I'll have a formal proposal for the project in the mail in a couple of days." After ending the call, I met with Bob Richey, my recreation assistant, and told him the good news. He already had a folder of ideas, ready to go.

I next met with Ave Thayer for a few minutes. He said the oil companies were considering adding a new well on the edge of the Swanson River field. We briefly discussed some stipulations we would require if they went ahead with the project, and then I turned to other things. Several pieces of mail on my desk needed answering, and while composing my replies over the next hour, I also took a few routine phone calls.

After a quick sack lunch at my desk, I drove with Bob the thirty miles to Skilak Lake to inspect a new campground our maintenance crew was building. We met with Rex Williams, the maintenance foreman, and the three of us decided on the location of several more picnic and camping sites. On the way back Bob and I took a short hike to an eagle nest that I had spotted from the air a week before. An adult was perched near the nest, and with my binoculars I saw the heads of two fluffy eaglets, probably less than ten days old. Now I would be able to update that information.

On the drive back to the office a lynx crossed the road, and we stopped to admire it for a few minutes. "This is the highlight of my day," I told Bob, who shared the sentiment. Even with all my time in the field, I rarely saw one of these shy creatures.

After arriving back at the office, I told my secretary I was going to make a late flight to count the Dall sheep on Surprise Mountain. The air had remained calm through the day, and I thought I had better take advantage of the good weather conditions. I drove home and told LuRue about the flight, saying that I would be late for dinner.

I gassed up the Cub, started it, and zoomed down the lake. Airborne, I climbed to three thousand feet as I approached Surprise Mountain. The sheep would be in the high country, so I cruised along the alpine zone looking for them. I spotted a large group and circled them repeatedly while determining there were forty-five

As a refuge manager, I was responsible for managing a variety of wildlife, including Dall sheep.

ewes and yearlings with ten lambs in the bunch. Continuing around the mountain, I recorded several small groups of rams. I carefully looked over four large rams with full-curl horns. I knew hunters would be seeking them in the fall, as the mountain had good foot access and was a popular hunting area for sheep. Though I had no plans to hunt them myself, I knew others would ask me what I had seen.

White spots appeared on a high peak. I pushed the Cub's throttle forward, made a few climbing turns, and leveled off near the top. I circled several times, counting sixty-two sheep scattered in the high terrain. I eventually determined there were fifteen new lambs. Five half-curl rams grazed on the fringe of the group. I continued around the mountain, counting a few more sheep before completing the survey. I had recorded 135 sheep and speculated that I may have missed a few rams, which often rest in rock crevasses. I called it good and turned the plane toward home.

I landed on the lake at seven o'clock and tied up the plane. Two of my kids, Janice, age ten, and Eric, age seven, were sitting on the bank. They had heard the plane and had come down to greet me.

"Daddy, Mom said dinner is ready and waiting," Eric said.

"Okay," I said. I grabbed each by a hand, and we started walking toward the house. "Let's go home and eat. I'm hungry."

"Mom's got a moose roast in the oven," Janice volunteered. That sounded delicious. As we walked into the house, I smelled the aroma and looked forward to dinner. But first I had to give little four-year-old Teresa a piggyback ride. A few minutes later we were all gathered around the table enjoying part of the moose I had shot the fall before.

It had been a productive day. Tomorrow I would leave early again—this time to drive the hundred miles to Seward. I had a meeting with the Forest Service about a planned hiking trail near the refuge boundary.

Chapter 18

Working for Wilderness

I had a panoramic view of the Kenai refuge as I sat on top of a mountain above Tustumena Lake. I had made the long, arduous hike into the Kenai Mountains the day before, and now I could sit back and enjoy the view. Just below me a group of Dall sheep worked its way along a rocky trail above Indian Creek; lambs exuberantly ran and played as they followed the more serious ewes. Sharp warning whistles from a nearby colony of marmots occasionally pierced the air, and farther down the mountain slope near timberline a black bear and several moose grazed peacefully, apparently oblivious to one another.

I directed my attention to the lowlands far to the north. With binoculars, I identified a few of the larger lakes in the canoe system that my staff and I had worked hard to connect with portages just a few years before. To the west of these lakes I caught the silvery glint of buildings within the Swanson River Oil Field.

As I gazed at the two distant, contrasting scenes—wilderness and development—I speculated about the future: What would the Kenai refuge look like a hundred years from now? Would more of it be broken up by roads, airports, industrial complexes, homes, and other modern developments that follow human population growth? As I sat on that mountain surrounded by a vast wilderness, I hoped much of this wildlife refuge would remain forever wild. And I knew I could help that wish come true.

In 1964 Congress passed the Wilderness Act, establishing a National Wilderness Preservation System (NWPS). It set aside large tracts of wild lands that were to remain forever wild and roadless. Most of the lands were within national forests,

Our family and friends enjoy a trek through part of the Andy Simons Wilderness Area.

but Congress had also directed the U.S. Fish and Wildlife Service to evaluate wild lands remaining in national wildlife refuges and to recommend areas suitable for the wilderness preservation system.

Government wheels usually turn slowly, and it was not until 1968 that the FWS was ready to hire someone to evaluate the wilderness potential of refuges in Alaska. The employee who took that job would have to study each Alaska refuge and recommend whether to include all or designated parts of it as a national wilderness area. My boss, Dave Spencer, knew of my interest in wild lands and asked if I would be interested in the position. The decision was not easy. I was just completing my fifth year as the Kenai refuge manager, a position Dave had convinced me to take. I had learned to love the Kenai and was definitely not ready to leave. On the other hand, I strongly believed in the wilderness program and did not want to see the job go to someone who was not committed to the cause. In addition, the new job would require that I explore many of the remote refuges in Alaska—areas that I would never see if I remained at Kenai. The allure of exploring new wild places was strong. After pondering the issue for several days and discussing it with LuRue, I decided to accept the job. I was not looking forward to moving to Anchorage, but LuRue was; it would give her the chance to pursue her dream of obtaining her university degree.

One of the downsides of the job was that I would again be jumping into a new controversy. When I had come to the Kenai, I had entered a conflict between wild lands and oil development. Over the years my staff and I had worked out our differences with the oil companies, and we now had a good working relationship with them. This new job would be full of issues involving wild lands versus development, but I would be dealing with many new people on both sides of the fence. I knew my work would be more political than biological. Many Alaskans wanted to see large parts of the state remain wild and undeveloped; they supported the concept of wilderness. But many others wanted to construct roads and develop all the resources in every remote corner of Alaska, regardless of the consequences. This job would not be easy, as I would be trying to find a reasonable path between the two extremes.

To lay some political groundwork, I immediately started to build a rapport with local and national conservation and outdoor groups, which supported wilderness lands in general. I also began talking and working with people who had doubts about or were opposed to conserving pristine lands for future generations. I hoped to change their minds or at least get them to compromise on some issues.

I quickly learned that I would have to become something of a public information officer. I would need to prepare reports and brochures and give public interviews. Public hearings on each individual refuge would be required before any recommendations could be submitted to Congress. Before long I was attending meetings, giving talks, and writing numerous articles for magazines and newspapers on refuge wilderness areas.

Many of the refuges had been actively managed for years. We knew enough about their wildlife resources to know how permanent wilderness status would affect them. Still, I would get to do plenty of the fieldwork that I loved. I was expected to become personally acquainted with all refuge areas in order to speak knowledgeably about them to the public. For some of the refuges more information about wildlife and other resources was required. To make good recommendations, I would have to gather biological data on many remote sea-island refuges that had not been visited by FWS employees for many years.

The long chain of islands in the Aleutian Islands National Wildlife Refuge was particularly challenging. The refuge had been actively managed for many years, but still more data was needed on most of the islands. It would take years to visit all these remote spots and gather the information. I received clearance to hire Palmer Sekora as my assistant in 1969. He would spend the next four years surveying the vast seabird and marine mammal populations of the Aleutians. I eventually hired additional people to assist me in the field studies and in the numerous office duties.

The least controversial areas would be the small sea-island refuges. Very few people had ever visited these isolated spots, and they did not have many mineral resources that could be developed. Dave Spencer and I decided that I should start evaluating these locations first. I began with Simeonof Island in the

Shumagin Island group and the Semidi Islands east of Chignik, both southeast of the Alaska Peninsula, as well as the small, precipitous Chamisso Island in Kotzebue Sound of the Chukchi Sea.

Once I completed the field studies, my staff and I prepared brochures and news releases for the public. I gave numerous talks about the importance of the marine resources the islands contained. I received considerable support and met little opposition at the public hearings when I recommended placing these small islands into the NWPS. In fact, the Alaska State Legislature passed a resolution supporting wilderness classification for the Semidi Islands group. Many state legislators probably embraced the resolution to enhance their conservation images; nevertheless, their support was appreciated by me and others who wanted to see the islands receive permanent wilderness protection.

On the political side I determined that the two most important and controversial refuges to be considered for wilderness would be the Kenai National Moose Range and the Arctic National Wildlife Range. The Kenai's proximity to a large urban population and the variety of recreational uses on the refuge, coupled with the current and future commercial development of some of its land for oil and gas, would make it a hot-button issue. The Arctic National Wildlife Range was very important to many outdoor groups because it is one of the largest and most remote de facto wilderness areas in the United States. But it was, and is, coveted by developers because of its potential oil and mineral resources.

In 1971, when I did propose a wilderness plan for the Kenai, my staff and I tried to forge a compromise that would satisfy the many interest groups, including developers, hunters, recreational users, environmentalists, and future managers of the refuge. The proposal we submitted eliminated large portions of the lowland areas from wilderness status to permit continued oil development and to allow habitat manipulation in order to improve the amount and quality of vegetation browsed by moose. We did propose that the NWPS include the forests and lakes within the canoe system and most of the mountain regions.

Not surprisingly, Bob Atwood of the *Anchorage Times* opposed any permanent wilderness areas in Alaska, and he became my biggest adversary over the Kenai. He published many editorials in his paper about the evils of wilderness, hoping to persuade the public and the U.S. Congress to oppose the Kenai wilderness plan as well as others proposed by the FWS and the NPS.

Atwood was so vehement in his opposition to the Kenai plan that I intensified my efforts to counteract his editorials. I gave numerous public slide shows, wrote articles, appeared on radio talk shows, and met with many individuals to neutral-

My son, Eric, enjoying a rest stop on top of Surprise Mountain.

ize his editorials, but I had no way of knowing how effective his media campaign would be compared to my efforts. I was nervous about the outcome.

A few days before the first Kenai hearing, which was held in Anchorage, we got a break. One of Atwood's young reporters interviewed me on the wilderness proposal. The reporter seemed genuinely interested in the program. I explained why the FWS had proposed a large part of the refuge for wilderness while leaving out sections to permit certain developments. I showed him pictures I had taken in the undeveloped portion of the refuge. These photos included expansive mountain views and close-up wildlife scenes, as well as images of people enjoying outdoor opportunities, such as canoeing, hunting, fishing, and hiking. He asked me if he could borrow them to use in the article. I gladly obliged.

After he left the office, I felt I had convinced the young reporter that the Kenai wilderness plan was equitable, something he could personally support. But what would his boss, Bob Atwood, do with the information and material? Would he somehow use my pictures and information against me? Would he kill the story? I was nervous about the outcome and scanned the paper every day for his response.

The day before the hearing, I opened the paper to the Outdoor section, and there, spread across a full page of Atwood's newspaper, were many of the pictures I had given the reporter! The accompanying article was fair and balanced.

The Kenai Mountains within the Kenai National Wildlife Refuge became part of the National Wilderness Preservation System.

My staff and I were elated. The story and photos could have only one effect, and that was to show the beauty of the pristine area. We were sure the feature would convince some readers to support the plan.

I found out later the journalist had submitted the article late in the day, and it had somehow slipped past Atwood without his knowledge. He later called the writer into his office and reprimanded him. Too late—the story and photos had enhanced the image of the proposed Kenai wilderness. For once, I had a scoop at Atwood's expense.

The day of the Anchorage hearing, the room was full. I glanced around and recognized many conservation friends who were there to support the proposal. I also recognized several developer types who were there to oppose it. Others were there whose motives I did not know.

When it was time to start, the hearing officer read a brief description of the FWS proposal and then invited people to come forward to testify. The first person to speak was an oil company representative. He indicated that the oil industry was not opposed to placing some lands into the NWPS but disagreed with portions of our proposal. Other individuals said they did not see any need for further land protection, fearing that they would be restricted from landing their personal airplanes on certain lakes or using their snow machines in designated areas. A representative of the Alaska Department of Fish and Game testified against the proposal because it would restrict hunters from using snowmobiles to enter the mountain foothills to hunt moose. But the largest majority of the people present were conservationists and outdoorsmen who either embraced the plan or proposed increasing the amount of wilderness we had suggested.

I was pleased at how the hearing had progressed. We received similar support at the hearing held on the Kenai Peninsula a few days later. I knew, however, that numbers were not the only thing that counted; some individuals had more clout than others. A number of businesspeople, including my adversary Bob Atwood, had ties with our congressional delegation in Washington, D.C. It was there that the final decision would be made on our proposals.

Bob Atwood continued his opposition to any wilderness proposals by the FWS and the NPS. Following is an example of one of his editorials, written several months after the public hearings for the Kenai plan were held:

Zoo Country
(Published on November 16, 1971)

Those Japanese tourists who have received an invitation from Gov. William A. Egan had better hurry if they want to do all the things that have been promised them in Alaska. Mr. Egan, participating in a business development trip to Japan under the auspices of the Alaska Visitors Association, told a Tokyo press conference the other day that Alaska isn't an unfriendly land of ice and snow, but a state in which tourists can ski and camp and have fun in the great outdoors.

That's true, of course.

But it won't be true if most of the state eventually gets socked away into wilderness areas in which man, by law, is to be regarded as an unwelcome intruder.

As it now develops, more than 25.5 million acres of Alaska—including some of the most accessible recreation areas as well as the most remote— are being eyed as potential lands in which the wilderness concept may be used to prevent entry by man—Japanese tourist or Alaska resident.

Public hearings on one of those proposals already have been held, covering 1.04 million acres of the Kenai Peninsula.

Hearings on two other proposed wilderness areas—2.2 million acres in Glacier Bay and 2.5 million acres in the Katmai region—are scheduled to begin Thursday at Alaska Methodist University.

If all of these wilderness areas actually are created, there will be no place for tourism development in Alaska. There won't even be many of Alaska's favorite fly-in fishing spots left, or for that matter even a place to drive campers in the summer or snowmobiles in the winter.

But there will be the world's biggest zoo.

My staff and I were unaware that we would have to wait nearly ten years for a decision on this controversial issue. On December 2, 1980, President Jimmy Carter signed the Alaska National Interest Lands Conservation Act (ANILCA). It placed nearly all of our Kenai wilderness proposals, as well as others we submitted, into the NWPS.

I sometimes found the hearings stressful, as we were often verbally attacked by people who opposed our recommendations. In retrospect these controversial hearings were a sharp contrast to the usually peaceful fieldwork required to gather information.

While I did not enjoy all aspects of my wilderness job, I have always been grateful for the chance I got to explore so many remote areas.

Chapter 19

The Remote Sea Islands

The engine of the *Aleutian Tern* droned on as it had throughout the night. Now at dawn the radar indicated we were rapidly approaching the Semidi Islands, a series of nine small islands that lie in the Gulf of Alaska about one hundred miles southwest of Kodiak Island. They reportedly had massive numbers of seabirds, and I had yearned to visit this wildlife spectacle for many years. I stood on the foredeck and strained for a glimpse of the islands through the mist that enveloped us. Then, ten minutes later, we abruptly emerged from the fog bank, and the islands appeared on the horizon as a dark band amidst a vast sea. Murres, kittiwakes, puffins, auklets, guillemots, fulmars, and cormorants speckled the surface of the water wherever I looked. It was a stunning sight, almost surreal—the largest display of seabirds I had ever witnessed! Those nearest us swam out of the way or dove as the vessel's bow cut through the sea.

Our sea charts indicated we were nearing Chowiet Island, one of the largest in the island group. Constant storms lash the shores of the Semidis, and the islands offer little protection for ocean vessels. For that reason people rarely visit them; to my knowledge no scientist had stepped on their beaches since Ira Gabrielson, an ornithologist and former director of the Fish and Wildlife Service, had done so in 1946. Now, some twenty-five years later, I was anxious to explore the area to see if the large numbers of birds he reported were still present.

To conduct the wilderness studies in the Aleutian Islands, I had hired Palmer Sekora, a seasoned biologist with knowledge of the area. Within a year it became obvious that he needed a large vessel to accomplish the task. In 1970 we acquired

The rugged coastline of the Semidi Islands offers nesting habitat for seabirds and shelter for marine animals.

a sixty-five-foot surplus military vessel and modified it to suit our needs. Each year Palmer and his crew spent the summer aboard the vessel *Aleutian Tern,* surveying the natural resources of the island chain. One spring as the vessel and crew left Kodiak for their seasonal work in the Aleutians, I tagged along for part of the trip. Palmer and I decided to divert the *Tern* to the Semidis for a few days to survey the wildlife in that group of islands.

As we approached Chowiet Island, I marveled at the sheer rock walls, the pinnacles, and the sea stacks that rose out of the sea, thrusting upward for two hundred feet or more. Diving and wheeling birds filled the sky, while rafts of them bobbed on the choppy waters. I felt as if we were entering a great city of seabirds. Jagged rows of murres and kittiwakes highlighted the rocky ledges, standing like soldiers in formation decked out in black-and-white parade uniforms.

The vessel circled the shoreline closely. Each time we rounded a point, swarms of surprised birds lifted from the bluffs in a great swoosh, myriad wings beating the air. They rose into the sky and milled in clouds above us. They dove and circled in great swoops and arcs, creating a frantic rush-hour madness of birds. It was amazing how they swept by one another without colliding. Thousands landed, clinging precariously to ledges; hundreds more splashed into the water, joining the rafts that dotted the surface for miles.

The Semidi Islands provide nesting habitat for millions of seabirds.

I had never encountered such large numbers of birds, and I was at a loss as to how to count them. Palmer, who had several years of experience recording seabirds in the Aleutians, came to my rescue. He showed me how to estimate their numbers by counting them in blocks of fifty, one hundred, or two hundred birds at a time as we moved around the island. It was a daunting job, and the tally soon surpassed a half million.

The steep cliffs gave way to broken, rocky points and sloping canyons colored with patches of grass. This was the terrain of fulmars. Hundreds sailed out of the canyons and effortlessly rode the air currents on outstretched wings. Their low, guttural calls were barely audible compared to the raucous cries of the kittiwakes and the murres.

As we rounded another corner, about three hundred startled sea lions resting on a huge, flat rock awoke and clumsily humped their way toward the sea, where they felt safer from our approaching vessel. One side of the rock had a twenty-foot-high bluff. A few reached the edge of it, paused for a moment to look down, and then plunged into the sea. The impact of their huge bodies sent great plumes of spray skyward. Those already in the water popped their heads above the surface and roared at us in defiance.

We occasionally spotted harbor seals resting on narrow beaches; they also quickly scrambled into the water as we approached. But not all marine mammals we encountered were such alarmists. We often found pods of bewhiskered sea otters floating peacefully on their backs in dense beds of kelp. These creatures rarely showed any concern. To them, we were merely a curiosity.

For two days we circled the islands, estimating and tallying birds and sea mammals as we cruised by. The bird figures were astounding; murre counts alone exceeded the million mark, and kittiwakes approached a half million.

Toward the end of the second day we anchored in a cove on the leeward side of a large island. I had been eager to go ashore to get into the midst of these vast bird colonies. I took a small skiff and rowed toward the rocky beach, which was covered with harbor seals. As I neared the shore, a swell carried my skiff on its crest and deposited me among the seals; they scattered to give me room.

I hiked up to a long, narrow ridge of the island and then followed it until I was fairly certain I was above some bird ledges on a high bluff. I peered over the edge and was greeted with swarms of flying birds. Combers crashed into the rock bluffs on the windward side of the island, resounding like great claps of thunder. Offshore, murres covered a spired rock so densely that it seemed impossible they all had room to perch. Kittiwakes dipped and turned in the air, and an occasional puffin flew by, its wings beating rapidly in its no-nonsense, beeline flight.

I moved farther along the ledge until I could see several chimney rocks that rose out of the pounding surf. Sea lions and harbor seals covered the small, flat base of the rocks. I sat down on a ledge and spent the next hour absorbing the rugged, natural beauty before me. At times I could hear the roar of sea lions above the crashing of the rollers. Fulmars rode the airwaves in graceful turns, and kittiwakes screamed as they circled above me. The scene was awesome. I hated to leave, but I knew the rest of the crew was expecting my return. Reluctantly, I retraced my path back to the skiff and then to the boat.

Gambling that the weather would hold, the skipper of the *Aleutian Tern* decided to anchor for the night in a marginally protected bay. I awoke in the dark of night and peered out a window. Shadows were darting around the anchor light. I stepped outside onto the deck. Small, dark birds were diving and twittering around the brightness of the light like graceful butterflies. I recognized these nocturnal birds as storm petrels, both Leach's and fork-tailed. Even with the wide variety of birds on and around these islands during the day, here was yet another kind that came out at night. I enjoyed their elegant aerial ballet for some time before returning to my bunk.

Murres use the rocky ledges.

The next day we left the bay. Our work at the Semidi Islands was done, and Palmer needed to continue on to the Aleutians. Standing on the stern of the boat as we headed southwest, I watched the remote Semidis disappear into the mists. I knew it might be many years before I would return, if ever, and I savored the view.

During the course of my wilderness work I visited several other small islands. Another favorite was Simeonof Island, the outermost island in the Shumagin Island group, which lies south of the Alaska Peninsula. In contrast to the rocky Semidis, Simeonof has a low shoreline, extensive grass flats, and long, sandy beaches. It had been set aside as a sea otter refuge in 1958. In the late 1800s and early 1900s it was used for fox farming, but more recently cattle had been introduced. I wanted to see what effect the cattle and fox still present were having on the wildlife and vegetation. On some islands in this region the introduction of fox had drastically reduced ground-nesting birds.

I decided to visit the island while I was working in the Izembek National Wildlife Refuge on the Alaska Peninsula. Reeve Aleutian Airways kept a pilot with a twin-engine Grumman Goose stationed at Cold Bay to serve the smaller communities in the area. I arranged to charter the plane for the one-hour flight to Simeonof Island. I was told the pilot was a bit crazy, but he would get me there.

Thousands of horned puffins nest on the Semidi Islands.

We lifted off from the Cold Bay airport on a relatively calm day and headed east to Simeonof Island. We had barely left the runway when the pilot leveled off at one hundred feet elevation. I was in the copilot's seat, nervously glancing at the pilot, when he removed his feet from the pedals, crossed his legs, and started singing a song. We skimmed along, barely clearing the tops of several small islands. I certainly had an excellent view of the seascape, though my thoughts weren't exactly on the scenery! About twenty minutes into the flight several high sea stacks appeared directly in our path. I thought the pilot would climb to go over them, but no...he kept heading right toward them. As we passed between two stacks, the sky filled suddenly with wheeling puffins and gulls that the plane had flushed from the nearby rocks. It was like flying through a swarm of bees. I threw my arm across my face, as I was sure a bird would be coming through the windshield; the sky seemed saturated with birds. But we somehow passed through the sea stacks without hitting them or any birds. I heaved a sigh of relief and looked at the pilot, who had a happy smile on his face. I was incredulous at his devil-may-care attitude. This guy was crazy, all right.

Tufted puffins also nest on the Semidi Islands.

We continued our low-level flight and eventually reached Simeonof Island safely. He circled once and then landed in the protected harbor and pulled out onto the beach. I was immensely glad to put my feet onto solid ground.

"Okay, now." The pilot paused. "When is it you want to get picked up?"

"In four days," I said, holding up four fingers, hoping he would remember.

Several buildings, including a small house, sat near the head of the bay. The cattle owners had a grazing lease and let the cattle roam over the ten-thousand-acre island in a semiwild state. Before leaving Anchorage, I had talked to one of the owners, a schoolteacher. He said he spent only part of each summer on his ranch, butchering a few head for the market. A hired assistant served as caretaker of the livestock on the island, but no one was present when I arrived.

I moved my gear into one of the old buildings, which contained a cot and a small cooking stove. It was not much, but at least it would keep me dry in case of a storm.

The next morning I decided to survey the wildlife and vegetation by walking the island's perimeter, approximately a ten-mile hike. A few low mountains occupied the center of the island, but mostly it was a lowland of grasses, sedges, and heather. Wildflowers, such as white anemones, yellow buttercups, and blue violets, covered

These buildings served as ranch headquarters for the owner of Simeonof Island's cattle.

these lowlands like a colorful blanket. The cattle had worn paths all around the island, so I followed these trails. Dozens of ground squirrels ran across the paths, and I occasionally saw blue arctic foxes, remnants of the old fox-farming days.

At one point I stood directly across from the small, flat Murie Islets, which lay just offshore. Their kelp-laden waters were a haven for sea otters. With my binoculars I counted just over two hundred of the floating animals. In the same area on Simeonof I passed several shallow ponds with nesting pintails and common teals. The teals winter in Asia and return to western Alaska to nest each year. Sea ducks, such as scoters and scaup, bobbed in the waves offshore, while many song and savannah sparrows flitted amid the short willows, filling the air with their short, cheery songs. Willow ptarmigan sat on heather hummocks and sent their cackling calls rolling across the tundra.

I approached a group of cattle grazing on a hillside. When I got closer, an old bull lowered his head, bellowed, and pawed the earth. Having grown up on a farm, I don't fear cattle, but I respect them, especially a semiwild bull. I did not care to test the belligerence of this one, so I retreated to the shore, preparing to swim out into the cold waters if necessary. Fortunately, he allowed me to pass along the beach.

In another hour I arrived on the windward side of the island. Here beautiful white sandy beaches intermittently decorated the shoreline. Some accommodated dozing harbor seals, which slid into the sea and swam offshore as I approached. The beaches were as pure white as I had ever seen in Alaska, and I wondered how valuable they might be in a warm climate near a large city. Occasionally, I saw a piece of bright green seaweed on a beach, its vivid hue contrasting sharply with the white sand.

I continued around the island and found more cattle. In all I counted about two hundred. Though cattle had been present for many years, they appeared to

White sandy beaches form part of the coastline on Simeonof Island.

have had only minimal impact on the shrub vegetation. I speculated that if they were removed, the natural plant life would recover quickly.

I was tired by the time I completed my circumnavigation. It had taken all day. I slept well that night.

The following day I found a small skiff and rowed to the Murie Islets. The rocky shorelines were interspersed with a few sand beaches. For the most part the islets were covered with shoulder-high grass, elderberry bushes, cow parsnip, and salmonberry—a nesting haven for song and savannah sparrows. I speculated their density was due to the lack of foxes, which often decimate ground- and low shrub–nesting birds. As I walked around one of the islets, I came to a kelp-covered point and startled a dozen sea otters that were spread out on the rocks, sleeping in the sun. They stared at me for a moment and then scampered into the water.

I spent the day rowing between the small islets. I explored each one, counting wildlife and occasionally catching a quick nap in the rare sun. Late in the evening I returned to camp.

During the night I awakened to the sound of brisk winds and the patter of rain. By morning the storm was venting its full fury; I could hear surf pounding the beach on the windward side of the island.

I love a storm, and after a late breakfast I put on my rain gear to walk to the ridge above the beach. The wind was gusting fifty to sixty miles an hour, and the sea was achurn with whitecaps and waves. Combers slammed into the shore and shot up the sandy beaches. The roaring sea drowned all other sounds. Off to my right breakers sent sheets of spray skyward for thirty feet or more. It was a wild, fierce scene. The tempest drove the rain into my face with such force that it stung like needles. I walked along the beach, at times leaning sharply into the wind to move forward.

The fierce weather made me appreciate the cabin. In these conditions a tent would have been blown away like an insignificant leaf. I spent the rest of the day reading and occasionally walking to the beach to watch the storm. I knew there would be no plane tomorrow, for storms in this part of Alaska usually last several days. Even a crazy pilot would not fly in this weather; at least I hoped not!

Though the wind was still gusting briskly the next day, I spent part of it beachcombing on the leeward side of the island. As I walked around the shore of the harbor, I picked up rocks and driftwood to admire, saving a few special items. I spotted an unusually round rock; I reached down and flipped it over. I was utterly delighted to discover a small but well-preserved stone lamp! Ancient Aleuts burned seal oil in these lamps to cook and to heat their sod houses, which were dug partially into the ground. The lamp was a little more than six inches long and about five inches wide. The center depression that had held the oil was slightly more than an inch deep. I ran my fingers over the lamp and into the depression, worn smooth by weather and years of use. A short trough at one end of the depression marked the wick ledge. I wondered at the age of the lamp and its history. Perhaps it had lain there for hundreds of years, perhaps thousands. How many days had an Aleut sat outside his hut and chipped away at the stone to form such a well-crafted lamp?

I walked on and discovered three barabara sites. As I stood near the ancient semisubterranean houses, now just small depressions in the grass, I thought about the Aleuts who had once lived and worked on this same spot. They were probably attracted to this site by the protected bay. As I turned the stone lamp in my hands, I imagined a village scene hundreds of years ago.

In my mind I pictured several bidarkas lying on the beach. A man and a boy in another bidarka were entering the bay, towing a freshly killed seal. Blood streamed from the carcass, coloring the waters in reddish streaks. Two women and several children stood on the beach watching the returning hunters. Inside one of the barabaras an old woman warmed her gnarled hands over the stone lamp, which was burning low, sending a small plume of sooty smoke up through a hole in the roof. A mother with a baby sat on a sea otter skin mending clothes with sinew and a bone awl.

Questions flooded my mind: How many generations of Aleut women had warmed their hands over the lamp that I now held? Why had such a perfect lamp been left on the beach? Had there been a battle, the residents dropping the lamp as they fled with their few possessions? Could some disease have taken all the Natives, leaving their belongings to be claimed by the forces of nature? I wondered about these things as I slowly walked back to camp, moving my hands over the smooth lamp.

For two more days the storm continued, dominating the island with roaring surf, gusty winds, and rain. Finally, during the next night, the winds died down. In the morning the skies were clear.

Soon after I had eaten breakfast, a droning sound announced the arrival of my plane. The pilot swooped over my cabin roof, circled, and then gently sat the plane down in the harbor.

"Hey, how you doing?" he yelled. "Ready to get aboard?"

After five days of stormy weather and a week alone on the island, I was so ready that I was willing to climb into any plane, even if the pilot was a bit loony. He took off and surprised me by climbing to five hundred feet. We flew back to Cold Bay without having to dodge sea stacks or birds, and I was grateful for the uneventful flight.

Today the stone lamp sits on my living room bookshelf. Every time I pick it up and stroke its smooth surface, I vividly recall the storm-tossed shores and white sandy beaches of Simeonof Island. I also see the ancient Aleut village that once occupied the harbor, the bidarkas moving across the bay, and an old Aleut woman warming her wrinkled hands over the seal oil lamp.

I visited many secluded spots in Alaska during the years of my wilderness work. Each was unique and had its own special magic. The small remote islands inhabited by myriad seabirds and mammals, however, bring back some of my fondest memories.

Chapter 20

Along the Arctic Coast

We had been flying for more than an hour since leaving Fort Yukon at the confluence of the Porcupine and Yukon Rivers near the Arctic Circle. The vast boreal forest appeared to reach from horizon to horizon at first, but as we followed the Sheenjek River north into the foothills of the Brooks Range, the solid forest gave way to the spruce-muskeg taiga with its spindly, scattered trees. The pilot, Ave Thayer, had been my former assistant on the Kenai and was now refuge manager of the Arctic National Wildlife Range.* Several times during the flight he pointed out a moose or small bands of caribou as we traversed the refuge.

We climbed higher and followed a pass through the mountains; cirque glaciers, snow-covered peaks, steep talus slopes, and rock canyons surrounded us. In another half hour the mountains fell away abruptly; we flew over the great northern plains that lay between the mountains and the Beaufort Sea. Lakes and ponds dotted the landscape, while braided streams with their numerous gravel bars flowed northward. Giant frost polygons lay scattered across the tundra, forming a great jigsaw puzzle. The scene was wild and primitive. For a minute I speculated on how different this region would appear if corporations developed the oil reserves that supposedly lay underground. What impacts would oil wells, pipelines, roads, and other structures have on the current pristine wilderness

---

* In the early 1970s the Arctic National Wildlife Range contained a little less than nine million acres of land. The Alaska National Interest Lands Conservation Act (ANILCA) doubled the size of the refuge and renamed it the Arctic National Wildlife Refuge.

Giant frost polygons and shallow ponds dot the North Slope tundra.

qualities? What effect would such developments have on the Porcupine caribou that drop their calves here each spring? I put these thoughts out of my mind as the Cessna flew on.

As we approached the coast, the pack ice appeared solid all the way to the North Pole, even though it was the first day of July. Offshore gravel reefs and low islands held the sea ice at bay; a narrow strip of water lay between them and the mainland. It was through these narrow waterways that my son, Eric, and I intended to paddle our small kayak.

Ave landed on a gravel beach in Demarcation Bay, near the Canadian border. Eric and I would begin our journey here. Now ten years old, he was old enough to help paddle, and I hoped this experience would instill in him an appreciation of the outdoors.

Before I started the wilderness studies in the Arctic range, I had spent some time with Ave discussing the diversity and importance of the natural resources and geographic features that lay within the refuge. He recommended various areas to visit so that I could understand and evaluate the wilderness qualities of this huge area. He particularly emphasized the importance of the northern coastal region for waterfowl, shorebirds, and caribou; he had suggested the trip we were about to undertake.

Eric and I paddled a kayak along the Arctic coast in the Arctic National Wildlife Refuge.

After saying goodbye to Ave, we spent the rest of the afternoon arranging our gear and assembling our folding, two-person Klepper. According to my plan we would paddle and pull the kayak along the coast for about a week to our pickup point at Beaufort Lagoon.

I did not expect to see other people along the coast as we traveled. We were the only humans for miles around, but that had not always been the case. Long ago whalers sometimes spent long arctic winters locked in the ice in Demarcation Bay and nearby Herschel Island in Canada. They endured this long, cold wait so that they could hunt the whales that arrived along the coast in the spring. The coast was also once the highway of the north for the Inupiat Eskimos. They had traveled via dog team along these shores for centuries, taking seals, fish, and caribou, which provided food, clothing, tools, and shelter. Remains of some of their old village sites are still present.

After assembling the kayak, we pitched our tent and then explored the surroundings. A pair of tundra swans nested in a nearby shallow pond. Numerous semipalmated plovers ran along the beach, chirping at us if we followed. A Lapland longspur, the bobolink of the north, gave its chiming call from the top of a tundra tussock. Glaucous gulls and parasitic jaegers skimmed through the skies, and several northern phalaropes fed on the insects that their spinning swimming maneuvers brought to the surface in a nearby pond.

We were grateful for our down jackets as a chill breeze blew off the ice pack. Time passed quickly, and though the sun was still high in the sky, my watch said it was ten o'clock. The constant daylight was something we had to cope with during our days in the Arctic. The sun never sets during the short arctic summer, and it was only physical tiredness that drove us to bed.

When we got up the next morning, we began exploring the offshore reefs by paddling through the shallow lagoons. These waters are rich in nutrients flushed in from the numerous streams that drain the land; this attracts the birds and fish that thrive along the coast. We stopped and walked across a low island. Gulls circled above us, screaming defiance at our presence, while common eiders scurried from their nests dotting the low shoreline. We recorded the number of nests and the eggs they contained before returning to our kayak. On a low ridge on an adjacent island we found the remains of several abandoned sod huts. The site was once the village of Kuluruah, according to our map. Later in the evening we discovered the ruins of more sod huts and decided to pitch our tent on the leeward side of one of them to give us protection from the wind.

That evening we climbed a nearby hill to get a view of our surroundings. We spotted two seals resting on the seemingly endless ice pack. We scanned the ice, hoping to see a polar bear, but no such luck. Several Pacific loons swam in the lagoons, and in the distance we heard the constant gabble of long-tailed ducks. Surf scoters skimmed across the water, and a few jaegers wheeled in the sky.

That evening as we sat around a driftwood campfire, I marveled at the fact that I was sitting with my ten-year-old son here at the top of the world. His questions about the sounds in the distance and the variety of birds indicated his keen interest in nature. He also wanted to know how the Eskimos survived the long, cold winter months. I thought of the thousands of other ten-year-olds who knew only the drone of city traffic and had never heard the call of a wild loon or camped in a true wilderness. I was pleased to share these wilderness experiences with him, and I hoped it would help shape his future.

The next day we continued to move westward, rhythmically dipping our paddles into the water, pushing our kayak forward. The wind off the ice pack again blew in our faces, chilling us to the bone and making progress more difficult. Near noon we saw a small rise on the shore. We stopped for a rest from paddling and climbed the hill.

"Caribou!" Eric called out. He had been scanning the tundra when he spotted some of the animals. We watched the distant scene come alive gradually with caribou moving eastward.

"Holy smoke, Eric!" I said. "That's a lot of caribou! Let's get our packs and cameras and see if we can intercept them."

We ran back to the kayak, grabbed our gear, and hurried toward the mass of animals. The caribou were moving rapidly. We walked and ran toward the herd for a half mile, trying to keep out of sight by following a low ravine. I stopped to catch my breath.

"Let's go up that little ridge and see where they are," I said, indicating a high point above the ravine.

When we climbed out of the draw, we found ourselves directly in the path of the oncoming animals.

"Wow! Look at that!" I whispered to Eric. "Let's hold real still and see what happens."

Only a few hundred yards separated us from the vanguard of the herd. The leaders spotted us and parted, veering slightly to our left and our right. The caribou moved past us like rapids flowing around a jutting boulder in a stream, uniting again once they were beyond us. For as far as we could see, the churning mass of caribou moved over the tundra like braided streams. On they came—bulls, yearlings, single cows, and cows with calves at their heels—now trotting along, and then stopping for a few moments to feed on succulent sedges before dashing forward again. Here and there some bedded down for a few minutes and then rose again to follow the herd. The caribou were constantly grunting and coughing. Calves bleated at their mothers. Even though the animals walked over soft tundra, we could hear clicking noises, caused by tendons in their feet rubbing against bones.

The herd appeared to flow as one organism, undulating like a giant amoeba— moving, spreading, retreating, constantly changing form. Some of the animals stopped and watched us for a few seconds before passing to our left or right. Velvet antlers flashed in the sun as the caribou tossed their heads or used the antlers to scratch their backs. Short-lived challenges broke out between individuals as they vied for position.

Run, stop, look, feed, lie down, jump up. The animals were constantly active doing a variety of things, but the herd always moved in the same direction. Eventually, I was able to break from my fascination of watching the behavior of individuals and survey the entire scene. Above the mass of animals I could see the Brooks Range in the distance, adding a majestic background to the already awe-inspiring sight.

"Hey, look, Dad! There's a calf suckling," Eric said, pointing toward a group of cows and calves. Many of the calves were less than a month old, but they could run almost as fast as the adults and had no difficulty keeping up with the herd. The scientist in me recognized this ability as an evolutionary strategy, but still I found it impressive to watch those babies move so fast.

The numbers were staggering. I had seen some impressive flocks of birds and groups of animals in my life, but I had never been in the midst of such a large herd as I was now witnessing. I glanced over at Eric and found him also enthralled in the spectacle surrounding us, a scene found few other places in the world. I had to wonder if later in life Eric would remember this as the way the Arctic used to be, just as we now talk about the great herds of buffalo that once roamed the west.

The suddenness of being engulfed by this massive herd held us for a time, entranced by its natural beauty, but gradually the spell wore off. I attempted to count the caribou but found the task impossible; I could not see the other side of the herd. I knew Ave Thayer and the Alaska Department of Fish and Game had conducted an aerial census and concluded the Porcupine caribou herd contained approximately 130,000 animals, but I wondered what portion of the herd we were seeing. I finally guessed that the group surrounding us contained between twenty thousand and forty thousand caribou. I got out my camera to photograph the animals, but the scene through my viewfinder looked pathetically small. I took many photos even as I realized they would not do justice to what we were seeing with the full sweep of our eyes.

As we watched the herd, I thought about where the caribou were in the seasonal cycle of their lives. Each year they scatter across the tussock sedge meadows of the Arctic's coastal plains, where the females give birth. Cotton grass sends up green shoots early due to very little snow, providing the caribou mothers with nourishment to produce an abundance of rich milk for their newborn calves. In addition, the flat plains have fewer predators than do the inland mountains and forested areas. For these reasons the coastal plain is critical to the survival of the Porcupine caribou herd.

When calving is completed, the caribou begin gathering in groups, which grow larger and larger until a large single herd is formed. I explained to Eric that the herd, such as the one we were now witnessing, then moves as one. The animals migrate southeast through the mountains and scatter onto their wintering grounds in the forests of interior Alaska and the Yukon Territory of Canada, where they can more easily forage for food during the long, harsh winter. It's a huge, far-reaching migration that has gone on for centuries; yet so many people know little or nothing of it. We were extremely fortunate to be in the middle of this natural phenomenon.

The animals kept moving past us, pouring over the low swales and hills. Finally they swung inland and away from us. Eric and I sat on a low hummock and watched them leave with our binoculars, still unable to fully comprehend the overwhelming experience.

"Well, Eric, I think it's over. Let's go back to our camp," I said.

Reluctantly, we returned to our kayak and pitched our tent. That evening as we sat around the fire, Eric asked, "How many caribou were there?"

I told him I did not know, but biologists had recently counted more than 130,000 in the whole herd.

"It seemed like a million to me," he replied.

I woke up several times that night and realized I had been dreaming about the thousands of caribou we had seen. Our experience would stay with me forever. I've been on the ground with several herds of caribou in Alaska since that episode, but I never again came into such close contact with that large a number.

When we arose, fog was enshrouding the landscape. It drifted by us in waves, driven by the wind. Even in our down-insulated clothes, we were cold. My thermometer indicated the temperature was thirty-four degrees Fahrenheit. To keep warm, we sometimes took a break from paddling and walked along the beach while towing the kayak. In the afternoon we came to the mouth of the Kongakut River. The delta ice had not yet melted, so we had to pull our kayak over it for more than a mile. Dragging it over ice was much harder than towing it in the water, but we eventually crossed the frozen delta.

We camped early and warmed ourselves by a roaring fire built from the abundant drift logs. Thank goodness for the driftwood! The Kongakut and other rivers that flow from the Brooks Range to the Arctic coast in Alaska lack forests; these logs had probably come down Canada's Firth River or the long Mackenzie River, floated into the Beaufort Sea, and finally drifted ashore in this treeless world.

While we slept, several inches of snow fell, covering our tent. When we woke, my cold boots reminded me to expect winterlike weather any time here on the edge of the ice pack. It was the Fourth of July.

The patchy morning fog drifted by us, partially obscuring the birds that fed in the lagoons. Long-tailed ducks occasionally swept low over our heads. Scoters and eiders swam in the misty water, while arctic terns flew above it.

Seabirds weren't the only birds to watch. In the marshes just inland we saw Pacific, red-throated, and yellow-billed loons patrolling ponds where they had built their nests. They kept an eye on us as they swam guard duty. Pomarine, parasitic, and long-tailed jaegers sailed in the sky, and occasionally we spotted the white sentinel of the north, the snowy owl, searching for a

Empty fuel barrels litter the ground at Beaufort Lagoon, which was the location of a former Distant Early Warning site constructed after World War II. Many years after our trip, Congress appropriated funds to have the eyesore removed.

meal. Golden plovers performed their broken-wing act to lead us away from their young, and the trilling calls of several species of sandpipers announced their presence.

The coastal area not only provides habitat for many nesting birds but serves as a migration corridor for others. In the fall thousands of snow geese gather on the coastal tundra to feed and fatten on the abundant cotton grass before moving on. Most nesting birds do migrate to southern climates, but a few, such as the rock and willow ptarmigan, the raven, and the snowy owl, remain to endure the harsh, cold winter.

We spent part of the day at the mouth of a river catching a few grayling and arctic char for our evening meal. We camped early on a dry ridge in the middle of a garden of flowers. Despite the coast's bitter cold, hardy arctic plants bloom in profusion. Dryas plants are common, pink moss campion abundant; blue forget-me-nots and yellow arctic poppies bloom everywhere. These flowers attract a variety of insects. I was surprised at the number of small butterflies flitting between them. Fortunately, one insect not present was the mosquito. Because of the wind and cold, the little beast was conspicuously absent; later we would encounter hordes of them farther inland.

The weather alternated between sunshine and fog for the next few days as we paddled and walked along the coast, finally arriving at Beaufort Lagoon, located about halfway between Demarcation Bay and Kaktovik, Alaska.

The remains of a sod house used by the Inupiat Eskimos inhabiting the northern coast of Alaska.

Near the lagoon was a sorry example of how modern man can ruthlessly spoil a wilderness environment. A cluster of buildings that sat on the edge of the lagoon was the remains of a Distant Early Warning (DEW) site constructed after World War II. These DEW sites, a Cold War legacy that once rimmed the Arctic coast across Alaska and Canada, were designed to detect incoming enemy missiles and planes. Thousands of large, empty barrels, used to haul fuel to these sites, lay scattered across the nearby tundra, empty and rusting. Steel buildings, cranes, graders, and Caterpillar tractors were strewn about, abandoned due to budget cuts and changing priorities.

I was appalled by the sight. As we explored the area, my disgust deepened. I fully expected these despicable remains to be a blot on an otherwise pristine environment for centuries. Many years later I was glad to be proven wrong. The effort took three decades, but the outcries of environmental groups and FWS refuge staff were finally heard. Congress appropriated funds to remove the eyesore. Only the airstrip remains.

The influence modern man has on his environment is quite a contrast to that of the Eskimos who inhabited the coast for centuries. The sod huts and other basic necessities they left behind eventually collapse, decay, and disappear into

Inland from the Arctic coast and near the mountains, mosquitoes were atrocious and head nets a necessity.

the earth, a process we had been witnessing during our trip. We were not sorry to leave Beaufort.

The next day Eric and I heard the drone of the plane long before it arrived. We loaded our gear into it and were soon skimming over the tundra, anticipating a few more days at two wild and remote lakes in the Brooks Range before we would finally head home.

En route to Schrader Lake, Ave and I discussed the kayak trip, and he quizzed me on our observations. He suggested other areas within the refuge that I should visit; I told him I would be only too happy to oblige. I was already anticipating other remote adventures that I would experience before completing the wilderness studies in the Arctic range.

Chapter 21

The Firth River Valley

T he first time I flew over the upper valley of the Firth River with Ave Thayer, he pointed out various geographic features and said, "This is one of the most remote spots in the Arctic National Wildlife Range. It's surrounded by mountains in the Brooks Range and is the only spruce-covered valley within the refuge in which the waters flow north through Canada into the Arctic Ocean. I don't know of anyone who has explored the area, but you should. I'd like to know what birds nest in this spruce forest."

As refuge manager of the Arctic range, Ave had a large territory to cover, and he attempted to gather as much data as possible. As we continued on our flight, he went on to point out that the area lacked any lakes or river gravel bars large enough to provide access for small aircraft, unless you landed far downstream in Canada and walked back to the headwaters. But that would take days.

His words immediately challenged me to commit myself to exploring such a remote and wild area. When I got back to the office, I began to study maps for possible access points and hiking routes. Eventually I had to conclude it would be a more difficult trip than I had thought, and it would require more time than I had. I reluctantly put it out of my mind.

One spring a couple of years later Ave flew photographer Wilbur Mills and me into the headwaters of the Jago River to spend two weeks documenting the caribou calving. Just before departing, Ave turned to me and said, "Remember when we were talking about the Firth River area? We really need some good photographs

A northern flicker at its nest site.

of that area—also some bird-nesting data. Would the two of you be interested in going when you get through here?"

"Man, I sure would, but how do we get in?" I asked. I looked at Wilbur; he was nodding eagerly.

"I'll see if I can figure something out before I pick you up," he replied. He jumped into the Cessna and took off.

I wondered what he had in mind. Several times during our stay at the Jago, Wilbur and I discussed the possibility of visiting the Firth. Both of us were keen to explore the valley, but the access problems appeared insurmountable. We came to the conclusion that it wasn't possible. We figured that Ave would realize this when he again scouted the upper Firth for a landing site.

But a deep-seated hope remained alive in me: perhaps Ave had thought of a possible access point and was keeping quiet until he could check it out.

Two weeks later Ave flew in to pick us up.

"I just flew over the Firth and found a few large snow patches that I can land on. Do you want to go? I brought some extra groceries."

"Well, ah, yes," I stammered. "But how do we get out if the snow patches melt?"

"Oh, we'll work it out," he answered, seemingly unconcerned.

Wilbur and I exchanged anxious glances.

"Oh, let's go!" I said. "We can always build a raft and float out as the last resort." Wilbur was grinning; he did not need persuading.

A few hours later we were circling over the headwaters of the Firth. I tried to memorize as many landmarks as I could before Ave put on the flaps and landed on a large snow patch. We unloaded our gear, and just before Ave took off, he assured us he would figure out a way to get us out.

"I'll see you in two weeks," he yelled as he climbed back into the plane.

I had a twinge of anxiety as I watched the plane take off and disappear south into the mountains. We were alone in this remote valley, probably more than a hundred miles from any other human. But I put my apprehension aside; we were committed now. Wilbur and I picked up our heavy packs and hiked over to Mancha Creek, a tributary of the Firth. After a bit of searching, we found a good camping spot near the creek with plenty of firewood.

Wilbur was a professional photographer. He had spent many seasons in the Arctic range carrying his large-format camera to record the many unique scenic and wildlife features of this remote area. At times he sat for hours looking through the camera viewfinder, waiting for the right light to capture the perfect image. I also took photographs, but I did not have his patience. I enjoyed Wilbur's company, and we usually camped together at night; but we spent our days apart, following our own interests.

From our camp we had a good view to the north of rolling foothills and higher peaks behind them. The streams were lined with fairly large spruce trees, but they grew more stunted as they crept up into the ravines. The higher ones were so small they appeared to barely survive the short growing season in the Arctic. The valley was still covered with patches of snow, but willows were already unfolding tiny green leaves. Life was bursting forth after a long winter of dormancy.

The woods were alive with singing birds; their music seemed to resound from every spruce tree, willow clump, and snag. The flutelike notes of the gray-cheeked thrush rang from the forest; robins and white-crowned sparrows sang cheerily, while olive-sided flycatchers called out for "Quick, three beers." An upland sandpiper atop a dead spruce snag chattered to establish its territory, and from the open willows came the soft, clear notes of tree sparrows and yellow warblers.

Other birds were sounding off as well: hermit thrush, rusty blackbird, yellow-shafted flicker, fox sparrow, and redpoll. Never had I heard such a variety of bird music coming from such a confined area. It seemed to me that they had all headed north to the last stand of spruce in Alaska and were singing their hearts out to notify the world of their arrival. Or perhaps they were celebrating the tranquility of this unmolested arctic wilderness. Either way, the songs were joyful music to my ears and to my spirit.

Each day I tramped through the woods in search of nesting birds. The work was enjoyable, and I identified a lot of different birds. The scattering fringe of each spruce clump contained at least one active nest and the remains of many nests from years past. Robins, gray-cheeked thrushes, and the secretive varied thrushes were all nesting close to each other.

A pair of pine grosbeaks regularly flew over our camp singing their liquid, warbling notes. One morning I followed them to their nest, which was tucked into a thick spruce branch fifteen feet above the ground. As I approached, four naked heads rose above the nest and cried for food. I stood motionless and watched as the parents shuttled back and forth with insects to feed the hungry youngsters. On another morning I found a flicker nest only five feet off the ground in a spruce tree. I placed my ear next to the hole and confirmed that it was occupied by chicks.

On a clear day I followed Mancha Creek upstream, walking through clumps of spruce, skirting wet muskegs, and enjoying the music of birdsong. The sweet warbles of tree sparrows rose from the short willows, and longspurs chimed from wet tundra tussocks.

After hiking for a time, I spotted several caribou bulls entering a spruce grove a short distance across the valley. They were moving toward me, so I slipped quietly behind a nearby tree and waited. After a moment a huge bull stepped out into the open a few hundred yards away, his body rippling with strength, his velvet antlers glimmering in the sun. He acted nervous and alert, looking around a lot. He may have detected wolf or bear scent in the area, but he failed to spot me behind the tree. A minute later two large bulls joined him, then another and another, until nine magnificent bulls stood out in the open, unaware of my presence. They fed slowly across the meadow while I admired their graceful beauty from my hiding spot.

Then the wind shifted slightly, and their heads came up in unison as they caught my strange scent. The lead bull shook his head and trotted away in a swinging gait, and the others followed. They stopped on a ridge to look back, nine huge animals silhouetted on the skyline; then they turned and were gone. I was thrilled to have encountered this band of large bulls, and I hoped I would see others.

I continued up the valley, walking along the graveled streambed. Moose trails were numerous, and I watched a young bull disappear into the willows. The occasional tracks of a wolf and a grizzly bear were written in sandy patches.

Rock spires near the Firth River.

I climbed a high bank, leaving the spruce behind, and got my first glimpse of the pinnacles several hundred yards ahead. I had read about these spires in the rugged mountains: craggy limestone fingers that extended along one side of a ridge for a quarter mile or so. I crossed a small draw and continued toward the rock spires. They were immense; they appeared so much larger than when I had first seen them from an airplane. I was immediately reminded of cathedrals in a large city. Some pinnacles jutted up into the sky for well over a hundred feet. A variety of heights and base sizes, they were partially covered with patches of yellow lichens and green moss that added color to the dull gray rocks. The forces of nature seemed to be gradually revealing the jagged formations hidden in the mountain range.

From the base of the spires I glassed this wild land. It was a serene setting, yet full of life. With my binoculars I followed the ridge and spotted a rough-legged hawk. It stood on a pinnacle, its scream piercing the air. Nearby a pair of peregrine falcons launched from an aerie. I watched as their quick wing beats carried them in ever widening circles above me.

I hiked along the base of the pinnacles and then climbed a ridge on the opposite side of a draw until I was level with the top of the spires. I looked past them to a pond below, its surface reflecting a stand of spruce trees. Everywhere yellow, brown, and red lichens colored the rocky ground, and flowers were already in bloom along the south-facing slopes. Shrubby rhododendron bloomed profusely, and their purple flowers gave forth a pleasant aroma. Pink lousewort also added hues to the hillsides.

It was a landscape of awesome beauty. I took a few photos and reminded myself to tell Wilbur about this place when I returned to camp so he could capture this panorama with his large-format camera. His equipment was better suited to do the scene justice.

I wandered around these ridges for another hour before dark thunderclouds began to gather over the valley. I decided to descend the ridge and head for camp. Before I got halfway down, my eyes caught the quick movements of an animal. A wolverine! This elusive animal has always fascinated me, probably because I have seen so few. They are often portrayed as vicious, but I am drawn to the beauty of their dark brown coats highlighted with broad light-yellowish stripes. I had a grandstand view of this one, and I was enjoying it breathlessly. The wolverine was hunting below the pinnacles, moving toward a small marsh. It checked each grass hummock, moving rapidly from one to another, until finally it found a prize—a bird nest with eggs—and ate a quick meal. I watched as it thrust its nose into two more clumps of grass, raiding more nests, before loping into a willow thicket. Spying on a wolverine added a special bonus to an already impressive day afield.

The clouds had grown more ominous while I was watching the wolverine. Now claps of thunder crashed across the valley, and streaks of lightning flashed in the heavens. I smelled the refreshing air of the approaching storm and ran for shelter under an ample ledge nearby. I caught a few drops before I reached cover, and then the rain came down in torrents. Thunder clapped and lightning continued to light up the sky for nearly an hour as I sat snugly in my refuge, thrilled by the sound and light show of the squall.

After it passed, I started back toward camp; the wet vegetation soaked my pant legs, but I did not mind. The time just after a storm is often extraordinary, and it was particularly so this day. The scent of flowers seemed to have freshened the air. Everything looked full of life; water from the rain enhanced the plant colors, making them especially vivid. Birds, quiet during the storm, burst forth with song. Their sweet caroling came from every tree and bush. This expression of renewed life infected me. I felt joyfully energized to be alive and part of wild nature.

I hiked back to camp rapidly as it was getting late. I lit a fire to dry my wet clothes, and as I sat warming myself, a few mosquitoes appeared. So far we had been free of these buzzing pests, but I knew they would eventually come in hordes, making life miserable. I had to admit I could not find beauty in all things natural.

About an hour later Wilbur came back to camp. We discussed the highlights of our days while having dinner, and then he retired for the night. I stayed up to enjoy the soft, red glow of the fire and to reflect on the day's experiences.

My thoughts turned to the history of the area. The Firth River was once an ancient trade route used by Indians and Eskimos. They probably drove dog teams through the valley during the arctic winters. The remains of an old cabin I had found the first day had contained several rusting shovels and gold pans, indicating that prospectors had once explored the area for minerals. At the turn of the century whalers spent the winter near Canada's Herschel Island and probably followed the Firth upstream in search of game.

I speculated on the possibility that someone might discover some valuable mineral in the future, and if so, pressures to open the area for development might occur. Would that bring hordes of people? Would it be wise to give this area wilderness status to prevent such a turn of events?

It was late. The sun, now low on the horizon, backlit the mountains, giving the sky a rosy glow. The arctic evening was hushed; the birds had finally quit singing. The hot coals warmed my feet. As I began to write in my diary, I heard the faint howl of a wolf. I forgot my diary, sat bolt upright, and listened eagerly. For some minutes all was quiet except for the gurgling of Mancha Creek. Then I heard the long, mournful cry again. Though faint, it seemed to flow through the entire valley. Silence again for a few minutes before the creature repeated his cry. It electrified me; the wild, lonesome call seemed to dominate the night. Several times this symbol of the wild howled, and each time I thrilled at the sound. I wondered if the caribou were still in the valley; were they nervous when they heard the call? Silence returned, and I sat by the fire for another thirty minutes hoping for an encore. But the wolf remained silent. It was the end of a remarkable day, and I crawled into my tent, ready for a night's rest.

Two days before our pickup date I heard the drone of an airplane. It was Ave; he circled several times and then dropped a note. I ran to retrieve it. The note said, "See if you can find a short strip to land on. I'm sending a hotshot Super Cub pilot to pick you up."

"Wow!" I said to Wilbur. "I've got a few thousand hours in Cubs, and I haven't seen any place I'd want to land one."

I spent the rest of the day looking for a landing site. I finally found a gravel bar a little way from our campsite. It was marginal, but by cutting down a few willows with my axe, I decided it was doable. I marked the short strip with some orange flagging that Ave had included in his drop. That evening I told Wilbur about my short airstrip.

"Maybe we'll get out of here after all if he sends a good pilot," I said.

Wilbur and I had both been expressing doubts about the pickup, but we were now a little more optimistic about getting out.

"It will sure beat spending a week building a raft and floating to the ocean," Wilbur said.

The next day we waited hopefully in camp. At about noon I heard a Super Cub. The pilot spotted our tents and circled. I ran out into the open and gestured broadly toward my landing strip. But the pilot cut his engine to land right away. I could not believe it! There was a short, rocky gravel bar in front of our tent, but I did not think anyone could safely land on it.

I watched in horror as the pilot sideslipped the plane down over the treetops and landed right in front of our camp! The plane rattled and bounced as its wheels rolled over the rocks, many the size of volleyballs. The pilot crunched to a stop about twenty feet from Mancha Creek, and then he turned around and taxied to camp. I looked at the landing gear, convinced that it must have been damaged in the landing, but it seemed fine.

"There is no way I'm getting into that plane for a takeoff," I told Wilbur.

When the pilot got out of the plane, he seemed a bit nervous. I would have been too after that landing! He seemed relieved when I told him about the airstrip I had hacked out. He told us he had been warned the landing would be tight, so he stripped everything he could out of his plane to lighten the load, including the radio.

"Great!" I thought to myself. "If we crack up, he'll have no way to notify anyone."

The pilot was from Fort Yukon and seemed to like a challenge. He told me that after he stripped down the plane, he had spent several hours practicing short landings and takeoffs on the banks of the Yukon River. That was somewhat reassuring.

I told Wilbur to head home first; he had been eager to leave. I helped him carry his gear to the other strip and, exchanging uneasy glances, we listened nervously as the pilot took off from his first landing site. Would he make it? When he flew over us, we let out a joint sigh of relief. Well, at least he had accomplished that much! He landed on my makeshift airstrip—a runway compared to that other gravel bar—and got out of the plane.

"Oh, this is plenty good—no sweat," he said, smiling.

He loaded Wilbur and his gear onto the plane, and I watched them take off and climb out of the valley. Staying behind by myself, I felt a little apprehensive. This would be a very remote corner of Alaska in which to become stranded.

I waited several hours and was beginning to experience some small disquiet. I wondered what I should do if he did not show up again. Should I wait, hoping someone would come, or should I start building a raft? I was pondering these questions when I heard the Cub. I don't think I've ever been happier to hear that familiar drone.

This time the pilot landed confidently on my strip, and I climbed aboard. He revved up the engine, and we bounced down the improvised runway. A couple of willow branches nicked the wings, and then we became airborne. A sense of release washed over me; now I could let go of all my fears and take in the splendor of the landscape below. I looked down at the valley where I had spent the last two weeks and realized that I was also a bit sad to leave.

The view from the air reminded me of the remoteness of the upper Firth River valley, tucked in the mountains along the Canadian border. It is a beautiful wild place, practically untouched by modern man. I hoped it would always remain that way.

Chapter 22

Birds of the Delta

A s I walked across the tundra flats, western sandpipers rose out of the heather like honey bees coming from a field of clover. Other species of shorebirds were calling from tundra tussocks; ruddy turnstones, phalaropes, plovers, godwits, and curlews all made themselves conspicuous by voice and presence. Gulls, jaegers, and arctic terns wheeled in the sky and protested my company. Various species of ducks flew low over a nearby pond, and from a small ridge I spotted emperor, Canada, and cackling geese sitting on nests. From horizon to horizon the land and sky seemed filled with nesting and flying birds.

I was in one of the greatest waterfowl- and shorebird-nesting regions in the world—the Clarence Rhode National Wildlife Refuge.* The refuge lies between Alaska's two largest rivers, the Yukon and the Kuskokwim. Most of the refuge is a broad, flat, treeless tundra plain that is less than one hundred feet above sea level. It contains thousands of lakes, ponds, and sloughs, stitched together with rivers and streams.

During the long winter months the wetlands are locked in snow and ice. Only a few hardy species of birds remain; the marshes seem silent and desolate. In late April and early May warm winds bring rising temperatures; open leads appear along the seacoast, and then rivers and lakes begin to thaw. As spring arrives on the delta, the barren land begins to throb and pulsate with

---

* The 1980 Alaska National Interest Lands Conservation Act (ANILCA) combined the Clarence Rhode National Wildlife Refuge with other refuges and renamed it the Yukon Delta National Wildlife Refuge.

Many of the bar-tailed godwits reared in the delta migrate to New Zealand each fall.

life. A faint musical gabbling fills the air as flocks of eiders and emperor geese arrive. They are the first migrants to return; they don't have far to come, as they have spent the winter in the frigid coastal waters along the Alaska Peninsula and the Aleutian Islands.

Thousands of birds have wintered in the Bering Sea in polynyas, openings within the ice pack. These open water areas are caused by winds and ocean current upwellings; rich in nutrients, they provide food for the sea ducks and the marine mammals that congregate there. From these breaks in the ice pack spectacled eiders find their way to the delta for the nesting season.

Soon others follow. The arctic terns, the greatest migrants of all, arrive after traveling for weeks on a ten-thousand-mile journey from their wintering grounds along the southern tip of Argentina. Another distant traveler is the bar-tailed godwit. It is thought to take the longest single-flight migration over water of any bird, traveling from New Zealand to Alaska, a distance of nearly seven thousand miles. The greater scaup leave their wintering grounds along the eastern shores of the United States and cross the continent in order to reach the delta nesting grounds. The Pacific black brant arrive from their winter sojourn along the western coast of the United States and Mexico.

They come from every direction and from many different parts of the globe with their unerring compasses set to this great nesting ground in Alaska. In a few short months they will build nests, lay eggs, and raise their young before again taking to the air to wing back to their wintering grounds. I have always been fascinated with this miraculous movement of birds. How did such a great

Ruddy turnstones nest in the delta

variety from so many far-flung places evolve to make these flights each year and arrive on these nesting grounds in Alaska at nearly the same time? It surely took centuries for each species to develop such migration routes and habits.

I had heard and read about the birds of the Yukon Delta for years. When I took the wilderness job, it was one of Alaska's bird wonders that I needed to see. I contacted my friend Cal Lensink, refuge manager of this waterfowl area, and asked for advice on when to visit the flats. He suggested mid- to late June, when many of the geese and shorebirds would still be nesting while others had already hatched.

I arrived in Bethel, the headquarters for the refuge, on about June 20, 1972, and contacted Cal. I had planned to fly with him for several days for an orientation to the region. Instead I found Cal at home, flat on his back.

"Gee, Cal," I said, "what happened to you?"

"Oh, I injured my back and can't fly, or do much of anything else, for that matter. I should've called you and told you not to come, but then I thought maybe you'd be willing to do some flying for me."

"Be glad to help if I can," I replied, but I had a few qualms about his proposal. I did not know the area and had limited flying experience in a Cessna 180.

Cal got out some maps and showed me where his research crews were located. "If you'll fly in some supplies and move my folks around, I'd sure appreciate it." He pointed out some of the major geographic features, such as a few large lakes and Cape Romanzof on the Bering Sea coast. The cape's elevation is a little higher than two thousand feet, far above most of the delta area. With good visibility, it would serve as a guiding beacon for me.

On my first flight the aerial views were astounding. The myriad shallow lakes, ponds, marshes, and sloughs surpassed the size of any other wetlands I had ever seen in Alaska. Water levels across the delta were high from melting snow and from floodwaters of the two major rivers. Numerous Native villages were scattered across the flats; they all appeared to be on the verge of flooding. Over many generations the Yup'ik Eskimos had learned to build their permanent settlements on higher ground, and I suspected they would survive the spring flooding this year as well.

The area contained few landmarks, and I had problems keeping myself oriented while flying. Eventually, however, I found Cal's crews. I spent several days flying in supplies and moving crews from one area to another. Gradually I began to recognize various lakes and other reference points. After I completed the supply trips, I arranged to spend several days at Old Chevak, one of Cal's field camps.

When I arrived, the delta was already green and abloom with flowers. Cranberry and crowberry plants covered the tundra; later in the summer their berries would provide an abundance of delicious morsels for man, birds, and mammals. The heather, mixed with lichens and mosses, provided a soft, springy cushion for my feet. I had not walked far when a pintail duck fluttered from underfoot. Quacking loudly, she landed on the other side of a pond. It took me only a moment to find the down-filled nest containing seven pale olive eggs.

Several hundred yards ahead, the mournful cries of a black-bellied plover caught my attention, and I spied a strikingly beautiful pair of birds standing on a crowberry tussock. As I approached, they both flew toward me, landed nearby, and attempted to distract me from their nesting site. Their heart-rending cries of *tu-lee, tu-lee, tu-lee* filled the air. They repeated this sharp, piercing whistle over and over. The very mournful, distressed cry typifies this lonely land. Their jet-black breasts bordered by snow-white plumage make them one of the more striking birds of the tundra. As I continued toward their nest, both adults returned and fluttered on the ground, feigning injury by dragging their wings and trying to lure me away. I obliged by altering course.

A few longspurs sent their melodious bobolink-like chiming songs rolling from hummocks. The sweet music of savannah sparrows now and then drifted from a low shrub, but it was the display of shorebirds that kept me spellbound.

As I skirted around several small ponds, many western sandpipers rose from the tundra. Gulls, terns, and long-tailed jaegers wheeled overhead. Then in a nearby pond several red-necked phalaropes swam from shore. The movements of these graceful little birds were reflected in the clear water as they spun around in circles, picking tidbits from the surface. They moved rapidly, their

Black turnstones nest in the delta.

heads darting back and forth in swift, jerky motions. While I was absorbed in their antics, a red phalarope, glistening in its bright plumage, swam into the open from a patch of sedge.

A few hundred yards to my right another large shorebird, the bar-tailed godwit, attracted my attention. As I started in its direction, the bird rose and flew toward me and then circled overhead calling loudly, *too-whoo, too-whoo!* Its alarm call became more agitated as I continued; it obviously had a nest nearby. I did not want to disturb it, so I changed direction.

I learned later that each fall approximately sixty thousand godwits reared in the delta congregate on the coastline before making their record nonstop flight across the Pacific Ocean to their wintering grounds in New Zealand.

I came to the edge of a large depressed bowl of about ten acres. The inside of the depression was fairly flat, covered with green sedges interspersed with puddles of water. A horseshoe-shaped pond formed the outer edge on one side. As I scanned the bowl with my binoculars, an abundance of brooding birds came into view.

Numerous nesting emperor geese occupied the hummocks, and I counted six cackling geese incubating their eggs. As I sat down on the rim above the pond, a red-throated loon slipped from her nest at the edge of the water and swam away, sounding her low, mournful call. Black turnstones, mew gulls, Sabine's gulls, and arctic terns rose from nesting sites and wheeled through the air. A dunlin and several species of sandpipers scurried along the edge of the pond stabbing at insects in the water and mud. I was excited and a bit overwhelmed to experience such a variety and abundance of birds in one place. As a biologist and avid bird-watcher,

An Emperor goose nesting on the delta.

I felt as if I had entered my own paradise of singing and calling birds of all colors and descriptions.

One brave emperor goose held her ground. I inched forward until I was only six feet away. She flattened her blue and white body on the ground and stretched her neck and rose-colored head across her nest, determined not to move from her throne. The bright plumage and yellow legs of this noble goose make it one of the most colorful geese on the continent; I took my time photographing her.

After I nearly stepped on a nesting long-tailed duck, I carefully picked my path around mew gulls, terns, and turnstone nests. Birds were screaming in alarm as they followed my progress across the bowl. My intrusion was not appreciated, and I decided that maybe it was time to leave anyhow.

The next morning I boated and then walked from camp to the edge of the Bering Sea, where mudflats, sedge-covered rises, and sandy knolls are surrounded by tidal guts, providing a different type of habitat from the marshes farther inland. Here is the nesting ground of the Pacific black brant.

When the young brant are grown, they migrate along the western coast of Alaska to the extensive eelgrass beds in Izembek Lagoon near Cold Bay. I had been at the lagoon several times during the fall to witness the gathering of nearly the entire Pacific black brant population. They feed and fatten on the abundant eelgrass until November storms send them flying across the northern Pacific Ocean to the coasts of Washington and eventually to California and Mexico.

As I walked near the shore, a cool breeze blew in from the sea, chilling the already bleak day. A thick blanket of fog hung offshore. Gazing toward the sea,

I saw a landscape covered with pairs, singles, and flocks of brant. Some were incubating, some feeding; others walked about with newly hatched young in tow. Every little sedge ridge seemed to contain nesting birds or empty nests still filled with down. As I approached, parents led their fluffy young away, anxiously bowing and talking to their offspring. Black heads thrust above sedge clumps as birds kept an eye on me, and small battalions flew overhead in wavering lines. I continued across the flats, unable to fully comprehend such a massive concentration of the black geese. I spied a large driftwood log on a small sand dune and climbed on top to get a better view of my surroundings. Through binoculars I counted hundreds of geese.

Without warning, the fog bank moved inland. In seconds the entire scene was covered with a dense, moist, gray blanket. Moments before, hundreds of geese had been visible, and now I could see only a few. The sudden limitation to my sight gave me an eerie feeling, and I dared not wander for fear that I would be unable to find my way back to my boat.

I sat on the log for some time listening to bird calls. From my left came a high-pitched *whoo-whoo*. Six great tundra swans emerged out of the fog and flew by in slow motion, less than twenty feet away. They disappeared into the gray mists like phantom white ships. I sat there as other birds flew by, some close and visible, others obscured in the haze. Off in the mist I heard the melodious yodeling of long-tailed ducks, the guttural calls of sandhill cranes, and the deep calls of eiders as they passed by with thundering wings. I couldn't identify all the birds' calls, but I enjoyed just sitting and listening.

Finally the fog lifted, and the landscape was again filled with families of waddling geese. Fearing that another fog bank would roll in from the sea, I returned quickly to my boat and followed the tidal channel back to camp.

For several more days I wandered over the delta, experiencing the lavish population of avian life. The array of painted wings and musical notes gave this land a pulse of life that I have not seen equaled in any other area of Alaska. In that sense, this area seemed to be a natural choice for wilderness designation.

But these wetlands are more than excellent bird habitat. The vast delta is also home to many Yup'ik Eskimos. They have lived here for centuries, thriving on the abundant fish and wildlife resources.

I was reminded of this one day when I came across a Native fisherman attending several huge racks of drying salmon. The split fish carcasses hung neatly in rows across the framework, their red flesh gleaming in the sunshine. I stopped to talk to the man, and he told me how many fish his family would need to survive the winter. He said he also did some commercial fishing for salmon near the

The abundant salmon that spawn in the delta streams are an important food source for the Yup'ik people.

coast. Commercial seasons, though short, provided some income to pay for the gas he used for his motor. In the winter he trapped mink and other furbearers to add to his cash income. The Natives also gathered goose eggs each spring to help support their subsistence lifestyle. I knew my staff and I would have to take all these things in consideration before we could come up with a reasonable wilderness proposal for any of these wetlands.

I returned to the FWS camp and spent several more days flying the Cessna and hauling supplies to the research crews before I returned to Bethel. I stopped to see Cal and fill him in on the status of his crews. I thanked him for the chance to gain a lot of knowledge in my brief stay.

Witnessing the annual explosion of life in the wetlands and marshes of the Yukon Delta during the spring nesting season had been a truly stirring experience for the bird-watcher in me. Working for the wilderness program had given me this opportunity, and I was grateful.

Chapter 23

Leaving the FWS

By the end of 1972 the wilderness program was starting to change; the Washington, D.C., office of the Fish and Wildlife Service was pressing us to accelerate the wilderness studies. After four years of almost constant fieldwork I now supervised eight employees. That meant more administrative duties—more unwanted time in the office for me. Dave Cline, Marv Plenert, and Dick Hensel had joined Palmer Sekora to help conduct the field studies. Our program also had four office workers, including office supervisor Sandy Dauenhauer. I was spending most of my time helping the office staff write brochures, hold public hearings, and prepare information for the legislative process. I hoped these efforts would eventually lead Congress to add many Alaska refuge lands to the National Wilderness Preservation System, but I greatly missed being out in the field. During the peak of the field studies in 1970 and 1971 I was spending as many as 180 days a year in the field, but by 1973 that had dwindled to only a few weeks.

As I had anticipated when I first accepted this job, it had given me an opportunity to visit many remote areas in Alaska. I had floated the Coleen and Sheenjek Rivers in the Arctic refuge. I had spent many days hiking and camping in isolated valleys in the Brooks Range and in the vast boreal forest to the south of the range. I had visited Nunivak Island several times, boating along its rugged coast and watching musk oxen grazing its windblown plains. I had spent weeks in the Izembek National Wildlife Refuge, known for its eelgrass beds, and I had been there in the fall to witness the greatest concentration of brant geese in North America. I had wandered over Unimak Island and stood on the shores of the Bering Sea while combers crashed onto those wild shores. I had explored other islands within the Aleutians and elsewhere and had revisited many of my favorite areas on the Kodiak and Kenai refuges. Most of those areas had once been only dreams of mine on the map. This job had made those dreams become a reality. These had been extraordinary years, and I was looking forward to seeing many of these areas become officially designated as wilderness.

But new political issues arose that brought Alaska's part of the national wilderness program to a halt. Oil had been discovered at Prudhoe Bay near the Arctic coast in 1967, and the oil industry wanted to build a pipeline from Prudhoe to Valdez to get the oil to market. At the same time many Alaska Natives were pushing for compensation for lands they felt had been unfairly taken from them. This political battle had been going on for some time, but some of these lands lay in the path of the proposed pipeline route. In addition, national and state conservation groups were anxious to set aside more conservation lands in Alaska before the initiation of any large industrial developments. The nation's hunger for oil heightened the urgency for some kind of settlement.

In 1971 Congress passed the Alaska Native Claims Settlement Act (ANCSA), awarding Alaska Natives monetary restitution and forty-four million acres of land, some of which lay within the wildlife refuges. A provision in ANCSA required the secretary of the interior to bring to Congress recommendations to set aside another eighty million acres of conservation lands. As the FWS was part of the U.S. Department of the Interior, they would be required to recommend important wildlife areas that should be included in these conservation lands. Some Natives were also claiming additional lands in refuges based on historical usage. These issues would have to be settled by the courts and Congress, and that might take years.

Officials at the FWS knew Congress would not establish any more wilderness areas in Alaska until these conflicts were resolved. We continued to hold some hearings throughout 1973 and in early 1974, but by the end of 1973 I was ordered to dismantle most of the wilderness program. My budget was greatly reduced; most of the staff that had not already transferred to other government agencies or sought other jobs soon did so.

This turn of events was heartbreaking for me and my former employees who passionately believed in our mission; we had devoted time and ardent effort to get many of the Alaska refuge lands into the NWPS. Now many of our proposals might never be implemented.

One of the best parts of ANCSA—the requirement to recommend eighty million acres of new conservation lands—also became controversial. A strong contingent within the FWS believed the refuge system should be confined to protection of waterfowl habitat. Some of the FWS personnel on the study team that was proposing new refuges agreed with this philosophy and initially chose only prime waterfowl habitat.

I and many other FWS employees believed that some lands in Alaska with large mammal populations should receive equal consideration. We were especially concerned with species such as the brown and grizzly bears that required large tracts of wilderness lands for their long-term survival.

Many conservation groups were also identifying and lobbying for lands important for their wildlife, scenic, and recreational resources. It was a daunting job for these private and often small associations with limited funds. They frequently turned to federal biologists and other resource managers for information and opinions regarding the most valuable lands that should be selected for new national parks, wildlife refuges, and national forests. I and other federal employees spent many evenings and weekends working with these conservation groups.

After identifying the areas they deemed important, the private conservation groups met with Assistant Secretary of the Interior Nathaniel Reed, who was a strong proponent of establishing more wildlife refuges and national parks in Alaska. They listed their new refuge and park preferences, and Mr. Reed agreed with most of their proposals, including a brown bear refuge on the Alaska Peninsula, which I had suggested.

In early 1973 FWS Alaska Area Director Gordon Watson was in Washington, D.C., and met with the assistant secretary. Mr. Reed immediately confronted Mr. Watson with the Alaska Peninsula bear refuge proposal that the conservation leaders had brought to his attention. He related parts of his conversation with Ed Wayburn of the Sierra Club and Stewart Brandborg of the Wilderness Society—including the fact that Will Troyer thought the FWS was making a big mistake by not proposing a refuge for brown bears on the Alaska Peninsula.

Assistant Secretary Reed apparently gave Mr. Watson quite a lecture for not including in the FWS proposals some of the lands that the conservation groups wanted to nominate. Mr. Watson, contrary to other agency directors, did not want any of his employees working with these groups that disagreed with the FWS proposals. It was unfortunate that Mr. Reed revealed my name.

Mr. Watson did not appreciate the reprimand he received, and when he returned to Alaska, he was livid. He called me into his office and berated me for working too closely with conservation groups. He was not in a position to fire

Palmer Sekora and I floated the Sheenjek River while working for the wilderness program.

me because the assistant secretary had approved of my efforts, but he could, and did, make things miserable for me.

My supervisor, Dave Spencer, approved of my actions but tried to remain neutral. On June 13, 1973, he received a memo from Mr. Watson with a copy to me. The memo restricted my travels in Alaska and elsewhere, stating in part, "I expect you to review each individual travel request by Mr. Troyer as to its absolute applicability to the Wilderness Program in Alaska.... Those requests you concur with should be submitted to the Area Director for further review and either approved or disapproved." The last sentence read, "Although Mr. Troyer's information and education efforts and his interest in other bureau activities in Alaska are very commendable, they appear not to be in the best interest of the Wilderness and FWS programs at this time."

Mr. Watson sent the memo to me in Europe, where I was vacationing with my family. He probably hoped it would ruin my vacation. It did; I was seething.

When I got back to Alaska, I demanded a meeting with Mr. Watson and got one. I told him what I thought of his travel restrictions; he had little to say except to state that he stood by his memo. Though nothing was resolved in this meeting, I at least had the satisfaction of venting some of my anger.

I followed with a long memo of my own to Mr. Watson on June 29, laying out my grievances. I related the efforts that my staff and I had made in working with

My camp in the Brooks Range while studying the wilderness resources in ANWR.

conservation groups. I described the many evenings and weekends I had spent working for the conservation cause in Alaska on my personal time.

"In this work I've supported parks and refuges," I wrote, "and one of my major efforts was to include the wildlife and scenic lands on the Alaska Peninsula, which were largely omitted by the FWS. As a private citizen I will continue to fight for these unique areas. If this is criminally wrong in the eyes of the FWS, then I deserve to be hanged, but I will go to the gallows with a clear conscience."

In the memo I demanded a written apology from him. I never received one.

I was convinced that this controversy stemmed from politics. Senator Ted Stevens opposed setting aside more federal conservation lands in Alaska. I was fairly certain that Mr. Watson had made a commitment to Senator Stevens to include only waterfowl habitat in the FWS proposals; I could not prove this, however.

Later the FWS did include in their proposals lands for the protection of some large mammals in Alaska, thanks to the influence of Assistant Secretary Reed. When President Jimmy Carter signed the Alaska National Interest Lands Conservation Act (ANILCA) in 1980, it included the Alaska Peninsula National Wildlife Refuge and the Becharof National Wildlife Refuge, also on the Alaska Peninsula. Both include excellent brown bear habitats and healthy bear populations. The act also added many other areas my staff and I had proposed to conservation groups; these areas protected habitat for other large mammals, as well as waterfowl. I was immensely gratified; I felt my efforts had not been in vain.

Some years later I was awarded the Alaska Conservation Foundation's Olaus Murie Award for my conservation efforts, but I never heard officially from the FWS. I did, however, receive personal thanks from many of my colleagues, including several in the Washington office.

My disagreement with Mr. Watson was not the only controversy I stirred up during my time at the FWS. This was the 1970s, and changing social mores were allowing people to speak up in situations they had previously endured in silence. Though normally an easy-going type, I did feel strongly about some things and was willing to take a stand.

In the early 1970s smoking was still socially acceptable. Our FWS office at the time was one large room with individual cubicles separated by head-high panels. Nonsmokers found it quite annoying to breathe the smoke that curled over the walls into their spaces. I wrote a memo to Director Watson, suggesting that smokers and nonsmokers be separated into different rooms. Most of my colleagues agreed with me, but some of the smokers on the staff were offended by my proposal. Current social norms prevailed, however, and smoking in the office was allowed for many more years.

During the same period few women in the FWS served in field positions. One spring Fred Robards in Juneau requested an assistant to help him conduct bald eagle nesting surveys aboard the vessel *Grizzly Bear*. Since most biologists were busy, I wrote a memo suggesting that my office assistant Sandy Dauenhauer would be a good candidate for the job. Sandy had taken many college biology courses and was an excellent birder. This suggestion raised a few eyebrows and even brought gasps from some. The idea of a man and a woman not married to each other but working on the same boat sent up a red flag to more than a few traditionalists. Mr. Robards, being more liberal than many, accepted the offer. Sandy did an outstanding job. She eventually finished her degree in wildlife biology and became the first female assistant refuge manager in Alaska, at the Izembek National Wildlife Refuge at Cold Bay.

Most people thought my recommendations were justified, but a few thought I was just trying to be provocative. LuRue stood solidly behind the positions I took and encouraged me to ignore the negative comments.

Dave Spencer discreetly avoided the controversial issues in the office, but he made it clear that he approved of my conservation efforts. After it became obvious that the wilderness program would end, he officially requested that I become his assistant. I expected Director Watson to block my appointment, but he did not.

I became the assistant refuge supervisor for all Alaska refuges. I had acted often in this capacity during the past few years whenever Dave was absent for short periods, and he apparently approved of how I handled these extra duties. I quickly grew restless in the position, however; it was almost entirely office work.

A couple of months into my new supervisory capacity I attended an inter-agency meeting. Also in attendance was Bob Peterson, assistant area director for the National Park Service (NPS) in Alaska. During a coffee break he approached me and said, "Hey, Will, remember when we were talking a while ago about your wanting to get back into brown bear work?"

"Yeah, I remember," I replied. "I definitely prefer fieldwork; an office job is not for me."

"Then why don't you come over and talk to us. We might have a job that would interest you."

That got my attention. The thought of spending most of my time in the field again was definitely appealing. But I would have many things to consider, and I needed to learn more about what they were offering. I let the idea simmer in the back of my mind.

A few weeks later I met with Bob and Stan Alright, Alaska director for the NPS. They told me that their area biologist was transferring; they thought I would be a good candidate for the position. The job would include, among other things, brown bear studies at Katmai National Park and Preserve and caribou work in Mount McKinley National Park.*

I was tempted, but I had spent my entire career of twenty-three years with the FWS in Alaska; I hated to leave. I had enjoyed most of my work, had many good friends in the service, and felt dedicated to the FWS cause. My friends urged me to stay. But was I ready to spend most of the rest of my career in the office? The fieldwork offered by the NPS was terribly tempting. It was going to be a tough decision.

I mulled the job offer over in my mind for several days and then discussed it with LuRue. Knowing how discouraged I had been at the FWS for the past year and a half, she encouraged me to take the NPS position.

I talked at length with Dave Spencer. He had been my boss for twenty years and had worked hard to make me his assistant. He did not want to see me go,

---

* The 1980 Alaska National Interest Lands Conservation Act (ANILCA) enlarged Mount McKinley National Park and renamed it Denali National Park and Preserve.

but he understood. In fact, he rather envied the fieldwork I would be doing. Dave told me that with the way things were going he might not stay much longer, either. He was eligible for retirement and thought that it might be the right time to leave since the FWS was becoming so political.

After much thought and discussion with various people, I officially applied for the biologist job at the National Park Service. I was hired at the end of September 1974. Making the decision was difficult, but I never regretted it. The change was good for me, and the NPS fieldwork included many new adventures.

Chapter 24

Dart Guns at Katmai

The bear trail wound through a maze of willow bushes and tall grass meadows. It was barely visible in the dim morning light. We had arrived at the riverbank without encountering a bear and now stood by a placid pool, watching pink skies come aglow above the mountains. The constant squawking of gulls and the splashing of jumping salmon heralded the coming day. Two bald eagles flew by, searching for salmon remains that might have washed ashore during the night. A rainbow trout leaped high and sent wide, rippling waves toward the riverbank.

I was engrossed in these sights and sounds when I heard the splashes of a bear wading in shallow waters upriver. I came alert and strained to hear and see exactly where the bear might be. I turned and whispered to my assistant, Martin Grosnick, "Listen, I think I hear a bear coming!" I cupped my hands to my ears. Martin stopped in his tracks and turned his head to listen intently.

"There are at least two bears," I added, still speaking quietly. Martin nodded his head in agreement. The splashing became louder as they moved downstream toward us, and then, around the bend of the river, silhouettes began to appear.

"A sow and two yearlings," I hissed. "Just what we want!" By putting a radio collar on a female with two cubs who would remain with her until at least the following spring, we would get movement data on all three bears instead of one individual. Martin raised three fingers and smiled.

We hunkered down beside a large willow bush. As the bears moved closer, we estimated the adult female at 450 pounds and loaded the dart with the appropriate amount of tranquilizing drug. The sow stopped for a few minutes, scanning the waters, and then she charged across a shallow riffle, sending sheets of spray into the air. A watery streak raced in front of her as a salmon swam for its life. The bear pounced, missed, and pounced again, but the agile fish escaped into deeper water. The sow returned to her cubs and continued along the shoreline, closing the distance between us.

"Get ready, she's coming!" I whispered. Martin checked the twelve-gauge shotgun loaded with slugs that we carried for protection, while I looked over the dart gun one last time. Everything seemed in order. Seventy-five yards, then fifty...I ticked off the ranges in my mind. Goose bumps were beginning to compete for attention with the pounding of my heart.

"Keep coming, keep coming," I pleaded silently. I caught my breath as she stopped for a moment. She lifted her nose to test the air.

"Now turn sideways," I thought, "and you'll be a perfect target."

She stood there for another minute without moving any closer, swinging her head from side to side while my pulse raced. I waited nervously for what seemed like an eternity. Then she took that hoped-for step and turned broadside. Quickly, I brought the dart gun up to my shoulder, braced my elbow on my knee, let the sight settle on her shoulder, and touched the trigger.

Smack! I heard the dart hit flesh. As she whirled to run, I saw the silvery flash of the dart dangling from her shoulder.

"Good shot!" Martin yelled.

Everything continued to go well. The sow went down, and we found her quickly. The yearlings didn't give us any trouble. Martin and I were able to get biological data from the sow, and we placed a radio collar around her neck. The whole operation was done within an hour. We had an additional three bears to track, and we felt good about our accomplishment.

Soon after transferring to the National Park Service, I met with Bob Peterson, assistant area director for the NPS in Alaska, to discuss wildlife research priorities. Since I was the only wildlife biologist in the Anchorage office and had only one summer field assistant, the projects I undertook would have to be limited. The NPS had two other employees doing biological work in Alaska; one was stationed in Mount McKinley National Park and the other in Glacier Bay National Park. Bob was a strong advocate of using aircraft for wildlife work.

"If you'll lay out research proposals, I'll see that they get funded," he said. "And I'll make sure you have a single-engine aircraft available to help you conduct your studies."

After consulting with the park superintendents, I finally settled on three major projects: a caribou study in McKinley, a brown bear study in Katmai National

Park, and aerial inventories of the large mammals in Katmai, McKinley, and Lake Clark national parks. These aerial inventories of various large mammals, such as moose and Dall sheep, would provide base data for measuring future population trends. In McKinley the caribou herd was at an all-time low, and the park managers wanted to know why. In Katmai I would study bears around Brooks River and do aerial inventories of brown bears throughout the park to learn more about their total numbers, distribution, and movements.

Bob kept his word about supporting my work. With proper funding and an airplane, I started the studies at Katmai.

This park in southwest Alaska was becoming popular. More and more tourists were visiting it for the excellent fishing and the chance to see and hike around the Valley of 10,000 Smokes. Interest was also growing in bear watching, and people began coming on day trips to watch the animals. All this increased human activity was causing more encounters between bears and people. The danger was especially heightened because fishermen and bears were often competing for salmon, and sightseers were sometimes becoming a little too nonchalant. Remarkably, only one or two very minor injuries had occurred.

The park service needed more management information on the bears at Brooks River; we would do the work in the fall, after the tourists had departed. The superintendent wanted the information gathered with as little harassment of the bears as possible. That posed a challenge since my past bear research on Kodiak Island had involved capturing bears by traps and snares. At that time, more than eleven years earlier, we had had to work through several steps. After capturing the bears, we temporarily anesthetized them, roped and hog-tied them by hand, and then administered another drug to put them to sleep. Dramatically better techniques and equipment had since been developed, but I had not used the new and improved methods.

The drug Sernylan was now available and much more efficient than the old two-drug method I had used at Kodiak. A single dose, delivered with a dart gun (also known as a Cap-Chur gun) into a large muscle of the bear, would immobilize the animal for an hour or more. Antidotes were also available, and if injected, the animal was back on its feet quickly. Collars with radio transmitters were used by scientists to track the whereabouts of the animals from the ground or a plane.

After researching these new methods, I decided to stalk the bears on foot and shoot them with a dart gun. Once the drug had taken effect, my assistants and I would put radio collars on the bears to track their movements.

I was primarily interested in getting movement data, so we needed to capture and collar only a single animal from a family group. The Cap-Chur guns permitted us to be much more selective in choosing which animals we would take, something that the use of foot snares had not allowed. Since cubs follow their mothers wherever they go, we had no reason to capture a cub, thereby traumatizing its mother as we had done at Kodiak.

My summer assistant, Martin Grosnick, and I worked as a team, and I often persuaded Alaska Department of Fish and Game personnel to form another team to assist us in capturing bears and putting on radio collars. The Brooks River has excellent rainbow fishing in late September and October, so recruits were easy to find.

We did most of our work in the early morning when the bears were most active; they were usually fishing for salmon along the shores of Naknek Lake and Brooks River. When we found a suitable bear, we stalked it until we were close enough to try a shot with the dart gun. If the dart hit its target, the animal became immobilized in about two minutes. However, in that short time bears are capable of running quite a distance, and they would often disappear into the woods.

At times a downed animal was difficult to find in the thick brush, so we had park rangers help us search. We would spread about a hundred feet apart and hike through the woods in the direction the bear had taken. Usually we found the animal within twenty minutes. The drug kept the bear powerless for about an hour, plenty of time to gather biological data and collar the animal.

Eventually our captures and procedures became routine. Still, we had some moments that got our adrenaline pumping.

Martin and I worked alone the first week of October 1977. One drizzly morning we left our cabin at the first light of dawn and walked to the shores of Naknek Lake to look for bears. As I glassed the shoreline, I spotted a sow and two cubs on the beach a couple of hundred yards away, near the campground. Two subadults were following the lakeshore in the other direction.

"Let's try for the sow," I said to Martin. Collaring this mother with cubs would give us information on three bears.

We ducked back into the woods and paralleled the shoreline toward the bear family. The wind blew inshore, sending short, choppy waves swishing up onto the gravel beach. The situation was ideal. From the woods we could approach upwind and let the lapping waves muffle any noise we might make. The rain also helped mute our movements. Rows of small cottonwoods and spruce helped conceal us as we crept through the trees.

Brooks Lodge is located at the mouth of the Brooks River on the shores of Naknek Lake.

We moved forward a hundred and fifty yards or so and then cautiously sneaked to the edge of the forest. I spotted the bear family to my left, less than a hundred yards away. I gestured toward the bears to alert Martin, and we slipped back into the woods.

"Let's make a semicircle and come in behind them," I whispered to Martin. "She's just caught a salmon, and her cubs are feeding at the edge of the water." He nodded, so we began our approach.

"This should work, if everything goes right," I thought. When we were directly across from them, we could see that the cubs were still feeding while the sow stood knee-deep in water looking for another salmon. I estimated her at four hundred pounds and prepared the dart. I slipped it in the chamber and closed the bolt.

"Do you want to take the shot?" I whispered to Martin, but he motioned me to go ahead while he double-checked the slug in the shotgun chamber.

I moved forward another ten feet behind a low shrub and then rested the barrel of the gun against a small cottonwood tree to steady my shot. The sow was standing at the edge of the water with her butt toward us and her cubs by her side. I judged her to be about sixty feet away, a comfortable distance for a shot.

Red salmon: 1, Troyer: 0. The fish fought hard and threw the hook—right into my cheek.
A flight to the clinic in Naknek followed. Photo by Rollie Ostermick.

I aimed at her rear leg muscle and fired. I knew the dart had hit home when I heard it smack on contact.

The instant it struck, the sow bawled, whirled, and then slapped the cub nearest her. The cub tumbled back, emitting a distressed cry. The sow evidently thought the cub had bitten her rear, and she punished it again by nipping its rump with her teeth. The cub got back on its feet and approached the mother, whining like a child that had been wrongfully punished. "I didn't do it, Momma." But with another sharp cuff she sent it scampering.

While all this was happening, I had retreated into the woods and crouched down. Martin and I had huge, silent grins on our faces from watching the antics; I was afraid one of us would explode with laughter. Then the sow turned and came toward us. She halted at the edge of the forest and rose to her hind legs to peer in our direction, sensing something suspicious. Our grinning faces suddenly turned somber, and we instinctively froze.

As the angry sow scanned the woods, I wished for something more protective than the dart gun I held. She dropped to all fours and came forward into the woods to within thirty feet of us, her nose testing the air. She had detected something amiss but was not sure where the danger lurked. She sniffed the air for a few seconds more and then turned and ran back to her cubs. When she got

Martin Grosnick with one of our radio-collared bears.

to the beach, she snuffed at her cubs, and they all bounded down the shoreline a short distance before turning into the woods. I breathed a huge sigh of relief.

"Gee whiz, that was too close for comfort," I finally confessed to Martin.

"Yeah, I had the safety off, thinking I was going to have to fire," he replied.

Researchers rarely kill bears to protect themselves while performing studies, but it does occur. Close calls, such as the one we had just had, almost always end safely for both bears and researchers as long as the people involved keep a cool head. I was glad Martin had the patience, even under pressure, to wait the situation out.

We walked back to camp and recruited two rangers to help us locate the bear. We found the downed animal, put a radio collar on her, and got the biological data we needed. The cubs stayed in the background during our activities, but they returned to the mother as we were leaving. We knew the family would be okay.

Spawning red salmon fill a small stream near Naknek Lake.

Later in October Martin and I spent several fruitless mornings attempting to capture bears. Each time we made a stalk, the bears eluded us or we missed with the dart. We became discouraged with our morning hunts and decided to try in the evening.

I preferred to dart bears in the morning when animals were more active and easier to find. During the middle of the day they tended to bed down and were difficult to locate. Bears became active again late in the evening, but capturing a bear at that time of day could sometimes create problems; darkness often fell before we could process the animal.

One evening, after several unsuccessful days, frustration overcame caution, and I darted a mature sow later in the day than I should have. I could see the dart hanging from her rear leg as she rushed from the river into the spruce and birch forest. We sighted her again, moving through a grassy opening on a ridge some two hundred yards away. We knew we had little time before the setting sun would spread dark shadows beneath the forest canopy.

We picked up the sow's trail in tall wet grass and followed it to the edge of the forest. We stood there, scanning ahead, but we did not see her and began

Brown bears fishing on the Brooks River falls in Katmai National Monument.

to move forward. From about fifty yards into the woods she suddenly lunged toward us from behind a tree, growling. Surprised, I stumbled back, but she collapsed before I could flee.

"She's not quite out yet. Let's give 'er another cc," I said to Martin.

I prepared a dart with another small dose of Sernylan and shot it into the bear's left shoulder. Once more she lurched forward with a loud bawl before collapsing as we jumped behind nearby spruce trees. If she was trying to instill fear, she was doing a good job. We retreated a hundred feet to avoid further stressing the bear and waited for the second dose to take effect. The sow finally lay down at the base of a spruce.

"I think she is going down for good this time," I called to Martin.

"I hope so," he answered skeptically.

After a few minutes we talked it over and determined that the drug must have had time to act by then.

"Let's go," I said. We were losing daylight fast, and I was concerned we would not be able to get data from the bear or collar it. We crept to within forty feet of her. She was breathing heavily. I was fairly certain she was down for good, but a voice inside me also screamed, "Beware!" I picked up a stick and flung it, hitting her side. She leaped up with an angry roar and took a few steps toward us, but then she folded in a heap.

We stayed back and pondered the situation. I was reluctant to give her any more drugs; by normal standards she had already had an overdose. We waited five minutes more and again hit her with a stick, getting the same results. She leaped up and stumbled forward as we ran for cover. This time she managed to amble into some heavy alders. I could barely see her dark form beneath the thick cover. I circled the alders to see if I could get a better view, but when I accidentally snapped a branch, she again jumped up and growled. By then I was really worried. We had a half-drugged bear in a thick patch of alders with darkness rapidly descending.

I retreated and circled around to where Martin stood. We looked at each other, frowning. It was not going well. Frankly, I was scared and did not relish going into the alders after a partially sedated bear, especially in the dark.

"I think we'd better let 'er go," Martin finally said. That gave me all the excuse I needed. I agreed, and we headed back to camp.

The next morning we checked to make sure she had recovered and had left the area, which she had. The sow was one of those rare bears that did not react to drugs as anticipated. After this incident we decided to quit darting bears late in the evening.

One day we had an unexpected adventure while accompanied by a guest. One of the seasonal rangers had asked to accompany us; he had never seen a bear darted. He, Martin, and I left our cabins in the predawn darkness and followed a well-used bear trail toward the Trout Hole, a favorite spot for fishermen on Brooks River. As we moved toward the river, I thought I heard a bear moving through the brushy willows to our left, and I gestured for my companions to halt. We stopped to peer through the willows and alders, and I could just make out a silhouetted bear coming toward us along the riverbank. As it got closer, I got a better look; it was an immense bear.

I quickly assessed the situation, noting that the bear was on our side of the river. If we hit him with a dart and he stampeded in our direction, we could be in danger. We were trapped on a peninsula with no easy escape. The big bear was less than fifty yards away and walking rapidly. At the rate he was approaching we would not have time to prepare the dart and make a shot. As he closed the gap between us, his huge size became even more apparent, and I spooked.

"He's too big!" I hissed at the two behind me. I picked up a stick and threw it at the bear less than one hundred feet away, hoping to scare him into another direction. The stick landed right in front of him, hitting the base of a tree with a loud whop. To my amazement, he gave no indication of having heard anything. He continued in our direction, still unaware of us.

A cabin at the Brooks River camp.

"Is he deaf?" I wondered. In seconds the bear was eighty feet away and fast approaching. Martin had moved to the riverbank and was trying to hide behind a small cottonwood, while I backed into an alder bush for cover. The two of us were less than thirty feet apart. The ranger had spotted the impending situation earlier and had hid behind a willow bush, thirty feet behind us.

Something had to be done quickly to stop the bear from blundering into one of us. I was carrying a rifle that morning, so I raised it and fired into the air. I hoped the loud crack would frighten the bear into the opposite direction. The shot sounded like crashing thunder in the morning stillness.

The bear heard the shot, and it scared him; but instead of retreating, he bolted toward us. Before Martin or I could react, the bear ran full speed through the thirty-foot opening between us and then right toward the willow bush the ranger was hiding behind, brushing past it. After the bear passed, I watched the ranger stumble from behind the bush, his face ashen. He was trying to say something but was completely incoherent.

Martin and I exchanged relieved glances, realizing we were lucky to have avoided a disaster. The ranger finally got his senses back, but he never again asked to help us dart bears.

By following our radio-collared bears, we collected valuable information on their movements. Using a handheld receiver on the ground, we were able to track

Photographing brown bears along the Katmai Coast.

the animals around Brooks for half a mile or so, depending on the terrain. From a plane, however, we were often able to pick up the radio signal up to five miles away. I learned that some bears spent their entire life within a few-mile radius of the Brooks River. Others traveled extensively, often moving across mountain ranges. I was unhappy to hear later that several younger bears we tagged had moved out of the park and into the King Salmon area, where they were shot and killed as nuisance bears.

Radio collaring and marking bears was only part of our efforts in studying the brown bears in Katmai. I spent the bulk of the summer and the fall flying repeated stream surveys, gathering data on minimum population numbers for each drainage, and classifying the bears into age groups. The number of new cubs and yearlings in the population provided information on whether the bear population was increasing, decreasing, or stable. After multiple counts, I found we had far more bears within the park boundaries than we had originally estimated and the population appeared stable.

During my studies at Katmai I became concerned that potentially dangerous encounters between bears and people were increasing on the Brooks River and around Brooks Camp. Tourists hiked to Brooks Falls to watch bears fishing, which often caused close contact with the animals. I recommended that a bear-viewing platform be built near the falls to help separate bears and people. This was done a few years after I retired.

The lodge and the cluster of cabins where most people stayed were located on a peninsula. My studies indicated that many bears cut across this peninsula to feed on salmon and thus walked right through camp, causing more conflicts. Because of my findings, the park service recommended that the camp be moved across the river and away from this natural bear corridor. The lodge owners, however, liked to be close to the river and the lake so their clients could watch bears from the camp. They opposed the plan and lobbied politicians to block the proposal. The facilities were never moved, and the conflicts continue.

The brown bear work at Katmai was fascinating and often exciting. I enjoyed darting bears each fall and flying the aerial surveys to count hundreds of bears while they fished for salmon or fed on sedge flats along the seacoast. The park service job had gotten me out in the field again and away from the office politics in which I had been embroiled during my last few years with the FWS. I enjoyed the fieldwork immensely, and I was never again tempted to take an office position.

Chapter 25

Turquoise Lake Calving Grounds

I gazed at the panoramic scene as we circled in the Cessna 180. To the east lay ice-covered Turquoise Lake, its eastern shore bordered by rugged mountains towering high into the blue sky. Fleecy cumulus clouds drifted lazily across the peaks, enshrouding some of the pinnacles like silk veils. Far to the west the rolling Bonanza Hills dominated the horizon, and directly below me a high valley lay between the two contrasting geographic features. I carefully studied the land below, which was covered with short willows, heather, sedge meadows, and a few small ponds. The Mulchatna caribou herd, attracted by rich forage, gathered here each spring to give birth to a new generation.

Several thousand caribou were scattered over the terrain. A few individual cows had already separated from the main herd to seek solitude before giving birth. Once the calves were born, the cows would spend a few days alone, nursing their offspring and letting them gain strength before rejoining the herd.

The Mulchatna caribou were receiving an increasing amount of hunting pressure by the mid-1970s. To keep an eye on the situation and assess the health of the herd, the National Park Service and the Alaska Department of Fish and Game undertook a study to monitor their numbers, movement, and productivity. As the NPS biologist, I was looking forward to spending some time on the ground during the calving season. By observing these caribou I could learn valuable information about their interactions with the surrounding environment during this critical part of their lives.

"Let's fly over the herd one more time before we land on the lake," I said to the pilot, Glen Alsworth.

Glen glided down and circled over numerous groups of caribou before landing the Cessna on the west end of the frozen lake. Dick Proenneke and I jumped out and unloaded our gear. Dick was a longtime friend. I had invited him to accompany me on this trip, and he had eagerly accepted. Turquoise Lake was just over the mountains from Twin Lakes, where Dick had built a cabin and now spent his days roaming the vast, wild landscape on foot. His life at Twin Lakes has been chronicled in *One Man's Wilderness: An Alaskan Odyssey*, a book he wrote with Sam Keith.

I handed Glen a walkie-talkie. "Here, take this," I said. "When you return to pick us up in ten days, I'll let you know the condition of the ice."

"Okay. Good idea," he said, taking the radio. He and I both knew the lake ice sometimes deteriorated rapidly in the spring.

After Glen took off, Dick and I pitched our tent and got the camp ready. At an elevation of 2,500 feet Turquoise Lake is above tree line. The area next to the lake has little in the way of depressions or hills, and the small willows and other low shrubs provide little wind protection. I knew windstorms sometimes lashed the area, but I hoped the calm weather would prevail during our stay.

"It's still fairly early," I said to Dick. "Let's see if we can find a few caribou."

"Sounds good to me," he replied.

We grabbed a scope, a tripod, and binoculars and walked to the top of a low rise. Numerous tree and savannah sparrows flushed from the bushes, a pair of ravens squawked overhead, and a northern harrier skimmed across meadows looking for voles or something else to eat. We had not gone far when I heard the cackle of a cock willow ptarmigan. He sat in the top of a willow bush, his crimson combs contrasting vividly with his white breast and wing plumage. This was his breeding territory, and a hen was probably hidden on a nearby nest.

We spotted a group of about thirty-five caribou feeding and moving slowly in our direction. Dick and I ducked behind willow bushes and waited. We saw no calves, but several cows had swollen bellies and extended udders, indicating they would soon give birth. We watched the band for about thirty minutes without being detected, but when we stood up to leave, an alert cow spotted us. All heads turned in our direction, and the entire group appeared surprised at our presence. They stared at us a few moments before the lead cow turned and trotted stiff-legged down a ridge. The others followed. They traveled several hundred yards and then stopped to turn and gaze at us again. Suddenly, they wheeled and ran, apparently deciding they did not trust us.

Dick and I hiked a bit farther. I found a knoll, set up the spotting scope, and began scanning the area.

Dick Proenneke in front of his cabin at Twin Lakes.

"Okay, Dick. I see two cows with calves in a small swale to the left," I said, pointing.

Dick raised his binoculars.

"Yeah, from the looks of their wobbly legs, they can't be more than a day old," he said.

We scanned the horizon for more caribou calves but failed to find any, so we headed back to camp.

"What's for dinner—dried stew?" Dick asked skeptically after we arrived back at camp. I had supplied most of the groceries, so he was probably suspecting I had brought my usual larder of dried food.

"No. I brought a surprise," I said, reaching into my pack and pulling out two venison steaks.

Dick's eyes lit up. "Wow! Is that ever going to taste good!"

"We're going to live like kings tonight. We'll get plenty of freeze-dried stew later," I replied.

We got the stove going, and Dick soon had the meat sizzling. Ten minutes later we were eating steaks and a fresh salad I had also brought.

After dinner Dick brewed a pot of Labrador tea, made from the plant of the same name. We sat on a low knoll near camp, sipping tea and watching the sun disappear over the horizon. Dick entertained me by relating some of his adventures at Twin Lakes. As we talked, a full moon rose into the sky, and a small pond in front of us reflected the scene. A light breeze whipped a few ripples across the shallow pond, causing the moon and mountains to shimmer and dance. We put our cameras on tripods to capture the dramatic moment. After taking several photos, Dick brewed up some more tea. We lingered over it and watched the evening skies before turning in for the night.

During the next few days we wandered over the vast valley, observing many bands of caribou. Each day we encountered a few cows giving birth, and each day we could see that the percentage of calves in the population was rapidly increasing. Caribou seemed to be everywhere, and the moving animals gave life to these wild, quiet lands. Like most caribou herds, the Mulchatna caribou wander over hundreds of miles of terrain, crisscrossing mountains, rivers, and valleys. But each spring in May they return to this particular spot, their calving grounds, to give birth to a new generation.

In the distance I spotted numerous animals, some alone and others in small groups. "Let's walk over to those two cows," I said to Dick. "It looks like one is restless and about ready to have a calf."

We headed to a small knoll and sat down to watch the two females with swollen bellies. In about thirty minutes one cow lay down on her side and rocked back and forth for several minutes until the front feet of a fetus appeared. The mother-to-be stood up and then lay down again before the head made its appearance. A few minutes more of rocking completed the delivery, and the rest of the calf slid to the ground. Giving birth had taken only about ten minutes. The cow immediately rose, turned around, and began eating the afterbirth from her newborn calf. This trait helps deter predators from finding newborn calves. The newborn lifted its head a few times as the mother licked it. Before long the calf struggled to its feet, immediately falling to the ground again. The mother continued licking the newborn, encouraging it to rise. Several minutes later it got to its feet, tottered toward the rear of the cow, and began to suckle the rich, warm milk. The calf fed for a few minutes before it collapsed to the ground to rest.

After watching the birth, we decided to leave. As we stood up, the mother turned to look at us nervously and trotted off in a swinging gait, away from her calf. The newborn lay quietly on the ground without moving.

"Let's get out of here before she abandons it," Dick said to me.

A newly born caribou calf suckles its mother near Turquoise Lake.

We did not need to worry, for as soon as we moved away the mother returned to her newborn. Caribou calves gain strength rapidly, much more so than many other mammals; in a few hours this one would be able to trail its mother. In a few days it would be capable of following the herd.

Near noon on the fifth day of our stay the wind picked up and increased rapidly while we were hiking the area.

"This wind is so strong I can't even hold my binoculars steady. Let's head back to camp," I called to Dick.

"Yeah, it looks like we're in for a big blow," he replied. We had to practically yell to each other to be heard.

The wind was gusting even harder by the time we got to camp. The tent flapped violently, and I noticed a small tear in the fabric near one of the tent stakes.

"We're gonna have to lay the tent down to save it," I shouted to Dick. He agreed.

We dropped the center pole and laid the tent on the ground. Just as we got one section secured, another would break loose. We hurriedly scrounged for several large rocks to keep the tent from flapping and tearing.

"Wow! I think that last gust hit sixty!" Dick yelled above the fury of the storm.

Nature seemed to have unleashed its demons. The wind picked up speed as it roared out of the mountains and raced across the lake. Dick and I both searched for some shelter to eat dinner but without success. Dick knelt down in a shallow depression and tried to light the small Coleman stove, but the task was futile. Our only recourse for protection from the storm appeared to be under the flattened tent, where we would be unable to cook. I found the grub bag and fished out some cheese and crackers.

"Here, take this. It will have to do for dinner tonight," I said to Dick.

We slid into the flat tent and into our sleeping bags that lay within. After eating our meager dinner, we tried to get some rest. I slept fitfully, constantly awakened by the howling wind. Toward morning my bladder was getting full; I was miserable, but I hung on for another hour, hoping the storm would subside. But there was no letup. In desperation I fished around in the murkiness of the tent for an empty can and finally found one. I emptied my bladder, searched for a hole in the tent entrance, and flung the can and its contents outside. Relieved, I went back to sleep.

When I awoke again, my watch told me it was seven o'clock, but the storm was still buffeting us. Two hours later, nearly fifteen hours after crawling under the collapsed tent, I finally heard the wind begin to diminish.

"Hey Dick, you awake?" I asked.

"How can I not be?" he muttered. "She's a regular banshee storm."

"Yeah, but it's letting up," I said. "I'm getting out. I've had enough of this for a while."

We crawled out from our prison to find that the wind had lost about half of its strength. I saw my empty pee can wedged into a willow bush, where the wind had blown it. I retrieved it and deposited it in our trash. Dick and I walked around stretching our legs and searching for a protected place in which to cook breakfast.

"Hey, Will. Come over here!"

I hurried over to find Dick squatting down in a depression behind a rock.

"I think we can get the stove going here and have some breakfast," he said.

We hunkered down behind the rock and soon had enough hot water for some cocoa and oatmeal. It sure tasted good after so many hours with only a few crackers and some cheese.

The storm continued to die down, and by midafternoon it was over. We erected the tent again, and then we pigged out with more food for an early dinner.

"Boy, I hope that's the last storm we get," I said.

"That was about the worst one I've experienced since coming into this country in the 1960s," Dick replied. We both knew, of course, that it had seemed a lot worse trying to weather a windstorm under a collapsed tent than in a snug cabin.

Later in the evening we were both eager to take a hike. I grabbed the fishing gear, and we followed the shoreline to the mouth of the Mulchatna River. The river was actually a small stream at the outlet, but we found a nice deep pool a hundred yards downstream. As we approached, four harlequin ducks in bright breeding plumage flushed from the water. I cast a small lure into the pool, and almost immediately a fish grabbed it and ran. It leaped out of the water several times as I tried to tame it. When the fish tired and came to the surface, I yanked it out of the water onto the riverbank to make sure we would have fresh fish to eat. It was a fourteen-inch lake trout. I smiled and handed the pole to Dick.

"You try," I said.

He took my pole and repeated the performance.

"Those will taste mighty good for breakfast. We don't need any more for now," he said, returning my rod.

Dick was whistling in jubilation as we walked back to camp. The storm had passed, and we had fresh trout—life was good! Since neither of us was eager to crawl back into our sleeping bags so soon, we sat around drinking tea until nearly midnight.

The next morning, after feasting on the two trout, we again headed out to observe caribou. Groups of them were scattered across the calving grounds, just as they had been before the storm. The strong winds apparently had little effect on these rugged animals of the north. More cows with new calves had joined the bands, and we estimated nearly a third of the adult cows now had calves. We spent the next two days taking photographs of caribou feeding, calves suckling, and groups of calves running and playing together. We were still finding a few newborn calves, but calving had reached its peak and was beginning to taper off.

That evening we dined on more fresh trout caught from the pool.

"Tomorrow is our last day at Turquoise Lake," I said to Dick. "Let's spend the day counting as many cows and calves as we can. I want to know the success of this year's calf crop."

"Good idea," Dick replied. "We know where most of them hang out, and we should be able to find several hundred animals." Most of these caribou would later wander over to Twin Lakes, where Dick lived, so he had a special interest in the herd.

The following morning we packed a lunch, grabbed our binoculars and spotting scope, and headed west. Before long we encountered a band of sixty animals. I set up the scope, and as I called out how many cows, calves, and yearlings I saw, Dick recorded the numbers.

After censusing that group we continued our trek, stopping often to count small bands, singles, and pairs. At about noon we topped a ridge and saw a

Caribou form into large herds after calving.

serene pastoral scene in a large swale below us. More than a hundred caribou were bedded down, peacefully chewing cud. Nearly every adult cow had a calf by her side. We sat and watched the animals for some time without being detected. The only sound we heard was a male Lapland longspur that repeatedly rose from a bush, climbed high in the sky, and then fluttered down like a butterfly, all the while sounding his chiming call as he descended.

We did not want to disturb the peaceful scene, so we sneaked down the other side of the ridge and continued our census. By the end of the day we had tabulated 603 cows and 409 calves.

"It appears we're getting a good calf crop this year," I said to Dick.

"It sure does, and I hope some of them will visit me at Twin Lakes later this summer so I can get more pictures."

The temperature continued to rise after the storm, and the lake ice was melting rapidly. Open water appeared on the far side of the lake. We were due to fly out the next day, so Dick and I walked out onto the frozen lake in front of our camp that last evening. We found spots where the ice appeared quite weak.

"What do you think, Dick? Shall we wave off Glen tomorrow and tell him the ice isn't safe?"

"Boy, I sure think so. He can go back and get the Tcraft on floats and pick us up in that open water."

I agreed. The ice was just too rotten to chance a landing with the heavy Cessna 180 on wheels.

During the calm of the evening we heated a freeze-dried stew and then sat around a small fire drinking tea and talking about what we were going to do when we got home. Dick was anxious to return to his cabin and see how all his wild pets had fared while he was gone. He always fed a few small animals and birds, such as gray jays, that hung around his area. I was eager to return to my family.

The weather was good the next morning, and we were sure Glen would arrive to pick us up on schedule. After eating breakfast, we walked out on the ice again. It was definitely unsafe for a wheeled landing. We decided to pack our gear but leave the tent standing in case we were stranded another day.

At about eight thirty Glen's 180 appeared on the horizon and circled overhead. I turned on the walkie-talkie. His voice crackled over the radio.

"How's the ice down there?" he asked.

"We think it's too rotten and recommend you don't land. There is enough open water on the other side for a floatplane landing," I radioed back.

"Roger, I hear you, but are you sure? It looks pretty good to me."

I looked at Dick. He shook his head. "Roger, Glen, but Dick and I both think you shouldn't chance it."

There was a short pause before he called again. "I'll just touch down a little and see how it feels."

Glen made another circle, reduced power, and gently let down until the wheels ran on the ice. I expected him to lift off and go around again, but instead he cut the engine. Dick and I glanced at each other apprehensively. We both held our breath, as we knew the ice was weak. The plane slowed as it rolled along the ice, which appeared to be holding. But just as the plane stopped, the left wheel dropped through the ice. Fortunately, the left wing hit the frozen lake, and its wide surface kept the Cessna from sinking deeper.

"Boy, oh boy! Are we ever in a jam!" said Dick.

I was speechless. Why in the world had Glen tried to land after we had warned him against it? Dick and I walked quickly out to the plane. Glen was still inside as we approached, and we could hear him talking on the plane's radio. I surveyed the stuck Cessna and wondered how we were going to get it out.

Glen finished his radio conversation and crawled out of the plane's passenger side, looking sheepish.

"Well, I guess I should have listened to you guys."

We did not reply. No point in saying, "I told you so."

A wheel broke through the ice when Glen Alsworth's plane landed to pick us up.

Glen said he had contacted a large airliner on the radio emergency frequency. The airliner pilot would call the Federal Aviation Administration (FAA) in Anchorage. They would relay a message to Glen's brother Bee at Port Alsworth, a small community on the shore of Lake Clark where Glen and his brother lived. Bee would arrange a rescue.

Glen was concerned the plane might sink farther into the ice and asked if we had seen any logs that he might slip under the 180. I said no, but told him we had found a cache of empty five-gallon gas cans that someone had left on the lakeshore. The three of us got the cans, tied them together, and slid them under the wings, the engine, and the right wheel. We all hoped that would keep the plane stable until it could be rescued.

In about an hour Bee arrived in a Tcraft on floats and landed in the water on the other side of the lake. Glen hiked across the ice to his brother, and they flew back to Port Alsworth to arrange for help. Before Glen left, he asked Dick and me to look around for a possible emergency airstrip near the lake.

Dick and I were discouraged. We had been looking forward to going home. Now it appeared we would be out another day, maybe longer. Despite our feelings, we had a task to do. Back at the tent I asked Dick if he remembered the flat ridge we had found a few days earlier while looking for caribou. We had taken notice because it was apparent that a few planes had landed on it.

"Yeah, it's right there," Dick said, pointing.

We started hiking toward the site, which was northwest of our camp. A short while later we got to the ridge and looked it over. We thought it might serve as an emergency strip if we moved a few rocks, which we did during the next half hour. I was sure I could land and take off on it with a Cub, but I was not sure about the larger Cessna 180.

We returned to camp. About an hour later two planes came in—Glen in the Tcraft on floats and Bee with a Super Cub on large wheels. Bee flew to the head of the lake and found a landing site on a gravel bar, while Glen landed on the ice using the Tcraft floats like skis. It saved a long hike from the open water on the other side of the lake. We didn't worry about the Tcraft punching through because it was lighter than the Cessna and the floats distributed its weight more evenly than wheels.

After landing the Tcraft, Glen told us a helicopter big enough to lift the Cessna would soon be on its way from Anchorage. I told Glen about the emergency strip we had found.

"I'll run Dick back to Twin Lakes," Glen said. "When I return, we'll hike up to inspect it."

I helped Dick load his gear in the Tcraft. We shook hands, and I thanked him for accompanying me on the trip.

"Yeah, it's been quite an adventure," he said, smiling. "I'll be glad to get back to my cabin and the quiet life, though."

Glen flew Dick back to Twin Lakes. When he returned, he landed the Tcraft on the ice near the Cessna again. We hiked up to the emergency strip that Dick and I had found. Glen was sure the strip was long enough to take off with the 180, but the surface of the ridge was rough. He decided to put larger wheels on the Cessna so it could better absorb the rough spots. When we returned to the Tcraft, Glen radioed Bee and asked him to go back to Port Alsworth to get a jack and the bigger wheels. In a few minutes we watched Bee take off from the head of the lake.

At about two thirty that afternoon the helicopter arrived and landed on the shore of the lake. Glen and I put a large sling, brought by the copter, on the 180 while the chopper crew placed a net over the wings to break the airflow while carrying the plane. The crew returned to the huge helicopter, and in a few minutes it was hovering over the 180. The crew lowered a cable, which Glen attached to the sling around the Cessna. In just a few minutes the chopper lifted the plane off the ice and carried it over to the emergency strip on the ridge.

The helicopter crew unhooked the Cessna and then flew back to Anchorage. Glen and I hiked over to the site carrying the jack and wheels Bee had brought. We jacked up the plane and put on the larger, softer wheels. At about that point something occurred to me. Glen planned to fly back to Port Alsworth in the 180

A large helicopter in the process of pulling the Cessna 180 out of the ice.

while Bee returned with the Cub, which was loaded with gear. That left only the Tcraft and me at the lake.

"Who's going to fly back the Tcraft?" I asked Glen.

"You are," he replied. "You told me you once flew Tcrafts."

My stomach sank. That was not what I wanted to hear, but I had suspected as much. I had not flown a Tcraft for nearly twenty years, and this one was on floats sitting on rotten ice. I voiced my doubts, but Bee and Glen both assured me I would have no problem. I had little choice.

"Okay, I'll give it a try," I said to Glen. "It's your plane!"

Bee agreed to wait until I was airborne, to make sure I took off safely. In the meantime Glen got the 180 off the strip without any problems.

While we had been rescuing the Cessna, the ice had continued to deteriorate; when I walked out to the Tcraft, my foot broke through the ice twice. That really made me nervous. I got into the plane, checked out the controls, and started it. After warming the engine, I gave it full throttle, but the plane would not dislodge. The floats had sunk into the soft slush a couple of inches. I got out, pushed on the struts, and rocked the plane. I managed to get one float out of the depression, so I got back in and gave the engine full throttle again. The plane still did not budge. Perspiration began running into my eyes. Frustrated and nervous, I revved the engine several times, and finally a float broke loose. Then the other. In seconds the Tcraft was scrunching along the crusty ice, gaining speed. Finally it became airborne. I exhaled mightily!

As I gained altitude, I turned and circled over the caribou. Large groups of cows with calves occupied the numerous ridges and swales. Calving was almost complete. I would retain many fond memories of the week Dick and I had spent with this remote herd of caribou.

The plane continued to climb until I was flying high over the mountains toward Lake Clark. I was still nervous, though, as I had not made a water landing with a Tcraft for nearly twenty years. When I arrived at Port Alsworth, I let the plane down gently and made a power landing. It was a smooth one, and I was one relieved pilot. I wiped the sweat from my brow, taxied to shore, and tied up the plane near Glen's house.

Dick and I had gone to Turquoise Lake to learn more about the Mulchatna caribou herd. We had gotten a lot of good information, and we had enjoyed one another's company. Spending several days in a picture-postcard setting had certainly been a treat, but, like Dick, I had had enough adventure for a while. I looked forward to getting back to my family in Anchorage.

Chapter 26

Danger in Our Business

Ross and I were floating peacefully down the Alagnak River as I watched an osprey glide and turn in the sky. High rock walls loomed on either side of us. As we approached a bend in the river, my ears caught the sound of a waterfall. I became alert and cupped my hand behind my ear to hear better. The sound became louder, and I yelled to Ross, "Waterfall ahead!"

He nodded and grabbed his oar firmly. Our raft shot around the sharp curve, driven by the increasing velocity of the current. My mind swirled with confusion as my eyes swept across the plunging river and the foaming white water below. When I saw our friends' raft floating upside down in the river below the falls, I knew we were headed for disaster.

Wildlife biology may not seem like a dangerous business, but over the course of my thirty-year career in Alaska many of my colleagues have been killed while conducting fieldwork. Others, including myself, have had serious accidents but were fortunate to have survived them. Most of these incidents were related to aircraft or boats. We often traveled in remote mountain regions or on open seas, areas which are exposed to windstorms, snowstorms, fog, and other hazardous weather conditions. Those of us doing aerial wildlife surveys frequently had to fly at low elevations, leaving little room for error.

During my early days in Alaska the U.S. Fish and Wildlife Service tried to improve the safety of the working conditions. The agency equipped its aircraft, boats, patrol cars, major offices, and field stations with radios linked by a common radio frequency for quick communication. Employees also had to go through intensive safety training. Despite these efforts, accidents happened. When they did, the esprit de corps among employees shone through. As soon as one of our planes or boats was reported overdue or missing, we rallied to the search. Finding our missing colleagues became our highest priority.

The last search in which I participated was for Jerry Fisher and Jim Erickson in late July 1970. They had been conducting aerial sheep surveys on the north side of the Brooks Range in the Arctic refuge. When the men were reported as missing, the FWS responded with three Beaver and two Grumman Goose aircraft. I flew as an observer in one of the Beavers, piloted by Dave Spencer. We had not searched long when a pilot ahead of us radioed that he had found the wreckage. Dave and I were over the scene soon after hearing the news. The plane was in a small canyon. It appeared that it had exploded and burned on impact. We circled but saw no survivors. Dave turned to me, shook his head, and said, "It doesn't look good."

We flew to Peterson Lake, where the rest of the search team was assembling. A helicopter with a state trooper aboard had already been dispatched to the scene.

We gathered around a fire, awaiting the helicopter's return. We had all flown over the accident and were despondent, expecting the worst. I wrote in my diary that evening, "Everyone is standing gloomily around the campfire this evening making small talk—each in our own thoughts. Many of us thinking it could just as easily have been me. All of us have conducted sheep surveys in rugged mountains, and all of us have experienced downdrafts or had other weather-related incidents that resulted in close calls. We are continuing to sit around drinking coffee late in the evening. No one wants to go to bed. One just can't sleep at such times."

Later the chopper returned with two body bags. As we had feared, there were no survivors, and the troopers confirmed the plane had exploded and burned on impact.

This incident was especially hard for me. Jerry Fisher, Ave Thayer's assistant, had flown me over part of the Arctic refuge only a week or so before. We had camped out together for several days at Schrader Lake.

I had many narrow escapes over the years, but there were three times when I was sure I had met my demise. The first accident happened in 1957, when Doug Haynes and I crashed at Tonki Cape, which I described in Chapter 12. The last two occurred in 1979, while I was working for the National Park Service. The first of these was the rafting incident.

Six of us were preparing to float the Alagnak River in three sixteen-foot rubber rafts to survey the fishery, recreation, and wildlife resources of this major drainage. My primary interest was to locate and map the raptor nests along the river. The Alagnak flows from Kukaklek Lake. Its other main water source is Nonvianuk Lake. These two lakes are each about thirty miles long and are located just south of Iliamna Lake, the largest lake in Alaska. The outlet river from Nonvianuk Lake joins the Alagnak about twenty-five miles below Kukaklek Lake. The Alagnak River meanders another seventy-five miles before it empties into the Kvichak River near the head of Bristol Bay. At the time of our float trip the area had not yet been added to the Katmai park lands, but much of it had been selected as an addition.

I had flown over the Alagnak River several times while conducting bear surveys and had seen a substantial waterfall on the northern branch below Kukaklek Lake. I was alarmed, then, to learn that the plan called for two rafts and four people to float this branch. Worried, I told the others what I had seen, but they assured me they knew a number of people who had floated the river and had gone over the falls without incident. They told me that singer John Denver had recently made a video of himself going over the falls, and that it appeared to be an easy drop. I was not convinced and protested more, so the others finally agreed to drop me off just above the falls. I would then hike around the falls and photograph the two rafts going over this rugged stretch of water. It would make a spectacular picture.

Four of us were flown with our gear into Kukaklek Lake on the morning of June 14, 1979. Bruce Kaye and his friend Dick were to fly into Nonvianuk Lake the following day. They would float the Nonvianuk River and meet us at an old cabin near the junction of the Alagnak and Nonvianuk Rivers. Dick Russell and his assistant Bill took off in one raft; Ross Cavanaugh and I followed in another. We floated the river, catching a few fish and enjoying the scenery. We camped about fifteen miles downstream from the lake outlet. That evening we delighted in a nice fish dinner cooked over an open fire.

The next morning we stuffed all our gear into waterproof bags and secured them to the rafts. I climbed in and took a seat at the back of the raft. A light mist was falling, so I wore hip boots, a wool jacket, and a light raincoat. Over the rain gear I wore a life vest that contained a CO_2 cartridge for quick inflation.

Not far downriver high cliffs lined the banks. I began to think about the falls and the plans to let me off to hike around them, but I wasn't too concerned. The river seemed placid enough.

As it narrowed, however, the current picked up speed, and I became a little anxious. Dick and Bill were a hundred yards ahead of us and had disappeared around the curve when I first heard the roar of the waterfall. Ross and I were moving rapidly along one of the rock walls and were pulled suddenly around a sharp bend of the river. That is when I saw the waterfall and the overturned raft, and I knew there was nothing we could do.

"Hang on!" I yelled to Ross.

I let go of my oar and grabbed the safety rope with both hands just before we dropped over the ten-foot falls. The raft hit a huge standing wave at the bottom and flipped before continuing down the river. I was now in front of the upside-down raft and still hanging on to the safety rope. As we were carried down the turbulent river, waves broke over my head. I was having trouble catching a breath. I tried to grab the pull tab that would inflate my life jacket, but I could not find it. More water washed over me, and I gagged as the river rushed into my mouth.

"This is a heck of a way to go," I thought. I was certain I was going to die, but even so I did not give up. Coughing and gasping for air, I fought to keep my head above the violent water. As I was swept around a bend of the river, I spotted two large willow bushes leaning over the edge of the bank. Convinced I could not survive in front of the raft for much longer, I let go and desperately lunged for the willows, about ten feet away. I missed!

Now being swept down the river like a half-submerged log, I tumbled and spun out of control. My energy spent, I was almost ready to give up, when my feet hit some rocks. Hope surged through me, giving me strength I did not realize I still had. I kicked and fought my way across the slippery rocks toward the riverbank, slowly getting out of the main current. Finally, I grabbed a bush on shore and pulled myself out of the river. Exhausted, I lay on the bank, coughing and spitting up water and even some blood. After several seconds I staggered to my feet in time to see Dick crawling ashore on the other side of the river, pulling his raft onto the riverbank. He had been caught in a whirlpool for a few minutes before it spit him out and sent him toward the bank. Our raft, still turned over, was being carried downstream.

I desperately looked around for Ross but could not see him. I did not know he was under the raft trying to keep his head above water in the air pocket. When he hit shallow water a little farther down the river, he got out from under the raft. I was relieved to see him alive and watched as he crawled onto the opposite shore. The raft was too big for him to pull out of the current, however. I heard him holler for help. He was hanging on to the raft, desperately trying to keep it from being swept away. From the opposite side of the river I could do nothing to assist. I yelled to Dick that Ross was downstream and needed help with the raft.

Eventually the three on the other side got together and poled the rafts across to my side. As we discussed the ordeal, we found out that each of us had been about ready to give up. After Dick had been thrown from their raft, he was sucked to the bottom and held there by a strong current. When his hand accidentally hit the safety rope tied to the raft, he grabbed it and pulled himself to the surface. Bill had been thrown from the raft and somehow managed to swim ashore. We all knew we were extremely lucky to have survived. The whole event had occurred within a few minutes, but in our minds it had seemed much longer.

After we recovered, we surveyed the damage. Our fishing rods were gone, as were three of the four oars. Our gear was still tied to the rafts, but water had seeped into several of the waterproof bags. Some of our food was saturated, and parts of my camera gear were ruined. Most of our extra clothes were also soaked, so there was little point in changing. Fortunately our sleeping bags remained dry.

The situation was not great, but also it was not grim. We had all survived, and we still had our rafts and most of our gear. Since we knew no other dangerous rapids were downriver, we decided our best course of action would be to continue our trip. We cut down three small spruce trees, fashioned them into crude oars, and then continued floating down the river to the junction, which we reached a few hours later.

Bruce and Dick were already at the old cabin. They had a fire going in the stove and hot soup simmering on top. Chilled and shivering in our wet clothes, we were extremely grateful for the fire and the soup, which warmed both our outsides and insides. We told Bruce and Dick all about the falls and again wondered how all of us had survived the plunge. We decided that when John Denver had made the video, the river had obviously been at a different level. We spent the evening resting and drying out our wet gear and clothes.

The next morning we continued our journey, mostly dried out but still using our makeshift oars. We had several more days to float to the pickup point near the Kvichak River before being flown back to King Salmon. Despite the accident, the trip was a success. We were able to continue surveying the resources of the river, and we had a heck of a story to tell when we got home.

And while I never got those spectacular pictures of the rafts going over the falls, I'll be content to see photos someone else has taken. That experience taught me some strong lessons: never raft over a waterfall, and always wear a life jacket that does not need to be inflated.

I had another brush with death later that year, this time in a plane. I had flown sheep, moose, and caribou surveys in McKinley park in a Super Cub for several years, and I had become familiar with the poor weather conditions that often develop rapidly in this high, rugged, mountainous region.

On November 27 I was flying moose surveys in the Riley Creek drainage. The weather conditions were good in the morning, but by noon the wind had picked up. At one in the afternoon I ended the surveys and returned to the park airstrip.

Two students from the University of Alaska had arrived that afternoon and wanted to be flown to the northern side of the park. They were researching winter feeding behavior of caribou.

"It's too windy to fly today," I told them. "I'll try to get you out tomorrow, weather permitting."

The following morning the wind was still blowing, but by eleven it had died down a bit, so I told the students to get ready. I left with the first student at about noon and followed the Denali Highway north toward Healy. I had a good tailwind through the pass and very little turbulence until I flew over Otto Lake. The wind there tossed the Super Cub around violently for a few minutes, but as I flew north toward the Stampede Trail, conditions improved. We spotted several hundred caribou near the Teklanika River. I landed on a small lake near them and unloaded my passenger and his gear. As I got ready to leave, I said, "I'll be back with your partner in about an hour."

On the way back I detoured farther to the east to avoid the turbulence around Otto Lake. I landed at the airstrip around one thirty, loaded up the other student, and was again underway. I flew through the pass and then east to avoid the winds I had encountered on the first trip. I landed on the lake and dropped off the student and his gear.

The wind increased on the way back and slowed my speed. The winds were playing with my plane that day, but they weren't throwing anything at me I hadn't seen before. As I approached the airstrip, I put on a notch of flaps and reduced power. The plane was at treetop height when I crossed the end of the runway. A violent gust of wind hit me from the side and turned the plane crosswise to the airstrip. I immediately shoved the throttle forward to give the engine full power. As the engine roared, I tried to turn the plane back into the wind, but it did not respond. I felt helpless as another gust hit me, tipping the plane on its side. I saw willow bushes coming at me.

The plane hit. A cacophony of crashing, ripping, and screeching rent the air as the Cub skidded through the willow bushes. The force of the impact slammed me forward. I barely registered the chaotic blur of bushes, rocks, plastic, and metal. I felt I was going through a tunnel of death; I had finally met my end. Then everything became quiet. I sat there for a few seconds before I realized that I was still alive.

Relief swept over me. Quickly, I began to survey the damage. A wing had been ripped off. The cockpit was crushed. The upper part of my body was outside the plane, the windshield having been torn away. The engine had been jammed back, trapping my legs against the control stick. I tried to pull myself free but could not.

I was lucky to survive the crash of this Piper Super Cub in Denali National Park in 1979. This picture was given to me by Theron Smith. Photographer unknown.

Martin Grosnick, my assistant, appeared at the side of the wreck and saw me move.

"My God, he's alive!" he said. "Sit still, Will. I radioed the office, and help is on the way."

Martin had been standing near the runway, awaiting my return. He had watched as the wind gust hit the plane and turned it crosswise. Then he saw the plane disappear behind some short trees and heard the impact. He immediately called the park office on his radio.

The plane was a mangled mess. The left wing, which contained one of the gas tanks, was now directly over my head and leaking gas onto my shoulder. I was lucky that sparks had not ignited it. I was not in pain, but when I reached down, I could feel that my leg was broken. The kneecap had a big knot on it, and I could feel a protruding bone. In spite of the fire danger Martin stayed beside me until the rescue crew arrived.

Within a few minutes an emergency crew began cutting and pulling the plane apart to get me out. My leg was still jammed under the control stick. I asked for a wrench and used it to unbolt the stick. I could finally pull my leg free. The crew splinted my leg, pried the instrument panel forward, and lifted me out. I remained conscious and calm during the entire ordeal. I think I was partly in shock, which probably helped.

I was rushed to Healy, where a medic confirmed that my leg was broken. The weather was too rough to fly, so an ambulance took me to the hospital in Fairbanks. I arrived at six thirty that evening, and by eight o'clock I was on the operating table. They wired my kneecap together, and then secured my leg in a cast.

I spent about a week in the Fairbanks hospital before my NPS supervisors, Bob Peterson and Paul Haertel, accompanied by LuRue, arrived in a government plane and flew me back to Anchorage. I was very happy to see LuRue and glad to get home to the kids again. Once again I had caused LuRue a lot of worry and nearly made her a widow.

The FAA team that investigated the crash said it was one of the worst airplane wrecks they had seen in which the pilot had survived. They attributed my survival to my helmet. A Piper Super Cub has two tubular bars that cross inside the windshield just in front of the pilot's head. Some years before, I had decided that I had a good chance of surviving a crash if my unprotected head did not hit those bars. Since I flew a lot of low-level wildlife surveys, increasing my chances for a crash, I began wearing a helmet even though it was not required. In the crash the helmet had been severely damaged when I was slammed forward into the bars. The investigators said that the helmet had saved my life.

I spent several months recuperating, but by May I was flying again. I continued to fly Super Cubs in my wildlife work, but the experience stayed with me. Whenever I got into severe turbulence, I became much more nervous than I had before the crash.

After surviving two bad accidents in one year, the possibility of being severely injured or killed while doing fieldwork was more real to me than ever. I think those incidents helped me decide to retire at the end of 1981. By then I had put in thirty years of government service; I had lived the explorer's life I had dreamed as a youth. I loved my work, but there were others things I wanted to do.

The Kenai Peninsula was calling me back. LuRue and I moved to Cooper Landing in 1982 to build our dream log home, the beginning of a whole new adventure.

Index

Note: Italicized page numbers indicate photographs.